SCOUSE MOUSE

SCOUSE MOUSE

or *i never got over it*

GEORGE MELLY

an autobiography

Weidenfeld and Nicolson London

For Tom

Acknowledgements

I would like to thank Marilyn and Jenny for typing this book, Diana and Tom for pointing out those passages which lurched towards pretension or sentimentality, and Alex of Weidenfeld and Nicolson for monthly lunches which shamed me into pressing on.

G.M.

1

Place of birth: Liverpool. Year: 1926. I was born a fortnight late during an August heatwave.

This took place neither in hospital, nor in my parents' tiny flat in Linnet Lane, but a mile away in my grandfather's large house, The Grange, on the banks of the Mersey. I was a rickety-looking baby with a wobbling head and didn't take kindly to my mother's milk. It turned my stools bright green and I had to be weaned on Cow & Gate. I survived however and the Mellys were delighted. It seems to me odd that they should set such store on an heir in the direct line. There were no large estates to inherit and the money they left was always divided equally between sons and daughters.

Great-Aunts Eva and Florence in their black, floor-length dresses came to view me a day or so later and I was carried out of the bedroom by the midwife for their inspection. My mother called for them to come and see her but they refused. According to their Victorian conventions it would have been improper to visit a woman so soon after an 'interesting event'.

Rather subdued at her breach of etiquette, my mother heard Florence remark to Eva in respect of me, 'What a good thing he's a Melly!'

My great-great-grandfather, André Melly, was born in Switzerland in 1802. He could trace his ancestry back to the early sixteenth century when one Jean Colombe had a son called Matthieu who later, for reasons connected with becoming a burger of Geneva, changed his name to 'Mesley ou Melly'. Family legend held that Jean Colombe was the son or grandson of a Genoese pedlar, in itself not much of a cachet except that he was meant to be a direct descendant of Christopher Columbus. Certainly, to substantiate this rather nebulous claim, the family crest is a pair of doves' wings while the shield depicts a dove in

1

an azure sky hovering above a ship sailing towards the setting sun. The motto, with no especial relevance, maintains that 'A Good Name is Better than a Golden Girdle.'

André Melly seems to have been an amiable young man if a little solemn. In his youth he was touched by the scepticism of Voltaire, and revolutionary enough to have incurred the displeasure, through some remarks overheard at a café table, of the Neapolitan Government. For several years afterwards, when travelling on the Continent, he was closely watched by secret police and put to some inconvenience. He later regained his faith and became a model of propriety.

In the 1820s he emigrated to England and engaged in business, mostly in Manchester and Liverpool. His probity was such that, during the financial crisis of 1825–6, he was able to ride out the storm supported by considerable loans from friends, secured without interest. He eventually married a Miss Grey whose father was his partner, and became a naturalized citizen through a special Act of Parliament, as was necessary in those days. He suffered from migraines, played the flute adequately and was a keen entomologist; a collection of beetles he assembled and mounted is still in the museum at Geneva. An engraving reveals a marked resemblance to Schubert: curly hair, small round glasses and a stock.

His business, which was to extend to railways, was at first confined solely to cotton. He had dealings with America, but his principal activity was in Egypt, a country which had always excited his interest and was to prove the place of his death. He became, in 1820s, the Liverpool agent to the Pasha, Mahomet Ali; a lucrative if anxious connection as it was forbidden for strict Muhammadans to insure their goods or to allow anyone else to do so. He was also commissioned to furnish a palace for the Pasha 'in the English style', a task he knew better than to interpret literally. His choice of ottomans with gold fringes, huge mirrors and extravagant chandeliers was well received.

In 1850 André himself set off for Egypt with his wife, his two sons, and his only daughter on an enterprise unconnected with commerce. It had long been his ambition to attempt to discover the source of the Nile, visiting its antiquities and adding to his collection of beetles en route. On their way back, on 1 January 1851, he was struck down by a fever from which, at 6.15 p.m.

2

some five days later, having first established the exact time by the angle of the sun, he died, and was buried in the native cemetery in the village of Gagee. His wife and family, after much difficulty and some danger, sadly returned to Cairo and embarked for Liverpool.

André's daughter, Louisa, never married, but his sons, Charles, the elder, and George, my great-grandfather, both did. Charles, a melancholy philanthropist with an interest in good works in general and an obsessional passion for providing drinking fountains for the working classes, bought a house for his mother and siblings on Mossley Hill, some five miles from the city centre. It was called Riverslea, and the original building was in a restrained and rather charming Regency Gothic, although Charles was to tack on a wing in the heavy Victorian revivalist taste with castellations and a tower. Riverslea stood in its own considerable grounds. Its owner, after increasing bouts of mental illness, eventually took his own life. He left eight children.

When Charles's brother, George, married in the 1850s, he deserted Riverslea and set himself up in a large and solid Georgian house in Chatham Street within walking distance of his place of business. He was of a very different temperament from his earnest father and gloomy, if worthy, brother. He became, until his financial interests made it impractical, the Liberal MP for Stoke-upon-Trent; he was a JP, a keen sportsman and a lively writer of amusing, if mildly snobbish, memoirs, privately printed and handsomely bound. He had seven children. His youngest son, Samuel Heywood Melly, was my grandfather.

By the time I was born the family had divided firmly, and not without a certain tart rivalry, into the Riverslea and Chatham Street Mellys; although the latter were in fact the cadet branch, they considered themselves top dogs. Both Riverslea and Chatham Street were still occupied in 1926 and were to remain so until the middle 1940s.

I don't know much about my mother's family. There are no records going back to the fifteenth century. There were rumours, not much aired, of a Polish pedlar, but unlike the Mellys' Genoese hawker this one was rather too recent to be a source of pride, nor was he believed to be descended from a famous explorer. But while the origins of my maternal grandfather, Albert Edward Isaac, may have been obscure, everything I have heard about him suggests an honourable, intelligent and very lovable man.

Teaching the piano didn't make him rich, but it provided a living sufficient to support his wife and three children in modest comfort and to employ a cook and a housemaid. His interests were broad. He was very well read – Dickens was a passion with him – and he delivered several lectures ('The Poetry of Robert Browning', 'The Modern Theatre') to the Liverpool Philomathic Society which were later published as pamphlets. He was also a keen amateur Shakespearian actor, an interest he shared with his wife and more particularly his daughter, and a considerable wit. His photographs show a handsome man with neat but luxuriant moustache. His expression is mild but alert.

My parents married about eighteen months before my birth after facing initial opposition from my father's family. There were three reasons for this. My mother was eight years older than my father. Her mother, a widow since 1912, had very little money; and she was Jewish. I don't know which of these objections was primary. The Chatham Street Mellys were not, so far as I know, particularly anti-Semitic by the standards of the twenties; their tradition was Unitarian and Liberal although, by that time, they had become both Conservative and c. of e. They were on the other hand rich, and the rich tend to favour 'a good match'. I dare say that at thirty-two they felt my mother was rather old to start a family. At all events they did what they could to break it up.

My father was then in shipping. He worked for Lamport & Holt, a firm of which his Uncle George had been Managing Director. The family arranged for him to be sent 'on business' to their office in South America for a year. He wrote to my mother on the voyage out, 'They are playing our tune – "Swanee".'

I asked him later what he remembered of South America. He only recalled, with some horror, an abattoir built like a helter-skelter; the cattle walking up a ramp snaking round the outside, to be slaughtered as they entered through a door at the top and dismembered by stages inside until their carcasses were carried out, ready to be frozen, at the base. As the animals, with their foreboding of death, were reluctant to move, they were sprinkled constantly with water and then touched with an electric prod at the base of the ramp, transmitting a visible blue flash along their

4

wet flanks right up to the top. The shock made them push, panic-stricken, forward and upwards to their doom. Although he enjoyed shooting and fishing, my father detested gratuitous cruelty and the image remained with him always; a glimpse of hell in the otherwise even landscape of his life, for he was still training in 1918 and never saw the trenches.

When he returned to Liverpool from South America he remained obstinate in his determination to marry my mother and eventually his family caved in. His Uncle George gave her a rather fine diamond spray as a peace offering. He said it was 'to bury the hatchet'.

There were no religious objections to their union. My mother's father had been mildly orthodox but he had died, much mourned, when she was nineteen. His widow and younger son, Alan, eventually became Liberal Jews. The elder son Fred gave up religion altogether, but my mother converted, almost instantly, to the Church of England, possibly because she was a passionate dancer and some of the best dances in Liverpool were held on Friday nights.

Although there was money in the background, my father at twenty-six earned very little. My parents took a tiny flat in Linnet Lane and could afford only one cook-housemaid, an almost unheard of privation for the middle classes in 1926. My mother grew enormous during her pregnancy. When she got into bed my father would say, 'The *Dreadnought* is now in dock.'

At the time of his marriage, as my father had shown no aptitude or liking for shipping, my grandfather bought him a partnership in a firm of woolbrokers, founded by his late Uncle Hugh, and registered as 'Seward & Melly'. Here he was his own boss but although well-liked, he never displayed much enthusiasm for business. He told me once that he would have chosen to manage a country estate but that the family wouldn't hear of it. Burdened by expectations – he was to inherit a considerable fortune from his mother only a few years before his own early death in 1961 – he did what was expected of him. His last words to me were, 'Always do what you want to. I never did.'

*   *   *

I was in Liverpool recently, singing for two nights at Kirklands, originally an elegant nineteenth-century bakery, now a wine bar with a music room above it. I stayed, as I usually do, with the painter and poet Adrian Henri and his companion, the poet Carol Ann Duffy. Before my second gig, Adrian having left to recite his poems somewhere in Cumbria, I invited Carol Ann to dine with me in a bistro in Lark Lane in the suburb of Sefton Park and as it was a fine evening in late March, I suggested we took a short bus ride to the gates of Prince's Park and walked from there. Carol Ann didn't know this part of Liverpool very well, but I did. It was where I lived until I left to work in London in the late forties.

We caught the bus opposite The Rialto, a 'Moorish' cinema built during the twenties and now a furniture store, and moved smoothly up Prince's Boulevard. There is a statue of a Victorian statesman at each end of the tree-lined yellow gravel walk running up its centre, and I could see the ghosts of the tramlines where the 33 used to rattle and sway from the Pier Head to distant Garston. My maternal grandmother always advised her friends to wait for a 33. It took, in her view, 'a prettier way' than either the 1 or 45 which ran to the Dingle through slums and dilapidated shops closer to the river.

Prince's Park, an alternative childhood walk to the far larger, almost adjacent Sefton Park, is long and narrow, surrounded by the backs of big houses and mansion blocks, and enclosing a chain of artificial lakes, duck-strewn and the colour of Brown Windsor soup, fenced in by croquet hoop-like railings. At the entrance to the lakes is a small gravestone commemorating 'Judy, the children's friend', a donkey which died at an advanced age in 1924. My mother, wearing a sailor's blouse and a wide straw hat, had ridden on Judy as a child. On the edge of the largest of the lakes is a disused boathouse in the style of a Swiss chalet; a mode much favoured at the turn of the century for park-keepers' lodges and other small municipal buildings connected with recreation. At the end of the lakes the park, shedding its shrubs and marshalled flower beds, widens out into a bare and scruffy valley with trees on the further slope. Carol Ann and I left the park and, crossing Ullet Road, entered the district of Lark Lane itself.

Ullet Road is, I was always being told, a corruption of Owlet Road and, given that Linnet Lane runs off it at right angles to meet Lark Lane, I think this is probably the case. At the other end of Ullet Road is the Dingle where the 33, leaving 'the prettier way' behind it, joined up again with the 1 and 45 emerging from the slums to service Aigburth Road. Ahead of us, enclosed within this rectangle, lay my childhood.

Most of the suburb consists of Victorian and Edwardian family houses with quite large gardens, but within it is a smaller, more consistent grid of streets and it was through these we strolled. Built presumably by a firm of speculative architects, the three-storeyed terraces are named after the novels of Sir Walter Scott and display late nineteenth-century romanticism on an absurdly miniature scale. Of red or yellow brick, detailed in local sandstone or ceramic tiling, bulging with bay windows, bristling with useless little towers and pinnacles, they pay homage to the fag-end of the Pre-Raphaelite dream of Medieval England. Crossing Tristram, Waverley and Bertram Roads, walking down Marmion Road, we emerged into Ivanhoe Road where my parents, having given up their flat in Linnet Lane before I had time to become conscious of my surroundings, had rented Number 22.

I pointed it out to Carol Ann, telling her that there used to be a dairy behind the house with its own cows. Born into the age of the great milk combines, she found this hard to believe so we turned the corner. There was the arch into Hogg's Dairy with the name still painted on a fading sign over the entrance and the cowsheds surrounding the small yard. Furthermore, although the cows are long gone, it is still in use as a piggery. We walked inside and the pigs, with their beady eyes, grunted and strained up at us from their odoriferous pens inside the sheds. A man in his thirties came out of the office built into the side of the deep arch. I asked him about Tommy Hogg who smelt sourly of milk and was something of a ladies' man, walking out successively with several of our maids. 'My Uncle Tommy,' he said. 'He died two years ago.'

The cows had lodged there only in the winter. It was one of the signs that summer had arrived to watch them, herded by Tommy and his father, lowing their way down busy Aigburth Road to graze in the fields of a small farm which lay between the river and Aigburth Vale. Despite the 'Picture Houses', trams and shops, little pockets of rural life persisted then at the ends of cobbled 'unadopted' lanes. We said goodbye to Tommy Hogg's nephew.

Repassing our 'entry', the local name for those narrow high-walled alleys skirting the back-yards, we crossed Ivanhoe Road. There was what used to be a fire station on the opposite corner, an elaborate little Ruritanian building. I once dreamt that my mother, screaming silently, gave birth to a child in one of its empty rooms with me present but unable to help. Another thirty yards and we were in Lark Lane itself, the great sandstone gate-posts to Sefton Park visible at the far end.

Lark Lane is a shopping street. Some of the shops I remember are still there, although most have changed their names: a grocer's, a fishmonger's, a florist's, two cake shops, several tobacconists and sweet shops, a saddler's (gone), a wine mer-chant's, an undertaker's, and a small Gothic police station. Most of the shops delivered. They knew their customers by name, and had pretended to admire them in their prams, and the under-takers measured them up when they died.

As we were still a bit early for dinner, Carol Ann and I went into The Albert, a handsome château-like public house built in the 1880s with a walled bowling green behind it. My father had used The Albert almost every day of his adult life and twice on Sundays. Inside some disastrous 'improvements' have been made in recent years. The old smoke room is now a smart cocktail lounge, the engraved mirrors are gone and so are the bronze horses rearing up on the high mantelpiece over a coal fire, but there is still the barley-sugar Corinthian column in the public, the fine mahogany bar, the elaborate plaster-work ceil-ings, orange with tobacco smoke. We had a couple of drinks and I thought of my father sitting with his circle: Jack and Maisy Forster, 'Boy' Henshaw, Copper and Donald Carmichael, 'the Major'.

Lark Lane had its quota of unfortunates when I was young: an errand boy with so large a goitre bulging from his neck that he had to lean sideways on his heavy bicycle to keep his balance; an old woman whose feet in their surgical boots were turned inwards so that she had to lift one above the other to move forwards; a huge man, the son of a police sergeant, who was simple and had been, so they said, castrated because he had molested children. Despite this he had alarmed my parents by

8

offering to take my younger brother to 'see some chickens', but Bill had sensibly refused and run safely home. There was another simpleton, harmless and much loved. He was small and wore a huge cap. His name was 'Silly Syd' and he would stand up in the local cinemas during the ice-cream interval and shout out, 'Give me a penny, I'm daft.'

Carol Ann told me that Lark Lane was becoming quite fashionable. There was a wine bar nearer the park. The bistro, a word and concept unknown to my parents, stands on a corner with big windows along both sides. It was a junk-shop in the fifties and before that a record shop. I had bought many of my first jazz 78s there in the holidays from Stowe and on leave from the Navy.

You 'come-to' as a child as if from a major operation. Pink blurs loom up, solidify into faces, become recognizable. Objects materialize. Continuity establishes itself.

Early memory is fragmentary: a boxful of unsorted snaps, many of them of people and places whose significance is lost; a few film clips of random lengths shown in no particular order. Nor is it possible to distinguish in retrospect between what you can really remember and what you were told later, and anyway many early memories are false.

I am sitting beside my mother in an open car. She is driving along a seaside promenade festooned with fairy lights at night. Everything is in shades of milky blue: the sea, the pier, the boarding houses. I am very happy. I smile up at my glamorous mother. The only flaw is that my mother never drove a car.

A real one. A maid, a friend of my nanny's, is hanging up sheets in a small garden on the side of a house opposite ours in Ivanhoe Road. A blue sky full of little clouds, blossom on a stunted soot-black tree, the sheets very white, the arms of the maid red from the suds, the whole composition cramped and angular, without depth. Why this image chosen from so many which have been forgotten? Why a white horse galloping across a green hillside in North Wales lit by brilliant sunshine under a dark sky? Early memory has no discrimination. When everything is equal, without associations, without any meaning beyond itself, there is no measure available, no scale. My mother drives her car; the maid hangs up the washing (wooden pegs bought from gypsies who came to the door); the white horse gallops under the dark sky.

9

I was a discontented baby. My mother, to amuse me later, would recreate her nights in that small bedroom in the flat in Linnet Lane. A whimper leading to a prolonged wail. Her leap from the bed before my father could wake up. Her walking the floor, rocking me in her arms, crooning one of two songs: Paul Robeson's 'Curley-headed babbie' or Harrow's 'Forty Years On'. My subsidence into silence and careful replacement in my cot. Her return to bed. The approach of sleep. A whimper leading to a prolonged wail. . . .

On my afternoon walk I would scream in my pram and could only be quietened by her drawing an umbrella along the railings. By the time we moved to Ivanhoe Road my parents could afford and had room for a nanny, and anyway I was beyond the screaming stage.

We spent my early summer holidays in Llandudno or Colwyn Bay, those adjacent Victorian seaside resorts on the coast of North Wales. My maternal grandmother was often with us. My nanny, Bella, always. My father would spend a fortnight there and commute at weekends for the rest of the month. Sometimes his parents visited us in their chauffeur-driven car. Still an only child I exercised an iron will, insisting on a rigid and rather extravagant routine: a visit to the pier to feed the seagulls, to watch them banking down out of the salt air, beady-eyed and sharp-billed, to grab the biscuits. The biscuits came from a special kiosk. There was a notice in its window, 'the biscuits the birds like'. The birds were selective in their tastes. The biscuits they liked were rather expensive. Soon it was time for Punch and Judy, for which I early developed a passion which has never left me.

The Professor was called Codman. He was a Liverpudlian who during the winter months performed on the steps of St George's Hall in the city centre, and in consequence Punch and his victims all affected a strong, if squeaky, Liverpool accent and always will have in my ears. I soon knew most of the script by heart, deriving deep satisfaction from the thwack of Punch's stick, and his raucous pleasure in his own wickedness. I didn't mind the crocodile, accepting that Punch could believe, until the very moment his nose was between its jaws, that it was a domestic cat, but when the ghost appeared to drag him gibbering down to hell, I demanded, panic-stricken, to be taken away.

The afternoons, while less crippling financially, were given over to equally obsessional activities. My projects were either the removal of innumerable stones from one part of the beach to another or the filling of a bucket from a rock pool and emptying it at a given point above the tideline. The first exercise was called 'Stones', the second 'Bucket-a-boat'. I was prepared to spend several hours alone engrossed in these monotonous tasks, but preferred to enlist an adult working under my direction. Few were amenable for long with the exception of my patient, if rarely available, grandfather dressed, as always, in a grey homberg hat the same colour as his full moustache and wearing a three-piece dark suit of antique cut with a watch-chain across the waistcoat, and a starched butterfly collar – his bare feet and rolled up trousers the only concession he was prepared to make to the sartorial licence of the seaside. While we worked he would whistle tunelessly through his false teeth, an habitual mannerism which used to drive my mother mad with irritation. He smelt, deliciously, of Turkish cigarettes.

There were other entertainments. The pier itself with its salt-corroded penny-in-the-slot machines. There was 'The Haunted House' and 'The Execution of Mary Queen of Scots'. Of these I preferred the latter: two doors slowly opening on the façade of a castle, the executioner bringing down his axe, the Queen's head tumbling into the basket, the doors banging shut. I was mystified as to how the head rejoined the trunk in time for the next penny. There was also a 'What the Butler Saw' machine. I enjoyed turning the handle very fast so that the fly-stained sepia image of a massive-thighed Edwardian lady was forced to remove her voluminous clothing at breakneck speed.

There was a concert party which, until I was old enough to understand the jokes, my parents enjoyed rather more than I did. What they liked was it being so hopeless. There was a sketch one year, an exchange between the 'light' and 'low' comedians about a family called 'The Biggers'. It described how the little Bigger had grown bigger than the bigger Bigger and so on. 'I see', said the 'low' comedian at the conclusion of this rigmarole, 'there's been a bit of bother at the Biggers.' My parents laughed so much at this that a young man, sitting alone in a deck chair in the row ahead of them, turned indignantly round and told them it wasn't kind to laugh at him just because he had red hair.

Sometimes I was put on a donkey but I didn't enjoy it much especially when the donkey man would run with it jogging me up and down on its fat, yet bony, back. Nor did I appreciate being taught to feed a pony in a small enclosed field in front of our boarding house. My maternal grandmother, who was fond of animals, insisted I did this, balancing the lump of sugar on the palm of my hand, bending back my fingers to avoid them being nibbled. I can still feel the pony's wet, warm, snuffling breath and see its dilating hairy nostrils. Often I would drop the sugar but she'd make me start again. She believed, unlike my mother, in discipline or at any rate didn't lack the courage to apply it. My mother feared unpopularity, however short-lived, even from a child. 'When did you last punish George?' my grandmother asked her once. She couldn't remember.

They were happy holidays. I was the centre of attention, my every word repeated later to others in my hearing as though a miracle of wit or perception, every pose recorded by my mother's Brownie: the birds were fed on the biscuits they preferred, the stones were shifted, the water transported, and Punch was dragged squeaking and whacking his way along the road to perdition on the pebbly beach against the grey horizon.

As to why Llandudno comes back to me in such sharp focus from a time when Liverpool still seems fragmentary and vague I have, although it is apparently a common experience, no explanation. Perhaps the frame of the holiday, its yearly repetition clarified by growing terms of reference, developed and printed it in the dark-room of memory.

2

Number 22 Ivanhoe Road – a three-storey terrace house with steep front steps set back in a tiny front garden with a low wall. Behind its ornate brickwork and sash windows I spent most of the first nine years of my life. There were six of us living there to start with. My mother and father, my nanny Bella, a cook and a house parlour-maid. Later there was also my brother and, for a short time, my sister.

Opening the façade as if it were a doll's house; thinking of it as a setting for a play described by the dramatist before the maid enters to answer the telephone; this is how it was arranged.

Behind the front door, to the right, a small pram-room with just enough space for the pram and later tricycles or fairy cycles. The pram an imposing object, its rubbery smell, deriving presumably from its concertina hood and clip-on cover, scented the room. After the war, unless very grand, it was rather 'common' to own a big pram; push-chairs, as battered as possible, became fashionable, but in the thirties the middle classes subscribed to these imposing objects, the insides of which could be adjusted later to accommodate sitting toddlers. Dark and highly polished, the pram, with its large spoked wheels, remained closer to a horse-drawn carriage than a motor car.

Facing the pram-room was the lounge. It was called that as a sign of modernity, implying gin before dinner instead of sherry, and the use of lipstick. My grandparents and great-uncles and aunts had drawing-rooms. There was a great deal of furniture in that small lounge: a 'baby grand' piano which my mother used to tell visitors was 'off a ship', its top covered with framed and signed photographs of actors and actresses she knew; a rather 'good' bookcase, glass-fronted shelves above, a cupboard below in which my father stored several cartons of Black Cat cigarettes in their tin boxes from which to fill his case. There were easy chairs and a sofa before the fireplace and, in front of the sofa, a long low oak stool with a webbed leather top with the *Radio Times* on it. In winter there was a coal fire in the modern grate, protected when the room was empty by a winged brass-netted guard, and the coal was kept in a beaten brass scuttle. There were two standard lamps, their bases in twenties black lacquer with gold dragons climbing up them and parchment shades.

In the space beyond was my mother's desk with its reproduction Chippendale chair and, within reach on a little round-topped table, the flower-like, long-stemmed telephone. Opposite the desk, between the tail of the piano and the windows, was a wireless set (eventually to be replaced by a radiogram), with its heavy acid-filled batteries and its fretwork cloth-backed front. There was a built-in window seat. The carpet wasn't fitted, the surrounding floorboards were stained a shiny black. The colour scheme, in keeping with calling it the lounge, was rather 'daring': cream wallpaper, oatmeal loose covers, and burnt orange curtains and cushions. There were no pictures in the room.

Next to the lounge, facing the bottom of the stairs, was the dining-room. It looked out over the back-yard, a scruffy little square of grass with an outside lavatory for the maids smelling strongly of Jeyes fluid, and a shed of the kind much-advertised in the back pages of the *Radio Times* against the far wall, next to a back door leading into the entry. You couldn't see the back-yard from the dining-room because there were net curtains covering the bottom half of the window.

The dining-room, unlike the lounge, was entirely traditional except for its hemp carpet. There was a polished table with two leaves, Georgian chairs, a small glass-topped carving table, a corner cupboard and a square piano, bought for five pounds in an auction and wrongly believed to be a spinet. On the square piano, leaning against the wall, was a tray, a wedding present, with a collage of different kinds of Brussels lace arranged symmetrically behind its glass surface. There was a grandfather clock in the corner by the window with a phoenix painted on the face. My father wound it up on Sunday mornings after lunch. It gave me great pleasure to watch the heavy weights ascending on their chains as he did so, and to see the adjustable pendulum swinging to and fro through the narrow open door in the case. In the corner cupboard were heavy cut-glass tumblers, engraved burgundy glasses in beautiful glowing colours, claret glasses and liqueur glasses. Yet my parents, unlike my grandfather's generation, never drank wine; indeed my mother never drank at all.

On the walls were early nineteenth-century hunting and shooting prints: 'The View', 'Gone to Ground', 'The Kill' and gentlemen in frock coats and top coats bringing down partridges, snipe, and pheasants. The dining-room was warmed by a gas fire with fragile clay elements which slotted in over the jets. Gas fires then tended to bang loudly when you lit them, and sometimes when you switched them off. I imagine some early experience of this must have alarmed me deeply as I still have a phobia about lighting gas appliances, allied to a reluctance to open, although not to drink, champagne.

The only other door off the hall was at the back and covered with a fringed brown curtain on a brass rail to show that it led to the kitchen. This was far from streamlined. The solid wooden cupboards and drawers had big wooden handles, primitively carved curly bits at the corners and were painted white. There was a big, old-fashioned gas-stove and two battered wicker chairs in front of the grate, a scrubbed wooden table with kitchen chairs, a clothes pulley which squeaked when you raised or lowered it and, hanging from the light bulb, a sticky fly-paper textured with the corpses of many a summer's bluebottle, plump on the manure of Hogg's cows. There was no fridge, but in the back kitchen, with its sink and draining-board, was a wooden wire-meshed meat safe. Bread, flour and rice were kept in big round enamel tins, raisins, tapioca and sultanas in smaller editions of the same, and most of the shelves were covered in gingham-patterned oil-cloth for 'easier cleaning'.

The hall itself had comparatively little in it. There was an oak 'footman's chair', rather out of scale and below the stairs a chest dated 1694 in which my father kept his rods and guns. On the chest was a little brass pestle and mortar and a small brass crinoline lady that was really a bell. Above it was a beautiful plate of the twenties, another wedding present. In brilliant blues, greens and gold, it represented some elves crossing a bridge in a landscape dominated by mushrooms. My mother,

15

when I asked her recently, could neither remember it nor imagine what had become of it. I expect it was broken in a move, and much regret it. It was the most magic object in the house. There was also a barometer you tapped to find out if it was going to rain and a useless and nasty little brass warming-pan.

On the first floor, up the dog-legged staircase with its carpet rods and a gate fixed across the top to stop us falling down, there was a different pattern of rooms. In the front were the nursery and the night-nursery. The night-nursery, where our nanny slept with us when we were still young, has become vague, but the nursery is as clear as if I had just left it. The floor was of dark green cork, the walls white, the furniture apple-green. There was a gas fire with a tall fender guard and in front of it a grubby, faded white rug with animals on it. There was a big toy cupboard, a table with cane-bottomed chairs, a child's table, round with four legs, and two little chairs; one curved with arms, the other with a rush seat like Van Gogh's. There was a shelf of books, mostly tattered copies of Beatrix Potter, a small sand tray with tin animals, and a big chest, once my father's tuck-box, containing a large number of wooden building blocks. There was a wind-up gramophone and a few old records, a framed print of Margaret Tarrant's sugary 'All Things Bright and Beautiful'. There were dark green blinds instead of curtains, and an ottoman in front of the windows.

Behind the nursery was my parents' bedroom which over-looked the back-yard and the roof of Hogg's dairy. The general effect was blue largely because of the shiny blue eiderdowns on the twin beds with their dark polished headboards rounded at the corners. Twin beds for married couples, like calling the drawing-room 'the lounge', were a further proof of being 'modern'. My grandparents' generation still slept in a double bed which my parents believed to be unhygienic. Between the beds was a cup-board with a chamber-pot in it and a small drawer below con-taining medicines; a far from hygienic arrangement I should have thought. Although the bathroom was next door to them, my mother and father always used the pot, though my mother, as a further proof of her modernity, emptied it herself every morning instead of leaving it to the maids as my grandparents did. Over the beds were two nineteenth-century lithographs: sly Pandora and her box, and Lady Hamilton looking rather distraught. The origi-nals were perhaps by Reynolds or Gainsborough. My mother believed them to be valuable because they were wedding presents from a rich woman. Over the gas fire was a water-colour, a gift of a local artist and 'rather modern'. It represented barges on the Seine. There was a tall mahogany wardrobe with mirrors, a quite good chest of drawers and a dressing-table in the window with silver hair brushes and a cut-glass scent spray with a bulb. My mother's jewel case had very little in it: a few rings, some art-deco clips, some ear-rings, a string of pearls, and Uncle George's 'peace offering'. There was a Coty powder box which was round and had a pattern of little black and orange powder puffs on it. This pattern was very important to me, but it wasn't until I saw one recently in an antique shop (£5), that I realized what the black and orange shapes represented.

The bathroom, with the only indoor lavatory, was pretty functional. My father used a heavy safety razor with a one-edged blade which he honed on a special leather strap. There was a loofah, a sponge and a pumice-stone on the wooden rack over the claw-footed bath. No bathroom was then complete without these objects.

My father's dressing-room built out over the back kitchen was tiny, although later I was to sleep in it in a child's wooden bed of Swiss origin that had been handed down from my great-grandfather. Before this it had little in it except a wardrobe and a chest of drawers with a mirror above. On the chest was a cedar-wood Chinese 'mess-box' full of collar-studs, stiffeners, golf-tees and, as I discovered later, a solitary French letter, surely by that time unreliable, which once I had learnt its function I used to show my giggling and impressed school friends. There were also some racing binoculars in a leather case, his crested hair brushes and a bottle of Bay Rum, a lotion he was later to blame for his bald patch. His use of Bay Rum with its spicy smell was untypical, imposed by a legacy of several crates left to him by a deceased acquaintance. He never used after-shaves or deodor-ants even after they became acceptable. He rated them on a level with carrying a pocket comb, one of his few serious taboos. There was a single picture in his dressing-room. It contained three stages of a cock fight, the cocks a collage of real feathers with only their beaks and claws drawn in. Along the walls of the bedroom floor were spidery etchings of harbours and shipping.

The top floor, under the fanciful eaves, contained the two

maids' bedrooms, mysterious, seldom visited territory with fluff under the iron bedsteads and worn parquet-patterned linoleum. There was a washbasin but no bath so I presume they used the one downstairs, but when and how often I could not say. The curtains were thin, the wallpaper dingy.

I can seldom remember fresh flowers in the house. Owing to the Depression, my parents felt increasingly badly off, but in the hall there was an earthenware jug with Cape Gooseberries and Honesty.

It would be absurd not to admit to the obsessive spirit in my remembering so minutely the contents and decoration of an unremarkable terrace house some fifty years ago, but I have always tended to understand people initially through the objects they accumulate and the manner in which they display or conceal them.

My father's discretion is for me implicit in the way he stored his rods and guns – the proof of his frustrated desire for a country life – in the chest in the hall, while the French letter he concealed in his 'mess-box' was indicative of his low sexual drive. Similarly my mother's thwarted theatrical ambitions, only partially alleviated by her involvement in amateur dramatics, were more openly expressed by the display of the signed photographs of past and present members of the Liverpool rep on the top of the piano 'off a ship', but these conclusions are of course retrospective.

It is impossible for an adult to paint with the naïvety of a child; the huge parents with their great heads and stick-like limbs, the neat formalized house, far too small to contain them, the grinning sun smiling down. It is equally beyond me to recreate how I saw my parents when I was very young, but there are two tableaux which do so for me.

The nursery at breakfast time: Bella and I seated in front of a different dish every day: fish cakes, grilled tomatoes on fried bread, kedgeree, eggs in various forms. My father liked to eat with me before he left for the office, standing in front of the window with a bowl of Grapenuts, and staring abstractedly into Ivanhoe Road. He usually said little but some mornings there would be the sound of intermittent muffled hooting from the tugs on the Mersey a mile or so away. His response to this was always identical. Joining the words together he would observe, 'It's foggy on the river.'

I have the impression that this response was not his originally, but something he remembered from his own Edwardian childhood. His life was much ruled by such formal responses. Many snatches of verse, the choruses of music-hall and popular songs, repetitive physical gestures (rubbing the skin between the base of the left thumb and forefinger with the thumb of the opposite hand), seemed to act as runes against the dangerous chaos of life. Potentially clever, it was as if he had deliberately trained himself to aim low. It made him an easy companion. His lack of competitiveness prevented any tension between us as I grew older. He was genuinely pleased at anything his children achieved but, on the negative side, offered us no incentive. 'As long as they're happy' was his reaction to whatever we did or didn't do. Good-looking and with an easy charm and a quiet wit, he was ruled by lethargy. My mother used to say, and he didn't contradict her, 'Tom's motto is never do today what you can put off until tomorrow week.'

She on the contrary was intensely ambitious and, I believe, very highly sexed. In neither direction was she fulfilled. Her ambitions were displaced; it was her children to whom she looked in order to realize them. Her sexuality was inhibited by her fear of the opinion of others. Only once, she told me later, was she nearly unfaithful to my father. In Chester at a dance (Tom must have been away fishing) a young man tried to persuade her to spend the night in an hotel. She was tempted to accept but finally refused on the grounds that she would have been forced to return home next morning in her evening dress. She sublimated her libido by a series of what she called 'affairs' with young homosexuals, revelling in their confidences and delighting in their company. This suited my father very well as there were comparatively few plays, and certainly no ballets, that he wished to see.

Every evening when my father was at The Albert I would be taken down to spend an hour with my mother in the lounge. She would put on a very elaborate performance for my benefit, reading a certain amount, *The Jungle Books* were my favourite,

19

imitating music-hall and cabaret artistes, and speaking of her early life in a rather indiscreet and grown-up way which widened its scope rapidly as I grew older and proved myself a precocious pupil at her knee.

I especially liked her to 'do' accents. Her Liverpool was perfect, her Cockney adequate, if stagey, and she could manage a fair approximation of Welsh, Lancashire, Scottish and Irish. It amused her to imitate a woman called Alice Delysia, who performed monologues in English with a French accent, but what impressed me most was when she recreated an American colonel she had met during the war.

'Lady,' she'd say with a broad twang, 'do you mind if I spit in the fire?' and would then swing round to face the grate and pretend to expectorate. For a long time afterwards I was convinced that all Americans indulged in this inexplicable custom.

In fact, despite her ear for accents, my mother had never been abroad except once, as a child, to the Isle of Man. She claimed, although a strong swimmer, to be afraid of the sea, but I believe it was more a question of insularity.

'Everyone says I'd adore New York,' she told me, 'and that New York would adore me, but . . .' Everyone in this case was a few of her more cosmopolitan friends. She did however go to London once a year and, on her return, loaded with toys from Hamleys, would paint it in glowing colours. 'I did five shows in four days,' she'd tell us, 'and had supper twice at the Savoy with Rex Evans.' Rex Evans was a night-club owner of the period, a plump and bespectacled man who performed sophisticated songs at the piano. He stood high in her pantheon. My father was delighted that Rex Evans should take my mother to the Savoy. He himself was rather intimidated by London and would never go there if he could avoid it. As to the Savoy, he would have considered that a waste of money as in some ways, and especially when it came to eating out, he was almost comically mean.

There was another aspect of those evenings I spent with my mother about which I had mixed feelings, and that was her recitation of several late-Victorian poems recalled from her childhood which she would send up in such a way that I soon realized that I was meant to be amused by their pathos, but which nevertheless moved me to furtive tears. One told of a cockney orphan girl returning to her sick little brother with

20

some flowers presented her by 'a bang-up lady' who had learnt of his plight. 'Flowers in 'eaven? I suppose so,' she replies in answer to his loaded question. Predictably, in the final verse, he is in a position to find out the answer to this theological conundrum. Starving waifs watching a banquet; 'naughty little Briar Rose' who saved a village from flooding at the cost of her own, until then worthless life; and a criminal, 'Burglar Bill', who breaks into a doll's house at the request of a winsome tot were others who figured in her repertoire. I dare say she knew she upset me with these mawkish poems but was unable to resist so receptive an audience. As a child, she told me, she had once recited a poem about the Boer War, then in progress, at a benefit concert. She had no idea what it meant but had even so reduced many of her audience to tears.

'You've seen them dragging the guns along at the Agricultural Hall,' she'd lisped. 'But nobody saw them at Ladysmith when the shells began to fall'; and as the widows and mothers who had lost husbands and sons 'in far Natal' sobbed into their black-edged handkerchiefs, she experienced a glow of pride.

While not beautiful or even pretty, my mother was both animated and vivacious. She should have been an actress, but her mother wouldn't have it. Once, and it was typical of my grandmother, she had taken my mother aged sixteen to an audition held by a Shakespearian actor-manager who was so impressed that he offered her an immediate position in his company. 'I wouldn't dream of allowing Maud to go on the stage,' said my grandmother; 'I just wanted to find out how good she was.'

My mother told this as a kind of joke at her mother's expense, but I believe it had upset her profoundly. She also maintained she wouldn't have liked acting anyway as she had too jealous and envious a temperament, but I didn't believe her, even then.

When my father came home from The Albert, he and my mother would go up and change for dinner and Bella took me away to be given Horlicks and ginger biscuits and got ready for bed. My parents always came in to hear my prayers and kiss me goodnight, and I fell asleep thinking of the dying boy with flowers and the drowning Briar Rose and the American colonel spitting in the fire.

21

Although my parents employed a series of house parlour-maids wearing black uniforms, aprons and caps, I can recall none of them during my early childhood. The people I remember clearly were my nanny Bella and the cook, Minnie Roberts, partly no doubt because they came and went several times throughout my childhood, sometimes on a temporary, sometimes on a more permanent basis, and remained in contact with the family throughout.

Bella had red hair and was given to what my mother called 'moods'. Nevertheless she was admitted to be 'superior', that is to say quiet rather than raucous, and with a minimal Liverpool accent, although she did say 'buke' and 'luke' instead of 'book' and 'look', and was so convinced this was correct that she tried to teach me to do the same. She was firm but fair and had a strong sense of humour although when she was amused she would compress her lips and shake with silent laughter as though reluctant to display her teeth. She was a strong believer in routine, insisting, before I was old enough to use the lavatory, that I sat on my pot until I'd been a 'good boy' or, if nothing was forthcoming, dosing me on syrup of figs. Every morning she cleaned out my earholes with a twist of cotton wool, its tip coated in vaseline, and examined my tongue. She tried to make me eat everything up, and put me reluctantly to rest every afternoon for precisely one hour.

My father, who was also fond of her, called her 'Mrs Spilsbury', after an eminent forensic expert of his youth called Dr Bernard Spilsbury whose close examination of the corpses of murder victims had sent several poisoners to the gallows. The reason for this nickname was that Bella was always bringing him food to sniff in order to confirm her opinion that it had 'gone off'. She was a strong swimmer and had once entered a contest which entailed battling against treacherous currents around the Great Orme in Llandudno. It transpired later that the other two entries were professionals and in consequence Bella came in very much last, but nevertheless finished the gruelling course. Bella stayed with us initially for at least five years, before she left to marry a long-distance lorry-driver called Jack, a gentle giant of a man who adored his small wife. Eventually they had a daughter called Beryl, who was very pretty and adept at tap-dancing in the manner of Shirley Temple. Unfortunately Jack didn't live very long and it was then that Bella returned to us.

22

One afternoon, when Jack and Bella were still courting and I was about three, instead of walking in Prince's or Sefton Park, she pushed my pram down Aigburth Road as far as the rather run-down district of Garston and off into a maze of streets which led eventually to the yard somewhere near the Mersey where Jack's employer housed his lorries. They loomed up all round me like elephants and Jack lifted me high into one of the driving compartments and allowed me to pretend to steer the great wheel. The yard was paved with cinders and had its own petrol pump. It was a hot summer's day, the sky was bright blue, the river sparkled and beyond it the Welsh mountains, some fifty miles away, appeared surprisingly close. That visit to Jack's yard remains loaded with inexplicable significance. I felt a party to their happiness, almost a conspirator.

Minnie Roberts and Bella were very close. Minnie was a lively woman with springy dark hair, strong glasses, and the rapid high-pitched cadences of her native North Wales. She was adept at creating a sense of excitement at the thought of treats to come, in particular of the promise of 'the beano' when my parents and Bella should chance to be absent at the same time. This didn't take place for several years, although she mentioned it frequently enough to keep me in constant anticipation. When 'the beano' eventually materialized, it turned out to be a very literal event encompassing baked beans on toast and staying up half-an-hour later than usual. 'Don't tell on me now,' said Minnie Roberts, but her conspiratorial manner and frantic gaiety were sufficient to dispel any sense of anti-climax. She encouraged me, and eventually my brother and sister, to call her 'Auntie Min'.

Auntie Min was married to an almost silent man called Tom who worked on the railways. Although Auntie Min lived in, they owned their own small house the other side of Sefton Park. The parlour was very clean and full of bric-à-brac, and had that mildly disquieting atmosphere of a room used for seances or psychic consultations although, despite her Celtic blood, Auntie Min was in no way 'gifted' in that direction. She was what was called 'a good plain cook', which suited my father who disliked elaborate dishes. Otherwise, apart from his insistence on finishing every meal with a savoury, he was not at all fussy. My mother on the other hand had a very sweet tooth. 'I put sugar on everything,' she'd say as though it were somehow a proof of her worldliness, 'even salad, and I love Chicken Maryland – that's a *banana* with *fried* chicken.' In fact however she was perfectly satisfied with Auntie Min's roasts, stews and over-cooked vegetables.

Apart from the anonymous housemaids, there was only one other creature in the house: a fat neuter tabby cat called Joey who lived entirely in the kitchen. My mother felt a cat to be necessary to discourage the mice, but she couldn't bear him anywhere near her. She put this down to a dream she'd had as a child in which she'd found herself lying on a bed of partly squashed kittens scratching and biting in their death-throes. Her mother had thought this phobia ridiculous and insisted on having her daughter, aged ten, photographed stroking, with a look of agonized repulsion, a kitten seated on a velvet cushion.

When I was three my brother Bill was born. Unlike me with my reluctance to leave the womb, he was minimally ahead of schedule. My mother's waters broke on the lavatory and I was rushed round by Bella to my maternal grandmother's flat a quarter of a mile away. Again, whereas I had been underweight and fractious, Bill was plump and contented, but it was not for a year or two that I recognized in him a distinct threat to my position. With his blue eyes, curls and sturdy body, he was an infinitely more attractive child. His nature too was sunny and his manner easy and agreeable but worse, from my point of view, he was adept at learning necessary skills. He could do up his shoelaces long before I could and whereas I was seven before I could read, he could manage it at four and a half. His socks stayed up where mine fell down. He enjoyed physical exertion where I detested it. Admittedly there was a tendency to smugness in his reiterated cry, 'I can do it easily', but then he usually could.

Nemesis paid him out in one direction only. We both ran through the gamut of what were known as 'childish ailments': German and common-or-garden measles, scarlet fever, chicken-pox, mumps and whooping-cough but, although I nearly died of influenza when I was about six, Bill was continuously plagued by recurrent and painful attacks of toothache and earache. Huge water blisters like army pill boxes erupted on his fair skin (they had to be pricked with a sterilized needle and the empty carapace removed with tweezers, an operation which gave me enormous

24

satisfaction). He had a hard time, frequently toddling into my parents' bedroom in the small hours sobbing, 'Why do I get everything?' Otherwise I suffered from the comparison, not from Bella or Auntie Min, although the former could sometimes become exasperated by my ham-fisted obstinacy in contrast to Bill's adeptness, and certainly not from my parents. My eagerness to show off appealed to my mother; my rebellious streak struck a suppressed chord in my father's nature. But most relations and certainly other children's nannies and their employers favoured Bill. I, who had been king of the castle, the centre of attention, the repository of lineal hopes, was entirely overshadowed by this golden child to such an extent that my mother felt obliged as some visitor lavished attention on him to cry out in defence of her less-favoured first-born, 'George has his fans too.'

My revenge lay in my discovery that Bill was a highly conventional little boy. On our walks, for instance, if he refused to agree to some whim of mine, I would threaten to pretend to have a fit in front of approaching strangers and would have my way. If I wanted some of his dinner I would tell him, while Bella was out of the room, that the source of the meat was a dead tortoise which had ended its life writhing with maggots and, as he had a queasy stomach, we would rapidly change plates. Although I was sometimes caught out and reprimanded severely for tormenting him, he never sneaked on me, partly because he had from his earliest years an understanding of the correct code, and perhaps also because he suspected, quite accurately, that I would invent other and worse revenges if he were to do so. We quarrelled continuously as children, but later got on much better. My mother chose to date this from his emergency operation for a ruptured appendix during which, for a whole night, his life hung in the balance – a typically dramatic explanation on her part. My own view is that our improving relationship was more gradual and due to my realization that our potentials were so different that we were not really in competition.

3

My mother and her brothers, Fred and Alan, usually called their mother 'Griff' when speaking to her directly and 'the Griff' when referring to her in the third person. This nickname was an invention of my Uncle Fred who had once introduced her, assuming the accent of a fairground barker or circus ringmaster, as 'The only Griff in captivity'. He was adept at such nonsense. When my grandmother and I played duets together at the upright piano, she inevitably and rightly critical of my lack of concentration, he would announce us as 'those famous virtuosi of the keyboard, Mr Umpty-Plum and Mrs Oochamacootch'.

'The Griff' suited my grandmother. It seemed to encapsulate her neat fastidiousness, her small but upright stature, her horn-rimmed glasses, her feet, permanently set at 'quarter to four' (another observation of Uncle Fred's), the result of a broken ankle sustained whilst playing golf. We children called her 'Gaga', presumably due to my early inability to pronounce 'Granny'. With its implication of senility she never liked this and was always trying to get us to amend it to 'Gargie', but we never did.

My mother and the Griff didn't get on all that well. Many women of the Griff's generation deliberately prevented their daughters from marrying so as to have the use of an unpaid companion and dogsbody. There were many such elderly and embittered spinsters in our neighbourhood whom we would meet whilst shopping and whose entire conversation centred nervously around 'Mother'. The Great War had helped to reinforce their ranks. They had lost sweethearts or fiancés in the trenches, and afterwards found themselves 'on the shelf'. The Griff hadn't succeeded here, nor in fairness had she wanted to, although my mother's comparatively late marriage at the age of thirty-four must have made it seem a distinct possibility.

Nevertheless she tended to treat Maud as though her main duty was to be at her beck and call.

She was also a skilful tease and my mother took teasing badly. The Griff's main weapon here was the assertion that 'Maud isn't a sport'. This gibe didn't only encompass my mother's refusal to play golf and bridge, both of which the Griff did, although extremely badly, but also her neither smoking nor drinking, her refusal to go abroad; and even her inability to drive a car. The Griff had once been to Knocke le Zoute in Belgium to play golf; had been 'finished' in Germany; and drove a Morris Minor very slowly and dangerously right into her early eighties. She would also ignore my mother's advice especially when she had asked for it. It wasn't beyond her to make my mother go round to her flat, some ten minutes away from Ivanhoe Road, to help her decide between two hats, only to settle inevitably on the one my mother had rejected. Furthermore when she was on holiday with us she would encourage my father, who needed little persuading, to linger at the golf-club bar so as to make them late for lunch, one of my mother's phobias which the Griff dismissed with a wave of her Gold Flake, although she herself expected punctuality from anyone lunching with her. Nor should one forget earlier traumas; the audition with the actor-manager, the photograph of Maud stroking the kitten. And of course, much as I loved her, it was not without some ambivalent feelings of pleasure that I would watch my mother rising to my grandmother's teasing, turning red with irritation, clenching her fists, leaving the room to conceal her repressed anger, especially as the Griff would enlist us children as conspirators.

I suspect however that at the bottom of their antipathy was my mother's grief at the early death of her beloved father and her resentment that during her childhood she had watched him treat my grandmother as though she were a precious piece of Dresden china, appearing to believe that she had done him an immense favour by marrying him. The Griff was, it's true, very spoilt. As the youngest of her family she had been pampered as a child and she had been equally indulged by her husband. Both her sons lived at home for most of her life and my mother was never far away. She had a maid and a cook who adored her despite her imperiousness. She would ring the bell and tell Mary, the quiet and pretty Irish parlour maid, 'You may poke the fire.' 'Suppose', said my mother, 'she said "I don't want to."''

As to why the Griff and my mother were on speaking terms, the reason was Maud's terror of rows, of being thought badly of whatever the provocation. What's more in some ways, and with good reason, she admired her.

The Griff had indeed many admirable qualities: generosity, a sense of fun, self-respect. Her chests of drawers and clothes cupboards were in apple-pie order, her household accounts correct to the ha'penny, and she had never been overdrawn in her life, even after my grandfather's early death had left her for a time in comparative poverty. My mother used to say, with a certain wistfulness, 'She has a very strong character.'

With children, while firm, she showed great empathy. Her toy drawer, as orderly as the rest, was full of treasures which she would get out one at a time rather than allow us to rummage; a technique which made playtime with her very special by removing the unsettling element of choice. She had scrap-books, a top which threw out multi-coloured sparks, games of snap and animal grab, spillikins, and a kind of bingo called Housie Housie. She would buy transfers where we damped a piece of paper bearing the faint imprint of an image, pressed it on the page of an exercise book and then peeled it back to reveal a brilliantly-coloured butterfly or rose. Teatime was always a treat. She would roll chocolate finger biscuits in thin bread and butter, or sculpt an apple to form a chicken with its drumsticks, peas and potatoes. She could also peel an apple so that the skin remained an unbroken spiral. She read to us well and patiently: the Blue and Red fairy tales, *The Wallypug of Wye*, *The Cuckoo Clock* and particularly the *Golliwog* books, large illustrated adventures, naturally in immaculate condition, in which the manly and ingenious Golly and some rather soppy wooden dolls emerged unscathed from terrible adventures. I still have a clear and anxious-making vision of them nearly drowning when the sea destroyed a dyke in Holland. Finally, and to the great embarrassment of my mother and our delight, she would sing and dance the favourites of her childhood: 'You should see me dance the polka', 'Tommy make room for your uncle, there's a little dear', and especially a rather frisky number called 'Now then, young men'. This went as follows:

Now then young men don't be melancholy.
It's my duty just to make you jolly.
Whenever things go wrong with me I never cry or pout.

At this point she would stick out her lip and rub the corners of her eyes, and then, after a pause, she would conclude with great emphasis,

For I *always* am, and I *mean* to be
The jolliest girl that's out.

During the last two lines she would raise an arm above her head and jig round on one leg.

And jolly she was most of the time, but the Griff was occasionally prey to bouts of deep depression lasting for several weeks or even months. She was then convinced that she had neither friends nor money. Her conversation excluded all other themes. No friends. No money. Round and round like a pet mouse on a wheel. This was not a recent development. She had apparently always suffered from these dark visitations known to her family as 'doing herself'. During the thirties it was suggested that she might benefit from psychological help and she was persuaded, much against her will, to visit several specialists. All they accomplished was to arouse her resentful contempt. She called them 'talking fools'.

One of her obsessions when she was 'doing herself' was that all she was fit for was to work as an attendant in a station lavatory. Her eldest brother, Frederick Harvey-Samuel, a distinguished London barrister, was apprised of this by my mother who was sent to stay with him several times before the Great War, presumably in the hope of making 'a catch'. Sweeping up the ends of his luxuriant moustache, a court-room mannerism he had carried into his private life, he passed judgement.

'It would have to be Lime Street,' he said thoughtfully. 'I couldn't afford to have a sister of mine working at Edge Hill. It might have a damaging effect on my practice if it became known that Edith was employed in this capacity at a goods station.' Frederic Harvey-Samuel died before I was born, but the Griff continued to maintain that working in a station lavatory was the only resort open to her in her friendless and penniless state.

After her depressions had run their course, she would wake

up one morning in the best of spirits. Life was agreeable once more. There was golf, bridge, 'runs' in the car, my mother to tease and badger, a gin and orange before lunch and a Gold Flake cigarette after it. The only lavatory she felt the need to resort to was her own. Her bathroom window was of particular dimpled glass and the same glass was let into the upper panels of the flat's front door. I have come upon this glass since, but it is only comparatively recently that I have recognized it as the source of an instant evocation of my grandmother. Despite her maid, she chose to answer the door herself, and would cry, 'Wait a minute!' (her entire conversation was punctuated by this phrase) as her blurred and faceted image materialized behind the panes. This same glass still produces a certain anxiety: Are my nails clean? My knee-length socks with their concealed elastic garters pulled up? My rebellious 'cow's lick' of hair combed back? She was very critical of such details. 'George is quite frightened of the Griff', said my mother. And so I was, but I was very fond of her too.

I was not, however, at all frightened by the hysterical barking of her current dog as she came to open the door, although I am in general as wary of dogs as of lighting gas appliances or opening champagne. I have no idea why this should be so. My father had a spaniel when I was a baby. He had bought it for when he was invited to shoot by his uncles but it turned out to be gun-shy and given to biting people so it had to be put down. It never bit me, however, and indeed I was told later that I was extremely fond of it and pulled its ears and tail with impunity. Nor, as far as I know, was I ever bitten or menaced by any other dog. Nevertheless for as long as I can remember I have felt apprehensive of them, and my brother Bill's only, but extremely effective, riposte to my teasing during our childhood walks was to threaten to pat strange dogs, a ploy which reduced me instantly to placatory behaviour.

The Griff's dogs aroused no such atavistic anxieties because although nervous barkers – 'good house dogs' is how she described them – they were without any aggression or indeed character. What they were was indistinguishably wet with brown sentimental eyes and perpetually wagging tails. As one died, it was replaced by another which, although temporarily appealing as a puppy ('Isn't it an Uncle Wuff,' said the Griff, an expression she used for anything sweet or cuddly), soon grew up to become indistinguishable from its predecessor. They were all rather basic animals of no known breed and yet lacking the grotesque collage effect of dogs conceived on vacant lots. They might have posed for the 'D is for Dog' entry in a rather unimaginative alphabet book, yet if anyone tried to please my grandmother by offering the cliché that 'mongrels are more intelligent' she would respond firmly by insisting they were cross breeds. They were given names as banal as themselves: Jock was followed by Zip who was replaced by Peter. Jock was the first I can remember. Peter was 'put to sleep' during the war because the bombing made him hysterical. None of them resembled or grew to resemble the Griff in either appearance or character.

The 'cross-breed' syndrome was typical of her. It tied in with her insistence that people coming to see her took the 33 tram instead of the 1 or 45. She also told everybody that the few mediocre Victorian prints she possessed were 'artist's proofs', although I doubt she had any idea what an artist's proof was. Her family came from Birmingham, but she would never admit it. She always maintained that she was born in Warwickshire.

The Griff's flat was in a three-storeyed Edwardian block called York Mansions in a street of the same period called Sandringham Drive. The building was of red brick with 'Tudor' eaves. There were six flats in all; hers was on the first floor to the right of the slightly pompous entrance. A caretaker and his family, the Polands, lived in the basement below the level of the square back garden with its large tree in the centre of the sparse lawn. The stairs of York Mansions were of uncarpeted granite which Mrs Poland mopped down every morning, polishing the tenants' brass bells and knockers *en route*. She was a pale thin woman who sighed resignedly when you had to pass her at her task. Mr Poland, equally lugubrious, did the garden under my grandmother's directions. She would point at the weeds in an imperious manner. She was an accomplished pointer at things for other people to do; my mother gave an excellent imitation of this trait. If a workman came to the flat she would stand over him and point at what needed doing until he'd finished. 'Then', she would tell my mother, 'I gave him a cigarette.' She'd say this with the magnanimous and gracious air of one who had awarded a major and much sought-after honour.

31

The Polands had a rather large, plump moon-faced almost silent son called Billy. We would play with him sometimes in the garden, but he was as conscientious and melancholy as his parents. We felt he had been told he had to play with us whether he wanted to or not. It went with his parents' job, like the stairs and the weeding.

The rooms in my grandmother's flat led off a very dark dog's leg passage. The rooms at the front (the dining-room, the lounge and 'the little room' for guests), and at the back (my grandmother's bedroom, the bathroom and the maid's bedroom) were well-lit, while those at the sides (the kitchen, and the 'boys' room') faced the walls of the adjoining houses and were almost as dark as the passage.

The Griff's furniture was solidly Edwardian and rather out of scale: great wardrobes, massive dining-room table and chairs of an unpleasing orange wood, 'nests' of occasional tables, but the lounge – and it was typical of her wish to be 'up to date' that she called it that – had a bright magenta carpet, white-textured wallpaper and sea-green curtains. Her bedroom was more conventional – faded pink chintz – while on her dressing-table were silver-backed hairbrushes and pretty little tortoise-shell boxes for hair pins and other necessities. She always took, even during her depressions, what my mother called 'a pride in herself'.

In the front hall by the coat stand was something rather odd, a cigarette machine into which she and her sons put money for their packets of Gold Flake. It was filled once a fortnight by one of those men to whom my grandmother, appropriately enough in this case, 'gave a cigarette'. On the chest which faced the hat stand were some comparatively large wooden carvings of two dappled horses with detachable huntsmen and a small pack of hounds. She had bought these on a holiday in the New Forest. On the wall behind them hung two rather busy etchings. One celebrated the great events of Queen Victoria's reign. In the centre of it sat the old Queen on the occasion of her Golden Jubilee while around her soldiers slaughtered natives, great ships were launched, and the Crystal Palace glittered in Hyde Park. The other was devoted to the events of the same year, and contained an image which both fascinated and appalled me. In a menagerie or zoo a roaring lion reared up, the bars of its cage snapping like matchsticks, the bustled and top-hatted crowd recoiling in confused panic. Perhaps my fondness for zoos stems from this corner of a small etching. I have always enjoyed being alarmed. The only other picture I can recall was a misty drawing of the young, long-haired Paderewski over the upright piano in the lounge, presumably a sign of my piano-teaching grand-father's admiration for that virtuoso. My grandmother was unin-terested in the arts although she very much disliked modernism. She referred to all modern works of art of whatever tendency as 'futurist'.

Her two sons, Fred and Alan, lived with her; Fred until he married in the forties, Alan until she died a decade later. They were not at all alike, as different in their temperaments as Bill and I. As children Fred had employed similar tactics to my own to get his way. On cold nights Fred would force his younger brother to warm up his bed before allowing him to climb into his own. If Alan showed reluctance Fred would begin to recite 'Wolsey's farewell', a speech which always reduced Alan to hysterical tears, and rather than hear it through, he would submit to his role as a human warming-pan.

They had both been sent to Clifton, the only public school with a Jewish house. The housemaster, a Mr Pollack, was a cousin of my grandfather's and both his son and grandson were to become housemasters in their turn. When my grandfather died there was not enough money for his sons to stay on there and they had to leave and go into business. Alan accepted this without rancour, but it made Fred both bitter and resentful and, witty and charming as he could be, there remained a mistrustful streak in Fred's nature which emerged strongly when he had taken drink. Alan was a much sweeter character and showed no rancour at Fred's teasing, which continued into their middle age. Alan for instance read very little while Fred was, like his father, a devoted Dickensian. During the thirties, in my hearing, someone asked Alan if he had read a particular book, I believe it was *Rebecca*. Fred put his head abruptly on one side, always a sign he was about to make a joke. 'I shouldn't think so,' he said, 'he hasn't finished *The Wouldbegoods* yet.'

Physically too there was little resemblance between them. Fred was quite short and plump with the face of a clownish baby; Alan rather tall with more defined and sensitive features, more conventional on the surface, and given to describing every detail of his daily life as if the late departure or early arrival of a train at Lime Street Station, or the menu provided at an annual dinner, concealed some essential clue to the meaning of the universe. It was almost as if he were bent on establishing an alibi to satisfy a particularly suspicious detective-inspector.

I believe that Fred, like my mother, would have chosen to go on the stage. He could play the ukelele, dance nimbly, sing adequately, and time jokes brilliantly. When very young I was taken to see him in an amateur production of a musical comedy called *Victoria and her Hussar* and remember the audience becoming hysterical with laughter at his performance. During the Great War, throughout which he remained, mysteriously for a public schoolboy, a private soldier, he had spent most of his time in a concert party, and I believe he had the talent to succeed if he had decided to turn professional. The need to help support his mother probably made him decide against it and perhaps reinforced his sense of grievance. The 'failure' of having to leave Clifton early gave him an obsessive determination to succeed.

He went into oil, a firm called Samuel Banner, starting as a commercial traveller; it was a period of his life about which he could be extremely funny, but which I suspect he resented strongly. He rose to become a director alongside his boyhood friend Cyril Banner who, as heir to the company, had no need to struggle as Fred did to achieve this position. He also, in middle age, became Captain of Formby Golf Club. Formby, one of the several clubs strung out along the sandy coast between Liverpool and Southport, was considered the smartest. To become Captain at all was an honour but for Fred, as a Jew, it was a formidable achievement. Golf clubs tended to be anti-Semitic. During the late fifties, dining with my father and Uncle Fred, I had raised the question. Was Formby anti-Semitic? My father, who was also a member, denied it. He hadn't an atom of racial prejudice in him; a quality he had proved in marrying my mother in the face of familial opposition. Not so Fred. 'They've got their own club,' he said, 'they don't know how to behave. They drink lemonade and bring out wads of money to pay for it. They discuss business.'

My father was rather shocked, and yet the anti-Semitic Jew is not uncommon, and usually Fred concealed his prejudice

34

behind a defensive humour. He told me once that he had been involved in a slight car accident with a Jewish man who, in a state of high excitement, had demanded his name. 'Isaac,' said Uncle Fred. 'This is no time for joking,' screamed his adversary. 'Vat's your real name?'

Fred had never kept up with Clifton but Alan, who had been removed even younger, had always done so and regularly attended the Pollack House old boys' dinner in London. One year he persuaded Fred to join him, putting him on his honour to behave. The dinner was held in an hotel in Park Lane. While the old boys were drinking their cocktails asking each other what had happened to Cohen minor who had been such a promising full-back, or whether J.R.Goldberg was still in Bangkok, a page boy opened the door in search of a guest for whom he had a message.

'Mr Smith please,' he shouted. 'Mr Smith please.'

Uncle Fred was unable to resist the opening. He hunched his shoulders and spread the palms of his hands upwards: 'Vat initial?' he demanded.

My mother's attitude was more ambivalent. She would often claim to be 'proud of her Jewish blood', but with her awareness of anti-Semitism, was very disturbed by any overt Jewish characteristics or any scandal involving Jews. She would express relief if a financier accused of fraud had an obviously Christian name and deplored, during the war, Jewish women wearing expensive fur coats in queues or talking too loudly to each other. Like Jonathan Miller in the *Beyond the Fringe* sketch, she felt she was Jewish rather than a Jew.

I don't think the Griff gave it much thought. She would occasionally serve gefilte fish, but otherwise her cuisine was in no way kosher. From time to time she would invite the Reverend Frampton to lunch. He was a rabbi, a man of great culture and charm, but very anglicized. He dressed like a clergyman of the Church of England, and I was disappointed the first time I met him to discover he had no beard or high-crowned hat. The Griff's main dilemma apropos her race lay in relation to her burial. Her husband was buried in the Orthodox Cemetery at Broad Green and she wanted to lie next to him. This however would involve being shaved and anointed with oil, and vain to the last, she disliked the idea of not 'looking her best' even in the coffin. In the end she had decided that the proximity of her much-loved Albert Isaac was more important than her invisible final bow. My mother used to say that the Griff's main regret in relation to her funeral was the thought of being unable to see who turned up.

What with Fred's resentment, my mother's nervousness and the Griff's indifference, it was Alan alone who involved himself in the Jewish community, especially devoting himself to Harold House, a Jewish Boys Club, and to the Jewish Lads Brigade of which he became Colonel. When we were small we were sometimes taken to watch the Brigade move down Prince's Boulevard with Alan, extremely smart in his uniform with its Sam Brown belt, marching at its head. It always seemed to be a clear grey winter's day on these occasions. I can hear the drums and bugles drawing closer and I felt proud of my Uncle Alan, so serious and precise, as they swung past. Yet this didn't stop me laughing when Alan had fallen asleep one Sunday after lunch and was snoring and Fred suggested that the noise he was making was 'ooorghh-cadetzzz'.

Alan had been a Lieutenant in the 1914–18 war and a casualty too. While demonstrating the use of poisonous gas the wind had changed, and as a result, throughout the twenties and thirties, he was in and out of a nursing home for major operations on his intestines. The scars on his stomach were as complicated as a railway junction but he never complained. The nursing home was in Gambia Terrace and overlooked a rather romantic graveyard in a steep valley of sandstone with the Anglican Cathedral rising slowly on the other side. Gambia Terrace was, like much of inner Liverpool, respectable Georgian architecture and, like the whole district, had already begun to 'go down'. In the late fifties John Lennon had a chaotic flat there. It was close to the Art School which was itself round the corner from the Liverpool Institute where Paul McCartney did less and less work as the two became involved with Rock and Roll. The Cathedral, of which my father had seen the foundation stone laid by Edward VII, was completed only very recently.

Between operations Alan worked on the Cotton Exchange and later for a large store called Owen Owens, but it was not until middle age that he was fit enough for long enough to pursue a steady career. He joined a firm which manufactured children's clothes for Marks & Spencer and eventually became a director. He was also involved in managing the Basnett Bar, a seafood restaurant near the Liverpool Playhouse much used by the theatrical profession and the slightly raffish set which included Brian Epstein. When the Basnett Bar was pulled down he became a partner in a restaurant in Chester and still goes there most days at lunchtime to welcome guests and check that everything is 'as it should be'. Alan has always been a meticulous believer in things being done correctly.

His other great passion was and remains The Ramblers, an amateur football club for Liverpudlian public and grammar schoolboys founded over one hundred years ago. He, as the longest serving member, was elected honorary President for the centenary year at the age of eighty-four and had to make a speech at the dinner, a task which occupied and obsessed him for three years before the event. He was especially worried that he might leave someone out from those who had to be thanked. But on the night it was a triumph, and he was much moved by the warmth of the applause. He was given a record of his speech on cassette but, while he was on holiday in the Isle of Man, it was stolen by a burglar. Happily, it was not the only copy and could be replaced. I believe that the Ramblers' centenary dinner was the high spot of Alan's life, all of it spent, with the exception of the 1914–18 war, holidays and trips abroad, within a quarter of a square mile.

Fred would never have taken three years worrying about a speech. He was a brilliant public speaker, much in demand for golf-club dinners. He never improvised, however, but would rehearse and time himself until he sounded entirely spontaneous. He had an equal talent for composing verses set to popular tunes for special occasions, which he and Alan would perform together accompanied by Fred's ukelele. At my parents' wedding reception they scored a great hit with Fred's version of 'It ain't gonna rain no more':

> This afternoon at three o'clock
> Our hearts were beating fast.
> My brother turned to me and said
> 'We've got her off at last.'

It was Fred who had been instrumental in my parents' meeting. He had invited Tom home to tea after a rugger match and

Tom had fallen in love with my mother immediately. It was not Maud's first engagement. Just after the war she had almost married a rich man called Jack Eliot Cohen, but had broken it off because he had no sense of humour. The Eliot Cohens were the reverse of upset at this: not in this instance because of my mother's race – their name alone would dispel this as a grounds for disapproval – but because she had no dowry.

When Maud eventually became engaged to my father she received, as was then the custom, many congratulatory flowers. Reading out the accompanying cards to the Griff she came to Mrs Eliot Cohen's contribution: 'We are delighted and relieved', she read. The Griff exploded with indignation until Maud told her that she had added the 'and relieved'.

She was adept at teasing the Griff by such means. It never failed. On another occasion she was reading out a pamphlet in connection with an appeal for the Liverpool Foot Hospital, an organization on whose committee she served. 'And thanks are due to Mrs Tom Melly', she improvised, 'for allowing her feet to be photographed.' 'You didn't!' shouted the Griff indignantly. My mother's feet had always been a disaster area of twisted joints and bunions.

Serving on charitable committees was very much an obligation for the middle classes between the wars. My father, despite his indolence, was chairman of the Foot Hospital committee, although probably only to please my mother; his own feet were rather elegant. My mother did several days' voluntary work a week for 'The Personal Service', a forerunner of the Citizens' Advice Bureau, in which Tom was also involved, and Alan, as I said, was very active in this direction. Fred however did very little – his cynicism dismissed charity as beside the point – but he did join the Masons. I was very curious about the Masons even when I was quite young. He showed me his trowel and apron, but refused to tell me what they actually got up to, although sometimes I heard him in the 'boys' room' reciting the ritual for his next step up the Masonic ladder.

My curiosity was intensified to an unhealthy degree after I had bought a pamphlet on the subject from a rosy-cheeked, beshawled old Catholic woman who came to the door. The cover showed some hooded figures about to commit a ritual murder; the whole text accused the organization of every kind of wickedness and

38

blasphemy. With an early taste for Gothic horrors, I was even more fascinated. Was it possible that Uncle Fred with his jokes and ukelele was involved in such things? I did not dare ask him, but I showed the pamphlet to my father. He dismissed it out of hand but added that he found the Masons both ridiculous and dubious in their support for each other in business.

Fred tried to interest Alan in the Masons but I don't think he succeeded. I should guess Alan would have been discouraged by the amount of learning by heart involved.

That Alan and Fred, both over thirty by the time I was born, should share and continue to share the same bedroom for many years, may seem odd today. It was less so then. Alan was and remains a bachelor, but Fred, on the contrary, was a great one for the girls. My mother frequently told me that she could remember him and his friend Cyril Banner, while still in their teens, going out to parade along the prom at Llandudno in the hope of picking up 'a bit of fluff'. Fred was, I discovered later, highly sexed and perfectly prepared to indulge himself, but he had no intention of marrying until he was good and ready, and living at home was no doubt a useful alibi. I suspect he was mostly drawn to shopgirls, barmaids and waitresses, although once, during the thirties, he had a serious mistress, a rather glamorous blonde divorcée with a child, who gave my grandmother some alarm. It didn't last, however, and he returned to more casual promiscuity. During the late fifties his sexual philosophy led to us quarrelling so severely that he cut me out of his will. Separated from my first wife, I resisted his instructions to divorce her before she 'takes every penny you've got'. 'Always wriggle,' he told me, 'that's what kept me out of trouble. I always wriggled.'

Despite what I feel to be dubious in his character, I much regret we never made it up. Apart from the laughter he gave me, he was extremely kind and generous to me during my childhood. He was the first to take Bill and me to restaurants; my father considered it an absurd extravagance. We went to The State, a grand establishment by Liverpool standards with art nouveau stained-glass windows, a string quartet and the rich smell of roasts and stews. The speciality was 'chicken on the griller', a delicacy I misinterpreted, genuinely the first time, as 'chicken on the gorilla', a sinister form of cuisine that I was eager to sample. Having scored a hit with this notion, I didn't hesitate to repeat it on every possible occasion. This I believe to be a universal vice in children and an extremely tiresome one. My subsequent malapropism, 'suggestive biscuits' for 'Digestive biscuits', was equally successful and I was guilty of looking on any lunch table as an excuse for reviving it long after I was aware of its inaccuracy.

If Fred was a bachelor from choice and the need to support his mother, Alan remained one from temperament. Several girls, according to my mother, were 'keen' on him but eventually turned elsewhere for lack of encouragement. There was one in particular who probably remained a spinster her whole life for Alan's sake. She was one of the 'Mother' brigade, but a woman of spirit and dry wit, usually encountered riding a large bicycle down Lark Lane with a shopping basket on the front and a back pedal brake. Her devotion to Alan was so obvious as to arouse Fred's mockery. He maintained every Christmas that she was crocheting a little net bag to support Alan's 'arrangements'.

'Arrangements' was the Griff's word for the sexual organs. I was first aware of it when she took me, as quite a small boy, to the Walker Art Gallery. We stopped in front of a Cranach. She looked at it with some distaste. 'You can't tell me, George,' she said, 'that ladies' and gentlemen's arrangements are pretty.' I had, at that time, no firm view on the subject, but at least I was more aware than most of my contemporaries as to what adult arrangements looked like.

This was because Maud and Tom had somewhere absorbed the theory that it was healthier for children to be exposed to their parents' nakedness from the start. This was comparatively unusual thinking for the time and was especially odd in that they were not particularly 'advanced' in any other direction. Nevertheless we were encouraged to accompany them to the bathroom to watch my father shave and my mother in the bath, or my father in the bath and my mother on the lavatory. I am unable to analyse the effect of this on my sexual development, nor to decide what they imagined it might be. All it gave me during my childhood was something, like the French letter in my father's 'mess-box', to swank about to my school friends.

*   *   *

40

As the Griff was one of twelve children she must have had a lot of relations and so, though on a lesser scale, had her husband. Nevertheless, although it is always said to be a Jewish characteristic, neither she nor my mother and uncles were at all obsessed by the structure of the family, and those I met or heard about existed in familial isolation. I didn't even know in most cases from which side they came. It was on the contrary the Mellys who were concerned with who was whose second cousin twice removed.

Of the Griff's childhood I knew nothing except that she had developed a precocious taste for wine, and that whenever she had asked hopefully what there was to drink for luncheon, her mother had always answered, 'Water, Edith.' Of her finishing school in Germany she was equally vague. She would sometimes recite a piece of doggerel about a miller's three sons, all she retained of what was once presumably a fair knowledge of the language, and the only other thing she chose to remember was a visit to a famous sculpture, the nude torso of Venus, which was exhibited in a dark-room hung with black velvet and revolved slowly on a podium under a flesh-coloured spotlight.

I remained in ignorance as to how she came to meet my grandfather or the setting for their courtship. Of their early days together in Ivanhoe Road she told me only that she had 'draped her own mantelpiece', an accomplishment apparently denied to the majority of her contemporaries, but that was all.

Of her eleven siblings I met only one, her sister Lily, who was married and lived in Monte Carlo. She was a small, vivacious woman who always referred to herself as 'Naughty little Auntie Lily', wore strong scent and seemed to me, on the one occasion she visited Liverpool during my childhood, the epitome of Continental sophistication. I suspect I first heard of her from my mother whilst walking past a particular house in Alexandra Drive, a long curving street of large late-Victorian houses which links Sandringham Drive to Ivanhoe Road with its more modest terraces. The house was of cream stucco in the style of an Italianate villa and with a glass porch supported on slender but ornate iron columns. The words 'Monte Carlo' have always projected this house like a magic-lantern slide on my mind's eye, while similar architecture, in the Holland Park area of London for example, has the same effect in reverse.

During the German breakthrough in 1940 Lily and her husband were trapped in Vichy France. Her husband too was Jewish and they were by then quite old. We heard after the war that they had died of malnutrition.

Lily, who loved comfort, had stayed at the Adelphi during her visit. The Griff put up very few people as the only route to her spare-room was through the 'boys' room' with its distinctive smell of cleaning fluid and shoe polish. Both Fred and Alan were very particular about their appearance. Nevertheless there was an annual visit from her middle-aged niece, Cis Pollack, who was married to one of the Clifton Pollacks and whose son Phil was to become housemaster there in his turn. No one could call Cis beautiful; she resembled an elderly Harpo Marx. But she was one of those rare people whose inner qualities are immediately discernible. Children were drawn to her like a toy-shop window. She had a great sense of fun and adored teasing my grandmother whom she always called 'Auntie'. She was involved with a charity for East End Jewish girls and was constantly being asked to their weddings. At one of these, she told us, the father-in-law of her erstwhile protégée stood up and asked, 'Who'll swop a bitta fat for a roast potater?' Cis lived to a great age, dying at her son's house in Clifton; a move she effected with some reluctance as she was devoted to her own little house in Cricklewood. When I was doing a gig in Bristol during the seventies I visited her only a week or two before she died. She was in bed, very frail, and wandering in her mind, but the sweetness, almost saint-like in its charisma, was as powerful as ever.

The Griff's only other regular guest was another niece, Lulu Davis, who lived with her sister Emmy in Birmingham, or Warwickshire as the Griff would have it. Lulu was my godmother and allegedly well-off. I thought of her as rather dashing, but this may have been connected with her name. One of Uncle Fred's pieces on the ukelele was a song of the twenties called 'Don't bring Lulu'. It was about a man who is giving a party. His friends are welcome to turn up with any companion of their choice – 'Rose with the turned-up nose', 'Peg with the wooden leg' – but the eponymous heroine is barred. She 'knocks things off the shelf'. She 'always wants to do just what we don't want her to' and generally creates havoc. Lulu Davis certainly appeared conventional enough in her behaviour, but for a child a song is as real as a person. After all if Uncle Fred could take part in ritual Masonic murders, there was no reason why Lulu, back in Birmingham, mightn't revert to knocking things off the shelf.

But this was only speculation. What I knew for a fact was that Lulu was extremely mean. She would give us sixpence where other relatives would hand over half-a-crown and, considering I was her godson, her birthday presents were so meagre that I was even more reluctant than usual to write her a thank-you letter. My mother, rather beadily, told me that it was 'worth keeping in good books' as I might well be mentioned in her will. I eventually blew it on my nineteenth birthday when she sent me a packet of Gold Flake. I was stationed in Malvern in a naval camp, and I wrote to her a postcard pointing out that as Malvern was quite near Birmingham she could have hitch-hiked over and saved herself the stamp. Naturally enough I never heard from her again and, when she died, no lawyer wrote to advise me to get in touch if I wished to hear something to my advantage.

My mother was a little more forthcoming about her relations, but only when they had amused her in some way.

There were three Jewish Irish cousins, elderly women as poor as synagogue mice who lived in London, and whom she liked to imitate. When she visited them, one of them would always press a pound in her hand and cut short protestations by saying, 'Now don't annoy me', in her strong Dublin brogue. They were upset when she failed to marry Jack Eliot Cohen, a match they supported on the grounds that 'it will please your Uncle Lou'. Uncle Lou was another, Liverpool-based, brother of the Griff's but I learnt nothing more about him, except that he had been married to a lady called Auntie Reb who had provided enormous Edwardian teas for Maud and her brothers, and was always worried that there wasn't enough to satisfy 'the de-ah children'.

When Maud became engaged to my father they went to London, and she took him to visit the Irish cousins. They had forgiven her for failing to please her Uncle Lou, but feigned indignation on Tom's behalf for having to meet them.

'What will your fiancé think of you?' they cried. 'Bringing him to meet all your relations!'

There was also a rich first cousin of Maud's, a girl called Joan Harvey-Samuel who later married a military man and who spent

43

her entire life complaining about everything. She had her own lady's maid whose shortcomings were a constant irritant to her. She would begin most of the conversations she had with my mother in their teens with the phrase 'that dreadful maid Rose!'

With all these I became, at one remove, familiar. They would figure briefly in my mother's entertainments for me in the lounge at Ivanhoe Road after tea. They would pop up like characters in a radio comedy series, recognized and loved for their catch-phrases: 'Now *don't* annoy me', 'the de-ah children', 'that dreadful maid Rose'.

More substantial were her tales of her Uncle Fred Harvey-Samuel, the barrister who had lived in Wimpole Street and who was so concerned that the Griff, if she was determined to work in a station lavatory, should only be employed at a main-line junction. Even the Griff occasionally mentioned him because he had 'passed out first in all England', a feat which put him on a level with the signed artist's proofs. He sounded an impressive, if somewhat intimidating, figure offering Maud, a nervous young provincial girl with her hair only just up, a temporary glimpse into the great world of London with liveried servants and a carriage at the door.

Maud told me of smart dinner parties where the sweets were enormous architectural confections which, despite her sweet tooth, she felt obliged to refuse in favour of milk pudding in case the insertion of an ill-judged spoon should cause the whole trembling edifice to topple off the plate and on to the carpet. She was, I gathered, in some awe of her Uncle Fred as he could be witheringly sarcastic.

He was a keen bridge player and one evening, when the only guests were another couple eager for a few rubbers, regretted her inability to make up a four. Maud was able to tell him that since her last visit she had in fact learnt to play, as the Griff had told her it was selfish not to. She and her uncle were partners. The stakes were high, and partly from nerves, partly from lack of ability, she played extremely badly. When the beaming guests had departed with their winnings, her uncle poured himself a stiff brandy and soda. After sweeping up his moustache, he turned to her and remarked mildly, 'Did Edith say it was selfish of you *not* to learn bridge?' She blushed crimson and burst into tears.

44

Yet she was fond of him and regretted, following his early death, that the life he'd shown her was no longer open to her, the door closed. On the rare occasions when she and Tom were in London together, and inevitably got lost, she would always say, 'I think we're somewhere near Uncle Fred's.' For the rest of his life, whether on a North Wales by-pass or the outskirts of Nottingham, if ever my father wasn't sure of the way, he would repeat this sentence to himself.

In Liverpool, by the time I was old enough to take in people, there were very few relations of my mother's living there. Off Lark Lane, in a small flat facing Sefton Park was a sad, freckled cousin called Dodo, a middle-aged spinster whose only companion was a small and harmless dog of puggish origins called Terror. Poor Dodo, like her aunt the Griff, suffered from deep depressions only, in her case, with no one close to turn to. In the middle thirties, shortly after it had become necessary to put down the blind and incontinent Terror, poor Dodo gassed herself.

Maud's other Liverpudlian cousins were two unmarried sisters, Winnie and Ethel Mussons. They both had sallow complexions, and high mournful voices tinged by the sing-song Liverpool accent. Ethel, in particular, had been Maud's great friend and confidante before the war. They had gone to dances together, and always met next morning at Sissons tea-rooms for what my mother called 'a thorough committee'. They discussed, with appalled relish, the outrages of one 'Racer' Marsh, so named because she was considered 'fast'.

'Did you see?' Ethel remarked at one 'committee' after a dance at the Wellington Rooms. 'Racer Marsh had *shaved* under her *arms*!'

Sometimes Ethel would ring up my mother, breathless to transmit some piece of scandalous intelligence. When Maud asked her who on earth had told her, Ethel, after a pause, would usually reply, 'Now I come to think it over – you did.'

Ethel and Maud went ice-skating together, played lawn-tennis at the Mersey Bowman in Sefton Park, and discussed men endlessly, if innocently; Maud believed until well into her teens that you conceived a baby by kissing, a theory which gave her many moments of anxiety. They were both 'keen' on a man called Jimmy Duncan who, for some reason, was considered unsuitable. Not long ago I asked Uncle Alan why this should have been so. He thought for some time. 'I can't imagine,' he told me eventually, 'he always struck me as a thoroughly decent feller.' Perhaps it was simply because he wasn't Jewish and my grandfather was still alive.

Maud told me that Jimmy Duncan, when he had friends with him, would sometimes ring her up at home to get her to belch 'God Save the King' down the telephone, an unladylike accomplishment of hers which occasionally featured at my request in her after-tea divertissements.

After the war and her eventual marriage, my mother and Ethel became less close. Towards the end of the thirties, presumably for financial reasons, the Mussons opened a cake shop in Lark Lane. It was called Sugar and Spice and was in competition with the long-established Miss Stephenson's a few doors up. My mother felt obliged to patronize Sugar and Spice but would furtively slink into Miss Stephenson's as well. Miss Stephenson herself, a formidable old lady with a striking resemblance to Queen Victoria, was noted for her brandy snaps for which Maud had conceived an almost indecent passion. Ethel's cakes, while pure and wholesome, had a somewhat amateur look to them.

The Griff, who unlike Maud didn't care what people thought of her, remained completely faithful to Miss Stephenson despite her family ties with the rival establishment. Her imperious behaviour in local shops was a continuous embarrassment to my mother. Once, in Irwin's, the grocers, when a plain assistant hurried forward to attend to her, she announced that she 'wished to be served by the pretty young lady'.

4

A first cousin of my father's, a plump, bespectacled, kindly, noisy, mildly pompous man called Willie Bert Rawdon Smith, devoted his later years, following his retirement to Coniston Water, to writing a small pamphlet called 'The George Mellys'. His object, given in the preface, was 'to enlighten the next generation about the last, who either never knew them, or only knew them when children and therefore more for what they had in their pockets than for what they were'. The main body of the work does indeed deal with the Chatham Street Mellys, but there is a section on the Riversleas, and notes on those servants who remained with the family over a long period. I must admit that from my point of view it's a very useful crib.

Willie Bert's mother was a Melly, but I believe his obsession with the family was not merely due to a desire to be associated with a more unusual name than his own. Of his mother Beatrice, he writes:

> In 1881 she married Francis Rawdon Smith (1851–1930), a member of a Liverpool family then living in Shropshire. He was an only child and thoroughly spoilt. The marriage ended by her leaving her husband in 1891. A deed of separation was drawn up giving her the custody of the four children. . . . Owing to what was then an invidious position she did not go into Society much.

Could it have been this which made him so much more obsessive about his connection with the Mellys than most of those who bore the name? Certainly my father, the direct male heir, showed no great interest in the minutiae of his family history. Nor was he beyond teasing Willie Bert on the subject.

When my Great-Uncle Bill died in the forties, leaving 90 Chatham Street to the University and the drawing-room furniture to the museum, there was one object which Willie Bert felt merited special consideration. This was a massive and enormous book supported on an elaborate if spindly brass lectern. It had been presented to my great-great-grandfather, George Melly, by the electorate of Stoke-upon-Trent after business reasons had forced him to retire as their MP. The tortoiseshell front was decorated with oval china plaques representing the crests of the Five Towns, and inside were stiff board pages, tile-like designs by local art students, much influenced by the Arts and Crafts movement, with affixed sepia photographs of the town halls and other places of interest. With its Gothic hinges and gilt edges, it was a grotesque monument to Victorian decorative excess. The museum, perhaps wrongly, were not interested in it.

Willie Bert wrote earnestly to my father soliciting his views as to what should be done with it. My father, who was in the navy stationed at Troon, replied on a postcard: 'I feel it should be returned to Stoke-on-Trent so that the sins of the fathers should be visited on the sons.'

Willie Bert was not amused and perhaps this accounts for his note on Tom in 'The George Mellys': 'He had an acute vein of humour.' There are several such concealed barbs in his pamphlet. Of his Uncle George, the son of the MP, he wrote '. . . he did not suffer fools gladly.' Had he perhaps been put in his place by George for his neurotic determination to insist endlessly on his close connection with the family?

Concerning my grandfather, Samuel Heywood Melly (1871–1937), there are no hidden gibes. The tone on the contrary is a shade patronizing. He describes him as '. . . a very small man standing at 5 feet 3 inches but very neatly made'. He remarks that 'His interests were the Territorial Army, fishing and shooting especially the former', but then adds, 'He never had a chance to make as much of a mark as he might have done in business being completely overshadowed by his more brilliant brother George.' He hints, too, at a psychological explanation: 'He also suffered from having five mothers in his babyhood; his three sisters who were from seventeen to thirteen years old when he was born, his own mother, and Libby the nurse.' He notes that he married my grandmother, Edith Matilda Court, in 1898.

To children all grown-ups are about the same height, and I never thought of my grandfather as a very small man nor, as my

48

mother maintained, decidedly plain. There was, however, no doubt that my father's good looks came from his mother, who remained exceptionally beautiful to the end of her life. She was also the dominant partner, keeping an especially beady eye on my grandfather's drinking habits. He was forbidden whisky but allowed sherry and sometimes, my father told me later, would secretly empty the sherry decanter and replace it with scotch. At the end of lunch or dinner he would walk purposefully towards the sideboard and pour himself a large Kummel, which his wife believed, incorrectly, to be comparatively harmless. To help defuse this moment he would make the same joke or, to be more precise, repeat the same ritual. No joke delivered twice a day can hope to retain that element of surprise which is the essence of humour. Between chair and sideboard he would ask a question.

'What was the name of that Turkish General?'

Nobody was expected to answer this enquiry, and my grandmother would stare at the table with an expression in which exasperation and resignation fought for supremacy. Then, as he helped himself to a generous measure, my grandfather would answer his own conundrum.

'Mustapha Kummel!'

I never saw my grandfather noticeably drunk but I dare say, like many of his generation, he was usually mildly fuddled.

Although he would occasionally visit the commercial district of Liverpool, he had retired from business in 1924 at the age of forty-nine. He had been Passenger Superintendent at Lamport & Holt, the shipping firm to which my father had been temporarily and reluctantly attached. My grandfather's older brother George was joint Managing Director but had resigned following a row with Lord Kylsant who had taken over the company. My grandfather had left as a sign of solidarity, overshadowed, even here, by his 'more brilliant' sibling. No great sacrifice was involved. He had some money of his own and in 1927 George had died leaving what was, in those days, an enormous fortune to be divided amongst his brothers and sisters. From then on, apart from some charity work, my grandfather resigned himself happily to doing very little.

Nobody ever called him by his first name, Samuel. Although his middle name was held in common by most members of the Chatham Street Mellys, he alone chose to be known as Heywood.

His wife often made it sound like a call to heel. To his older brothers and sisters he had apparently been known as 'Pup', but I never heard any of those still living refer to him by this affectionate diminutive. My father called him 'Guv'nor'.

Collectively my grandparents were nicknamed 'Mumbo' and 'Jumbo'. As neither of them were in the least elephantine, I suppose this to have derived from the parents of the hero of the then popular but now taboo children's book, *Little Black Sambo*. Bill and I called them 'Gangie' and 'Gampa', obviously a childish mispronunciation of Grannie and Grampa. The Griff was irritated that we should call my other grandmother 'Gangie' as, unlike 'Gaga', it carried no suggestion of senile feeble-mindedness, but she was in general jealously competitive of Gangie, a failing we were well able to exploit.

When speaking of him to servants and tradesmen Gangie referred to her husband as 'the Colonel', and his correspondence was addressed to 'Colonel Heywood Melly'. He had indeed followed the family tradition of commanding the 4th West Lancashire Brigade, but in his case only from 1914 to 1916. He had led the regiment to France in 1915, but the following year was invalided out on account of acute dysentery. He was awarded the Territorial Decoration. It was hardly a glittering military career but he, or perhaps his wife, chose to retain the courtesy title.

On the eve of leaving for France, the 4th West Lancashire Brigade held a day of manoeuvres on a plain outside Liverpool. A tea-tent was erected on a nearby hill so that the Colonel's lady and the wives and families of his brother officers could watch their husbands charging about below; a picture which bore little relation to the filthy, lice-ridden trenches which were their destination. Due to the hostilities the regiment had trebled its size and among the men were many volunteers from the Liverpool docks, a class far removed from the clerkly respectability of pre-war days.

Among the lieutenants was a very young man called Tom Todd who had never been exposed before to six hours of strong language on such an insistent level. During the tea interval, seeing my grandfather in conversation with his wife and without a cup, he hurried over to make good this deficiency. 'Have a cup of fucking tea, Colonel,' he proposed politely. The effect was that of an animated H.M.Bateman cartoon. This was a favourite after-dinner story of my grandfather's, and my father would sometimes repeat the invitation as he poured himself out a cup from the dumb waiter between returning from the office and leaving for The Albert.

Until I was about five Gangie and Gampa lived in the large house where I was born. It was called The Grange and was built on the banks of the Mersey in the Parish of St Michael's, a small pocket of *rus in urbe* which lay unexpectedly concealed behind the bustle of Aigburth Road with its small shops and noisy trams.

Even then I was charmed by the abrupt transition. You turned off Aigburth Road down the side of the Rivoli Cinema and walked along one of those two-up two-down terraced streets built of yellow brick with lace curtains and holy-stoned steps. This eventually petered out, and there were perhaps six semis of the early twenties, speculative building on a decidedly unambitious scale, and traversed by a very small street along the side of two of the houses but of great interest and pride to me in that it was called Melly Road. I imagined then that this was due to the proximity of my grandfather, but realize now it was probably named after the family. If so it was a very modest acknowledgement of a century of public service and commercial acumen.

Beyond the semis was the entrance to a lane, its surface unmacadammed, partially cobbled, dusty in summer, muddy in winter. It was, according to its street sign 'unadopted', which meant that it was not the responsibility of the Liverpool Corporation. It was darkened by great Arthur Rackham-like trees and there were fields behind its tangled hedges and sandstone walls. At the end was a tiny lodge which served the four or five houses which surrounded it. The lodge keeper was a gnomish, startlingly white-haired Welshman called Mr Griffiths, who would emerge suddenly from his pointed nail-studded door to identify visitors, cackling high-pitched forelock-tugging greetings at those he recognized.

The Grange, shielded from its neighbours by tall shrubberies, was a long low grey house of restrained early Victorian Gothic. It had a large walled garden which ran down to the river. There were old fruit trees and little twisted walks. I found it enchanting if a shade sinister. The rooms of The Grange seemed,

51

in contrast to Ivanhoe Road, enormous. My mother always maintained that 'Mrs Melly has no taste', by which I suppose she meant that she made no concessions to modernity. There were several good pieces of eighteenth-century furniture, polished floors with faded Turkish carpets and old glazed chintzes. It's true the pictures weren't up to much: mediocre water-colours in wide gold mounts and engravings of Arabs around an oasis, but my parents didn't collect masterpieces either. There was one engraving I really liked. It showed an elderly but robust gentleman in eighteenth-century clothes toasting his beaming white-haired wife at the other end of a dining-room table. On the wall above the fireplace hung two oval portraits of them in their youth. I believed, despite their wig and lace-cap, that it represented my grandparents. Gangie, apart from her sternness over drink and frequent irritation at my grandfather's unwavering devotion to the habit, was extremely fond of him. He for his part worshipped her; her very strictness compensating no doubt for the loss of his 'five mothers'. He wasn't wholly in awe of her however. He would occasionally stand behind her chair while she criticized some aspect of our behaviour, making his false teeth pop in and out of his mouth – a course which, much to her uninformed surprise, reduced us to instant hysterics. I, for my part, was much less intimidated by Gangie than by the Griff. She was more easily diverted from course, less severe in her standards.

There were only two indoor servants at The Grange, both of whom were there before I was born and who remained with my grandmother, heavily exploited and frequently abused, until her death in 1959. Her maid was called Marjorie, a large, rosy-cheeked, heavy-breathing woman who retained the slow rural burr of her native Shropshire. She had caught my grandmother's feudal fantasies and whenever I went to call on Gangie, at however short an interval, would greet me with a cry of 'Welcome home, Master George', as if I were the young lord returning to his great estates after completing the Grand Tour. When I was small this seemed merely peculiar. I knew that my real home was 22 Ivanhoe Road. It was later that I found it absurd, and especially after my grandparents had left The Grange, which at least resembled a modest manor house, and moved into a semi-detached facing Aigburth Boulevard. After my grandfather's death Gangie rented a flat, but even this didn't modify Marjorie's ritual. Dressed during the war as a temporary post-woman, she would still evoke wide parklands and rolling acres.

Over the years she had developed several eccentricities which Gangie either failed or affected not to notice. When serving vegetables, if anyone, even for a moment, was slow to notice Marjorie's heavy-breathing presence at their side, she would nudge them quite sharply with her elbow. Her obsession was tree-felling or, failing the opportunity for that, the illegal collection of firewood from public places, an activity she pursued with Freudian intensity. Once, on discovering my father cutting down a small tree, she warned him in words which seemed loaded beyond their overt meaning. 'You be careful, Mr Tom,' she said, 'or you'll do yourself a *bad* injury.'

In the late 1950s, when Gangie was senile and almost speechless, Marjorie used to wheel her from her flat into adjacent Sefton Park in an invalid chair. My mother, meeting them by chance one windy afternoon, noticed that my grandmother seemed to be perched unnaturally high beneath her rugs. Marjorie had been thrusting all available branches and logs under her charge, jacking her up several inches.

Marjorie's greatest friend was the cook, Annie. They had been engaged the same week and were to share a flat together after my grandmother's death some thirty years later. Annie was almost a midget and badly crippled. She had a sweet face, always smiling, and rolled about her duties on her bowed legs with cheerful vigour. She was also an excellent and consistent cook which in no way deflected Gangie from cursing her roundly for any minor shortcoming or misunderstanding, referring to her on such occasions as 'Silly Little Annie'. Annie was especially skilled at soups for which Gampa had a particular liking, sucking them up with noisy appreciation from the side of one of the large crested spoons, a habit which set my mother's nerves on edge but had no effect on my grandmother beyond impelling her to raise her voice. For Bill and me, however, it was Silly Little Annie's puddings that won our enthusiasm, and in particular a creamy combination of rice and jam known as 'Freddie's Delight'.

The Griff, aggravated by our constant and maliciously appreciative references to Freddie's Delight, badgered Gangie for the recipe, a word she always pronounced 'receipt'. Gangie wasn't having any. It was 'her' pudding. They were on very formal terms anyway, never progressing beyond 'Mrs Melly' and 'Mrs Isaac'. Rather than admit defeat the Griff ordered her cook to try and create Freddie's Delight from our description alone. Week after week we were faced by variations of rice pudding, some so congealed as to form a mould, others so runny that they were almost a drink, but none of them even approximating to the delicious original. Eventually, and to our relief, for we had in effect been penalized by our own mischief, the Griff gave up.

With two dailies, Marjorie, Silly Little Annie and a gardener five days a week, The Grange might have been considered adequately staffed, but my grandfather also employed a uniformed chauffeur. It was not that he went in for very grand cars. His Chatham Street brothers, his cousin, the shipping heiress Emma Holt, owned huge old-fashioned Daimlers with the chauffeur like a stuffed animal in a glass-case taking his orders through a flexible speaking tube, freesia in little vases and sal volatile and smelling salts in silver-topped glass bottles slotted into the upholstery, but Gampa preferred a more modern if solid motor car, a maroon Armstrong Siddeley. It was also his habit to sit by his chauffeur, with whom he chose to establish an officer-and-batman relationship, a military illusion reinforced by his being addressed as 'Colonel' and the obvious pleasure he derived from casually but inevitably returning the obligatory salute of passing AA men on their three-wheeled motor-bicycles.

There were three chauffeurs during my childhood. The first, whom I can only just remember, was called Burscoe, a name that in itself sounded like the noise of an old-fashioned motor-horn. He was a small, thickset man like a sturdy little bull and apparently extremely randy. My father told me, although it may have been apocryphal, that Gampa once discovered Burscoe in the kitchen of a country house in Yorkshire where they were staying, rogering the cook from behind while she continued, impassively, to peel potatoes; a tableau which could well have come from 'My Secret Life', and formed part of my grandfather's stock of mildly indecent after-dinner stories when the ladies had left the room. Burscoe was not dismissed for this peccadillo. Like Tom, Gampa had apparently a tolerant view of sexual behaviour.

After Burscoe retired he was replaced by Kane, a big ebullient man with an open mobile face as innocent as Tommy Cooper. He was married to a small woman with unfashionably long hair and the looks of a beautiful gypsy. Kane was marvellous at amusing us on long journeys. He would recite a string of gibberish which he pretended to be the Chinese alphabet. He told us that RAC stood for Running After Chickens. He kept us in such stitches that I even forgot to feel car-sick.

Kane was succeeded by Jenkins, a friendly but silent Welshman and perhaps rather more to the liking of adult passengers, who knew what RAC really stood for and felt less need of continuous distraction. When Gampa was dying he sent for Marjorie, Annie and Jenkins and asked them to 'look after the Missus', a request they felt, in the circumstances, unable to refuse. Jenkins continued therefore to drive my grandmother about until the last few months of her life.

Gampa, like my father, died of a perforated ulcer in his sixties. Gangie, like the Griff, lived on well into her eighties. She was a practical-minded woman with nothing sentimental in her character but with a strong imaginative streak. Her childhood was odd. She was brought up by her grandmother, although from which side of her family I never discovered, in a dark old house called Denham on the Cheshire marshes near the mouth of the Welsh Dee; a bleak landscape criss-crossed by deep and treacherous irrigation ditches, and within sight of those fatal sands where the doomed Mary was sent to call the cattle home. As my grandmother was born in the 1870s, her grandmother must have grown up during the Regency and Gangie, in consequence, used several expressions of a vigour and directness denied to her Victorian contemporaries. Moments of exasperation would be met by a cry of 'Dash m'wig!' People who bored her were 'dull dogs'. Those who annoyed her she would threaten to shake until their noses bled.

She had a varied repertoire of old songs and snatches. Her speciality was a mysterious ballad called 'Marjorie sat on the bowling green'. She was unaware of its origin. Her grandmother used to recite it to her on stormy winter nights, and afterwards she would be very reluctant to take her candle and go up alone to bed along the creaking corridors of Denham. My father had excited my interest in this poem when I was very young, but

Gangie refused to recite it to me until I was about eight, and even then in broad daylight. I didn't think I'd be frightened. For one thing I found myself imagining Marjorie to be my grandmother's maid, and for another the only bowling green I had seen was in Sefton Park where, on summer evenings, the old men in their waistcoats frequently accused each other of cheating, angrily demanding that someone 'fetch the string' to settle a dispute. The idea of lugubrious heavy-breathing Marjorie in her cap and apron seated on the turf of the Sefton Park bowling green was an absurd rather than a sinister image.

My grandmother sat me on her footstool, fixed me with her fine dark eyes and began. The ballad was set to a lugubrious chant in the minor key and went like this:

> Marjorie sat on the bowling green, the trees grew all around.
> Twas in the middle of the night she heard a frightful sound.

(and here, after a long pause Gangie gave vent to two long low groans)

> 'Is that my father dead, or is it my Uncle John,
> Or is it Willie, my long lost love, who from the sea has come?'

(two more groans)

> 'It is not your father dead, nor is it your Uncle John,
> But it is Willie your long lost love who from the sea has come'

(two further groans)

> 'And have you brought me any fine clothes, or any fine things to
>   put on?'
> 'No but I've brought a long winding sheet to wrap your dead
>   bones in.'

And at this point my grandmother, who had appeared to be in a trance, leapt out of chair, flung her arms wide, and gave a sudden piercing scream. I almost fell off the footstool with terror.

The low chant, the repeated groans, the lulling effect of the tune all of course contributed to the shock of the finale, but it's quite a chilling little piece even on the page. I remembered every word instantly and could hardly wait to get home and recite it to Bill. I did so that very evening in the dark nursery with a candle on the little table between us. It gave him frightful nightmares.

Gangie was fond of acting in general, keen on organizing

56

charades and dumb crambo. Her party piece at family gatherings was one of 'Mrs Caudle's Curtain Lectures', drawn from a popular Victorian book of that name, which she performed with my grandfather on a bed improvised from armchairs or a sofa. Mrs Caudle nags her husband non-stop about his shortcomings during the day without allowing him any defence; a role that suited Gampa very well as he remained entirely silent throughout and yet was able to engage the sympathy of the audience. His own speciality was a recitation of 'The Village Blacksmith' as performed by a man with an articulated wooden arm and gloved hand which he appeared to manipulate to illustrate the imagery of the poem. I never saw Gangie act in a stage play but my mother, who was not altogether fond of her, said that her idea of acting was running about a great deal and flapping her arms.

My mother's antipathy towards her was based in part on Gangie's habit of saying exactly what came into her head but more especially on her insinuation that Tom wasn't looked after properly. That she should refer to him more often than not as 'poor dear Thomas' was a constant irritant. She implied too that 'poor dear Thomas' was primarily her son rather than Maud's husband and that we were her grandchildren rather than Maud's children. In fact she applied this proprietorial attitude to everything she was connected with. In her later years she became completely hooked on *Mrs Dale's Diary* and was always furious if interrupted while listening to what she called 'My Dales'.

She came from an old Cheshire family and told me that her grandfather had fallen in love with her grandmother when he had seen her, from his horse, swinging on a gate. The Courts had once been considerable landowners but most of the estates had been lost by some profligate over the gaming tables, and all that remained was an old manor farm near Nantwich. Gangie's younger brother Percy, after several years in Canada as an engineer, had returned to manage this, but he was a very unlucky farmer, and Gampa had felt obliged to lend him several fairly substantial sums over the years to help him out. In the large hall of the farm hung a reminder of former prosperity; an enormous picture in very bad repair showing a park with a substantial hall in the background. In the foreground were several men in tall top hats and tight breeches, women in *directoire* dresses, children bowling hoops or mounted on hobby horses and a toddler in a donkey cart.

Whatever its financial shortcomings, for us children the farm was a magic domain. There was a large duckpond in front of it, still referred to as 'the moat'. There was a priest's hole in the huge chimney. The building, with its exposed beams and yellow-washed walls, stood in gentle rolling country under wide skies. Uncle Percy, who was also known as 'Pip', although given to occasional unconvincing explosions of exasperation, was a courteous and charming man, physically remarkably like my father. His wife Isobel was not a beauty – she resembled Flora Robson – but she had startling blue eyes and a fascinating voice like a dove cooing. She had been a suffragette.

While specializing in Friesian cows, it was very much a general farm. There were rather intimidating geese and a few turkeys as well as scratching hens, several pig-sties, and a great bull in a dark dung-scented shed rattling its chain and rolling its baleful eyes. The bull had been awkward to start with until Percy realized it was lonely, and from then on spent several hours a week talking to it. The cows were milked by hand and sometimes, if he spotted us watching from the entrance of the shippon, the farmhand would aim a jet of warm milk at Bill or me with ribald accuracy. He also took us ferreting, although most of the time was spent digging out the mean-faced snake-like albino creatures from deep in the warren and there were few rabbits to show for it.

Sometimes we went down for the day in Gampa's Armstrong Siddeley. The ride itself was a great treat as it involved crossing the muddy Mersey on the Runcorn Transporter, a huge nine-teenth-century cable car big enough to carry across many cars and lorries on each journey. Sometimes we would stay for a few days, being met at Crewe by Uncle Percy in an old van smelling of meal. We fell asleep in the attics listening to the owls hooting, were woken by the rooks in the great elms. We helped Aunt Isobel feed the poultry, watched Percy and the hands getting in the hay and visited the animals. Once there was a litter of pigs who had lost their mother and had to be fed by hand. Bill and I discovered a cruel but irresistible trick. If you picked up one of the squealing piglets and squeezed it immediately after it had been fed, it would shoot out a stream of milk at one end and piss

58

at the other. They soon got wise to us and whenever we entered the outhouse would run hysterically under a pot-bellied stove called 'the cheerio'.

The interior of the farmhouse, while rather run down, was very beautiful in its simplicity. Isobel had a charming faded drawing-room looking onto a walled garden full of cottage flowers. There was a great linen press on the landing and old brass beds. The Courts ate extremely well. On one early visit with Gangie and Gampa we had lunch on a wooden table which stood outside the main door in front of the moat. There was a goose and a very rich chocolate pudding and I was disastrously car-sick on the way back. There was home-made bread and unsalted butter churned in the dairy. Bill and I called this 'country butter'. We always took some home with us.

They were still there during the fifties. I once took Mick Mulligan to tea when we were playing that evening at the Nantwich Civic Hall. We ate at the same table in front of the house, much intrigued by a sinuous little brown creature leaping and weaving on the other side of the moat. Suddenly there was a loud explosion. Percy had fired both barrels of a shot-gun over our heads from his office window. 'A damn weasel after the water hens,' he explained mildly as he rejoined us.

When Isobel died, Percy sold the farm and went to live with his son Peter and daughter-in-law Dot in a small house outside Leicester where Peter practised as a vet. I visited him there once. He seemed to have shrunk and looked out of context in that modern setting, but his smile was as warm as ever, his manner as gentle and old-fashioned. The sale of the farm had been sufficient to repay my grandfather's estate with interest. Dot wrote to me recently to say that the new owner had pulled it down and built a new house on the site.

Percy was still active enough to come to Gangie's funeral. But at the graveside it was noticed he was missing. He had fallen asleep in the back of Peter's car outside my grandmother's flat and been forgotten in the confusion of deciding the protocol of the limousines. He was still there and still asleep when they got back from the cemetery.

Gangie herself would have been amused by this absurd incident. She took a robust view of death due, I suspect, to her unquestioning belief in a personal afterlife. She was a steady church-goer, a keen if garish arranger of altar flowers and heaper-up of vegetable produce at Harvest Festivals, and on Good Fridays spent the three hours of the Passion on her knees in Christ Church, Linnet Lane. Unlike the Mellys, with their Unitarian background, she was drawn towards lace and incense, and keen on entertaining the odd canon.

When Gangie's sister-in-law Florence Melly died in 1928 my mother, who had been fond of her, arrived at 90 Chatham Street for the post-funeral baked meats wearing a rather tearful expression which she felt appropriate. The first member of the family she encountered was her mother-in-law in high spirits. 'Come in! Come in!' cried Gangie. 'The party's just getting going.' Maud was very shocked by this, and brought it up quite frequently over the years as a proof of Gangie's insensitivity.

A dedicated if apparently rather bossy committee woman, Gangie served for many years on the Ladies' Committee of the Liverpool Hospital for Women. When I was about seven, the hospital moved into a large new building in 'bankers' Georgian' style, and one morning Gangie took Bill and me over it. On a trolley in an ante-room was a shrouded object. Gangie strode briskly towards it. 'Look at our corpse!' she cried, whisking back the sheet. We nearly fainted with horror, but it turned out to be no more than an articulated life-size model on which student nurses practised their splints and bandaging.

When Gampa died so unexpectedly in 1937, Gangie came back that evening from the nursing home with 'poor dear Thomas' to Ivanhoe Road, and sat in the nursery looking a little dazed. Bill and I, who had not been told yet, were building a Roman Coliseum out of the wooden building blocks which were kept in my father's old tuck-box. The point of doing this was in order to push it over when it was finished and my mother, assuming what we were later on to call her 'church voice', asked us not to because Gangie was 'feeling rather upset'. She'd have none of it. 'Don't mind at all,' she said. 'Push it over. Knock it down!'

Next morning my father told Bill and me; my sister Andrée at five was considered too young to understand. We both howled and sobbed, and I had the sensation, as always at moments of emotion, of watching myself as if on film. Gampa was the first person near to us to die. It seemed dreadful that I would never

60

hear him drink soup again, or whistle through his teeth, or imitate a man with a wooden arm reciting 'The Village Blacksmith'.

Gampa had filled in the pools almost from their beginnings, but had never won a dividend. When Gangie got back to Dunmail (they had moved there from The Grange some years previously) there was an envelope from Littlewoods. Inside was a postal order for half-a-crown.

I suppose they left The Grange because it had become too big, but their choice of Dunmail was curious. It was a substantial, half-timbered semi-detached, built during the twenties and facing Aigburth Boulevard. This was a continuation of Aigburth Road, admittedly more residential and lined with Japanese cherry trees with the trams partially concealed behind low hedges, but even so ill-fitted to Gangie's mild delusions of grandeur. There was a dark little morning-room on the ground floor which the previous owner had hung with hideous embossed Spanish leather. Gampa spent most of his day there, coughing over his Turkish cigarettes, snoozing, and reading large leather-bound illustrated volumes with titles like *Through Africa with Rod and Gun*. Otherwise the rooms were arranged very like The Grange only, in that they were far smaller, the furniture looked rather cramped. In the hall was a big dinner-gong suspended from a yoke supported by two elaborately carved Indian deities. When it was time for lunch or dinner Marjorie, as had been her custom at The Grange, would strike this several times with deafening effect in so confined a space.

The only advantage of Dunmail was that it was a few hundred yards from The Dell where the Leathers lived. Dorothy Leather was Gangie's only living daughter. We called her 'Auntie Golly'. She was a kind, pretty, rather nervous person with a talent for water-colours and writing sketches some of which were printed in *The Lady*. She suffered terribly from migraines. Her husband, Ronald Fishwick Leather, was an energetic forthright man, who went bald early and wore a black moustache. He was very practical and used to make elaborate mechanized table-centre decorations every Christmas. The year Disney's *Snow White* came out, he designed one in which the seven dwarfs emerged from their mine, crossed a bridge over a looking-glass stream and vanished into a wood, returning, concealed and upside down, to repeat the exercise. It was powered by a small electric motor.

Uncle Ronnie was a keen business man, and became Executive Manager of Pilkingtons, the glass-manufacturers, in nearby St Helens. Unlike my father who was only mildly Conservative, Ronnie was extremely right-wing with a deep loathing for the trade unions. He was rather short-tempered but good company. The Dell, like The Grange, was built at the end of another unadopted lane leading down to the Mersey. It had a large steep garden, which gave it its name, in which Ronnie worked fanatically. He was an obsessive perfectionist.

The Leathers had two children, John and Gillian. John was a few years older than me. He had a lopsided grin and had inherited his father's biting wit; a kind of Noel Coward of the nursery. I was in some awe of him. Gillian was my brother's contemporary and mad on horses. She pronounced her name with a hard 'G'. They had a strict, rather handsome nanny called Cadwallader. In their nursery was an old glass-fronted music-box with huge flexible metal discs for different tunes. There was also a small wall-cupboard with a leering wizard painted on it mixing a spell from bottles and phials of poisonous coloured liquids. It was an image I found disturbing.

Bill and I once went to the pictures with my mother and the programme included a 'short' featuring Wilson, Keppel and Betty, a well-known variety act. Wilson and Keppel performed a lugubrious sand-dance dressed as unlikely looking Arabs. Betty just wiggled a bit wearing a yashmak. Bill and I became hysterical at this performance, not only because of its innate absurdity, but also because Wilson and Keppel bore a strong resemblance to Uncle Ronnie. When they next appeared at a local music-hall we were taken to see them in the flesh. From then on we always referred to Wilson and Keppel as 'The Uncle Ronnies'.

When I went with Gangie to put flowers on Gampa's grave, I discovered for the first time that Tom and Dorothy hadn't been her only children. On the stone, under my grandfather's newly-chizzled name, I read that he lay next to Mary Melly, a daughter who was born and died on the same day in 1914. I found this inexplicably sad.

A mystery I never solved was why Gangie was brought up by her grandmother. Not only had she a mother then, but she was still alive in my childhood. She was known as 'Tiny Granny', a very pretty little person like a Beatrix Potter mouse and in full command of her faculties in spite of her great age. She had a flat just round the corner from Christ Church, Linnet Lane and we used to be taken to call on her after 'Children's Service'. Tiny Granny lived with my grandmother's younger sister, my Great-Aunt Gwen, her husband Guy Watts and their eighteen-year-old son Newton.

Gwen, who had pince-nez and dyed red hair piled up into a kind of mad bird's nest, was considered something of a caution. When she was driven anywhere in my Grandfather's Armstrong Siddeley she would imperiously order the chauffeur to drive faster or slower, to raise and lower the windows as if the car were hers. 'You devil Burscoe!' she used to shout, much to my father's amusement. Guy, a large, rather boisterous man, had been very rich at one time but was more or less ruined in the Depression. Their son Newton was incredibly spoilt. He was usually still in bed when we arrived about eleven o'clock, reading a risqué magazine of the thirties called *Razzle* which had a striking front cover in art deco lettering. My father maintained that Guy had indulged Newton ridiculously during his childhood, allowing him to take school friends to the Adelphi and sign the bill. No wonder he lay in bed and read *Razzle*. Later on Newton was always getting into scrapes. He had a mistress and a child, which everyone thought very shocking, but when Guy and Gwen were old and poor it was Newton's mistress who went and looked after them.

I only discovered this much later when she turned up and introduced herself and her daughter at a club we were playing near St Asaph, North Wales, during the middle seventies. She had long left Newton. There was a question I was longing to ask her. Tom and I had once discussed fetishism, or at least I'd brought the subject up and he'd asked what it was. I'd mentioned rubber, fur, boots and shoes.

'I wonder if that explains your Great Uncle Guy,' he said. I asked him if what explained my Great Uncle Guy.

'He was always buying Gwen kid boots', he told me, 'and he used to clean them all on Sunday afternoons. She didn't even have particularly pretty feet.'

63

I said it sounded like it, but he wasn't entirely convinced. Fifteen years after my father's death I asked Newton's mistress.

'Was he not!' she told me, 'and right up to the end. A perfect old nuisance. I used to have to sit on my feet when I was reading to him!' I wish I could have told Tom.

Newton, of course, was one of those people that Gangie wanted to shake until their noses bled.

5

One afternoon, above the yards with pigeon-lofts and the tall garden walls which faced the shops in Aigburth Road, I watched a small aeroplane sky-writing the word 'Rinso', a form of advertising quite common in the thirties. The wind had blurred the letter R before the O was completed. As I still couldn't read, I asked my mother what it said. She told me. I knew Rinso was the name on the soap-flake carton by the sink in the back-kitchen but the concept of writing it across the sky as a commercial exercise was beyond me. I believed that what the aeroplane was doing related to our packet, a private message to me alone. When we got home, before even taking off my galoshes, I ran into the back-kitchen to look at it. I was surprised not to find the letter R blurred.

I demanded constant explanations. 'Why? Why? Why?' I nagged, tugging at my mother for attention, but her answers often confused me further. There was a middle-aged woman we sometimes met when we were out walking or shopping. She was usually on the corner of Ivanhoe and Parkfield Road, where a brick wall, banked high on the other side with earth, bulged dangerously outwards and a brass plate, screwed to the front gate, announced the practice of a certain Dr Mary B.Lee. The woman wore a purple hat with cloth violets hanging from it. Her face was heavily painted and she talked in an excitable and disconnected way. I usually got very bored when my mother stopped to talk to people in the streets and shops, but I was fascinated by this lady and didn't, as was usual, pull insistently at my mother's coat to get her to come along. On the contrary it was she who appeared eager to break away. Once, after an especially long and disjointed monologue, I asked my mother why the lady seemed so different from everyone else. She told me that she drank. This made no sense to me at all. Everybody drank but they didn't all wear purple hats and talk with smeared red mouths and lipstick on their teeth.

Rather precocious in some ways, I was incredibly backward in others. Anything which didn't interest me I ignored. Why bother to learn to read boring stories with short words when grown-ups could be wheedled or bullied into reading me about Mowgli carried off through the jungle by the Banderlog, or Peter and Benjamin crouching terrified in the bone-littered darkness outside Mr Todd's kitchen? I was seven before I could read at all but then, almost overnight, I could read everything. I couldn't add up, however; I simply shut off when anyone tried to teach me. I developed like one of those crabs with a tiny body and one huge claw.

I worried sometimes that when I grew up I would have to make a living, presumably by going into business. The only thing was that I couldn't understand what 'business' meant. I knew it was how my father and uncles 'made money' and that it took place in offices in the city, but even after visiting them I was none the wiser. My father's office was quite small. It was high up in a tall narrow building near the pier-head. The hall was dark and had a board on the wall saying who was on each floor. There was a lift with open iron-work and a man in uniform with one arm pulled it up and down with a rope. The names 'Seward & Melly' were painted on the glass door of my father's office. Inside sat a lady typing. The office smelt damp and pungent. This was because there was a little back room with big brown paper parcels with dirty black and yellow-grey wool bursting out of them. Did he sell the wool? No. They were what were called 'samples'. My father was a wool-broker. What he tried to do, he told me, was to buy wool, which he never saw, when it was cheap and sell it to people when the price went up. I stopped trying to understand although I pretended I did. The lady, whom he called his secretary, gave me biscuits and let me bang away on the big old-fashioned typewriter.

Then my father took me to have my hair cut in a brightly-lit basement under a shop. It had tiles on the walls and lots of mirrors. If you stood in the right place where one mirror faced another you could see yourself over and over again getting smaller and smaller. The barber's chair went up and down on a foot-pedal and tipped backwards like the chair at the dentist's.

There were lots of pretty bottles of hair oil on the shelves with names like 'Honey and Flowers'. A respectful but cheerful man in a white coat cut my hair. When he'd finished he brushed the back of my neck with a soft brush which felt nice, but some little hairs from the clippers always got down the back of my neck and tickled. It was easy to understand what barbers did, but not wool-brokers.

Uncle Fred's office at Samuel Banner was even more mysterious. It was round the corner from my father's but in a much grander building. There were lots of offices in Samuel Banner and several secretaries. Uncle Fred had an office of his own with wooden panelling and photographs of ships. He sat behind a big desk. There was no room at the back with samples, only a little carved mahogany rack on his desk with test tubes in it each containing an oil of a different viscosity. Uncle Fred took me out to lunch. I was introduced to lots of big noisy men as his nephew, or 'Tom's boy'. He was always very funny in the restaurant. Afterwards my mother, who had been doing her voluntary work at The Personal Service, picked me up and we went home on a tram.

Would I really have to be a business man when I grew up? I'd rather have been a shopkeeper because I could understand what they did, but then all the shopkeepers had Liverpool accents. When Mr Arnold rang up every day to ask what meat we wanted he said, 'Arnold the butt-cher'. There were other jobs people did. There were policemen, soldiers, park-keepers, tram-drivers and conductors, carpenters, decorators, ice-cream men, waiters, watchmakers, but all my relations, except for Uncle Percy and George Rawdon Smith who was a doctor, seemed to be in business and so did all my father's friends. Later on I found there were other things I might do. I could become a barrister like my mother's Uncle Fred, or an architect or a vicar, but all these meant years of study. I wanted to be something you could become at once. Above all I wanted to be famous.

Some of my mother's friends were famous. Most of them were actors and actresses who appeared at the Playhouse. Their photographs were outside, taken by Burrell and Hardman in Bold Street which my mother called 'the Bond Street of Liverpool'. The photographs were very dramatically lit with velvety backgrounds. One actor, wearing a soft hat, was pretending to light a pipe. The actresses all held their heads at funny angles like the ducks on Sefton Park Lake. They were the same photographs we had on the piano. I knew all their names because my mother said them so often in a special kind of casual throw-away voice: Bobby Flemyng, Geoffrey Edwards, Ruth Lodge, Harry Andrews, Michael Redgrave, Marjorie Fielding, Ena Burrill. There was also the producer, William Armstrong. I thought he must be even more famous because my mother mentioned him most of all. She always called him 'Dear William Armstrong'. He was bald and funny and had a high-pitched Scottish accent.

I met all these people when I was very young because I was allowed to stay up and see them when they came to supper on Sunday nights. A bit later I saw them on the stage too, at first in the children's plays which were performed in the afternoons at Christmas. They were usually very exciting with secret panels and children getting the better of crooks, but sometimes they were about animals like Toad of Toad Hall. What really made me feel special was that after the curtain came down, my mother took me 'round behind'. There was a funny dusty smell. The actors and actresses sat in their tiny dressing-rooms up steep stone steps. They wore dirty dressing-gowns and took off their make-up with cold cream. I was sometimes allowed to go onto the stage and was surprised but somehow pleased how, with the curtain down and the lights off, the set looked so unreal and sloppily painted. Sometimes the stage hands would be hauling up the backcloths and flats into the air and lowering others for the grown-up play in the evening: a drawing-room with French windows or a garden with a swing and a lake in the distance.

My mother didn't only know the actors and actresses at the Playhouse. She was a friend of Douglas Byng and Ronald Frankau. Douglas Byng pretended to be a lady and sang songs about being Doris, the Goddess of Wind or someone called Flora Macdonald. Ronald Frankau was a comedian and was often on the wireless. I had records by them in the nursery and could imitate them. Sometimes when my parents had a party, I'd be woken up and brought downstairs in my dressing-gown to sing their songs. I didn't mind being woken up at all because everybody laughed and clapped, especially when I imitated Douglas Byng.

'Flora Macdonald', I'd sing, 'Flora Macdonald. Heavy with haggis and dripping with dew . . .'

'You'd almost think he knew what it meant,' someone would say.

I didn't, of course, but I had listened very carefully to the intonation and, by exaggerating it, unconsciously emphasized the *double entendres*.

Once, when I was brought down, Ruth Lodge was sitting on an actor's knee and kissing him.

'Not in front of the child,' wailed William Armstrong.

My mother was also friendly with the ballet. When they were touring Robert Helpmann and Freddie Ashton would always come to the house. She'd met Freddie Ashton first because he'd been asked to do the choreography for one of the big amateur reviews in which my mother took part, but Helpmann was her favourite. She always referred to him as 'darling Bobbie'. My father sometimes called him 'darling Bobbie' too, but only when my mother wasn't there so I knew this must be a joke. My mother 'adored the ballet', which I couldn't understand as she didn't like classical music at all. She divided it onomatopoeically into two schools which she called 'mini-mini' and 'boom-zoom'. Mozart for example was 'mini-mini', Beethoven 'boom-zoom'.

I was taken to the ballet when quite young and was amazed to see 'Darling Bobbie' twisting and leaping in a way that appeared to be against nature, but I felt no urge to become a ballet dancer because I was told that it was necessary to start very early, that the training was long and arduous and that even when one had become a star, daily practice was essential. More curious was that I didn't set my heart on the stage, an obvious escape from the worrying idea of becoming a business man and a possible way to become famous easily. I think the explanation was that my mother constantly impressed on me that it was 'an insecure profession'. If anyone else – my father, Uncle Fred, my grand-parents – had taken this line I might have resisted their advice but that my mother, who adored actors and actresses, was against it forced me to affirm that I didn't want to go on the stage.

The only other class of person whom my mother spoke of in her casual throw-away voice indicating their high place in her Pantheon, were titled, although these were much sparser on the ground than members of the theatrical profession. In fact there were only two. One was the widow of a judge, a kindly rather boring elderly lady whose observations were, in themselves, completely banal but which my mother nevertheless aired so as to be able to introduce the source of their origin. The other was infinitely more dashing; a certain Lady Peggy Lacon. Maud had known Peggy when she had been married to a plain Mr Duckworth. Then she divorced Mr Duckworth and married Sir George Lacon, a ruddy-faced, almost silent Norfolk squire whose principal interest was shooting pheasants. Lady Lacon was a very glamorous platinum blonde in the manner of Jean Harlow. She occasionally came to stay with us and what made this both worrying and yet fascinating was that Bill and I were always warned several times in advance *that she didn't like children*! This had the effect of making me determined that she should like me. I followed her around and fawned on her throughout her visits in the way that a dog or cat will often make for the one person in a room who dislikes animals. She looked at us with indifferent dislike but confused us further by bringing us very expensive presents. The one I can best remember took the form of a black dude on a little plinth. There was a tiny microphone attached to the plinth and when this was placed near the horn of a gramophone the vibrations caused the dude to appear to tap dance. My father thought it was a ridiculous present and must have cost well over a pound. Although he found her 'decorative', his favourite word to describe a pretty woman, he didn't care much for Lady Lacon.

After the war, Maudie would frequently tell me that the thirties, her forties, were her best time. Although there was not much money, there was enough for her to entertain whenever she felt like it and her social life was full and busy. This centred around the Playhouse and the Sandon Studios Club, the Liverpudlian equivalent of the Chelsea Arts. The Sandon occupied a wing of a very beautiful eighteenth-century building called the Blue-coat Chambers in the centre of Liverpool. It had been built as the Blue-coat School and was of red brick with stone detailing, enclosing a large cobbled courtyard and separated from the street by fine railings and elaborate iron gates. At the back of the building was a garden surrounded by painters' and sculptors' studios and indeed the original purpose of the club was, as its name suggested, as a meeting place for those exclusively connected with the arts. By the twenties, however, an alleged interest was considered sufficient justification. There was a long narrow unlicensed dining-room with a stained floor, oak tables and chairs and earthenware water jugs. It had a coal fire in the winter and the food, while simple, was excellent and cheap. The head waitress carried on like a grumpy old nanny and was much loved. When my mother was shopping in the centre of Liverpool or 'town' as she called it, she would usually have lunch there and would often take us with her. I was fascinated to meet painters and sculptors in their rough tweed suits, blue or rust coloured shirts and knitted ties. It was proof of another world unconnected with business.

From our perspective the point of the Sandon was the annual children's party. It was held on New Year's afternoon and called the Hogmanay. It took place in the huge room on the first floor of the main block facing the street. The chief attraction was an enormous slide which you rode down on rather prickly door mats. After tea there was always a conjurer called S. Le Kessin, who wore evening dress. We didn't only get to see S. Le Kessin at the Sandon; the smarter mothers used to hire him for their children's birthday parties. To be frank his tricks, multiplying billiard balls and pulling chains of multi-coloured handkerchiefs out of his mouth, were rather tame, but he did eventually produce a ventriloquist doll called Tommy who sang 'Show me the way to go home', while S. Le Kessin drank a glass of water. At the time I didn't realize that the conjurer's name was made up of an initial, the French definite article and a surname. I thought he was called 'Esslerkessin'.

The Hogmanay party was fancy dress; the usual motley of pirates, clowns, arabs and wild men. One year, when I was about five, I had an ambitious and major failure. I was addicted to a children's strip in the *Daily Mail*. It was called 'Teddy Tail', and the hero was a rather wet mouse. His side-kick was an even less distinguished duck called 'Douggie'. That November the *Mail*, to which the Griff subscribed, offered a series of dressmakers' patterns representing these creatures, and I persuaded her to send off for Douggie Duck. It was duly made up from yellow towelling with a cardboard beak and eyes. I went to the party full of hubris, but nobody seemed to know who Douggie Duck was or even that I was meant to be a duck at all and I was much mocked and soon reduced to angry tears. My only recompense was that when my father came to pick me up it was pouring with rain, and I was able to provoke his laughter by running up and down the gutter outside the Blue-coat Chambers shouting, 'Fine weather for ducks.'

As a family we were not very lucky with fancy dress. Tom himself had once gone to a party, for which the invitation had proposed a choice between fancy and evening dress, disguised as a snowman, only to find all the other men in dinner-jackets. As a very young man he had elected to dress as an Italian organ grinder and, for the sake of verisimilitude, had gone to the trouble of hiring a live rhesus monkey from a Mr Rogers, who at that time kept a pet shop but was later to open the small and rather unsuccessful Liverpool zoo. When Tom took the monkey back to The Grange, it had broken loose, run along the mantelshelf deliberately throwing a rather good clock into the fireplace, bitten my grandfather quite badly on the hand, and run up the curtains to take up a position on the pelmet from which it refused to be dislodged. Mr Rogers had to come round, recapture it and take it away.

The year following my failure as Douggie Duck, I elected to go as Mickey Mouse and was reassuringly successful. I was so delighted at restoring my credibility among my contemporaries that I insisted on a permanent record. I was photographed one January afternoon at a local studio staring solemnly at the big camera on its tripod, its operator concealed under a black velvet hood. I stood next to a toy Mickey Mouse as a proof of my authenticity.

Later the same evening, the children's Hogmanay was followed by a New Year's Eve party for the members themselves. There was a special licence and, judging by my father's groaning recourse to Alka Seltzer every New Year's morning, it was not wasted. In preparation for this bacchanalia, huge murals, painted by the Sandon's artists, were already in position during the afternoon. They showed, in caricature, the more notorious associates cast in the role of classical deities or historical figures, and engaged in activities just this side of decency. I was fascinated, not so much by what they were up to, as how it was possible to retain a likeness by means of such grotesque distortion. These men and women, whom I had seen lunching soberly in the club's dining-room, were here presented as skeletal or pendulous monsters, writhing or monolithic, as bald as eggs or hairy as apes, and yet remained instantly recognizable. My interest in the 'truth' of distortion was born from speculating on this mystery during S.Le Kessin's less riveting illusions.

Yet for my parents the most important annual event at the Sandon was not the Hogmanay (indeed my mother's mistrust of drink and my father's enthusiastic indulgence in it on these occasions, 'spoiled' it for her more often than not) but the annual 'cabaret'. Both of them took part, but my mother's suppressed theatricality was given full rein, and she was always the star of the night. These cabarets were no casual stringing together of acts, but specially written reviews with proper songs and sketches. The former were largely the work of a man called Alfred Francis who worked, without marked enthusiasm, for his family bakery business and managed the large central tea shop which provided an outlet for its products. He was an urbane, slightly plump man, handsome in the manners of the period, with horn-rimmed glasses and a neat moustache. His passion was popular music and he was something of a jazz *aficionado*. He could play the piano well, conduct and orchestrate, and his songs, with titles like 'High School Hattie' or 'Don't Play Jazz on the Bechstein Grand', while clearly influenced by Noel Coward and Cole Porter, were memorable and amusing in their own right.

Most of the sketches were written by a remarkable woman called Maud Budden. She was the wife of the Professor of Architecture at the University and one of my mother's best friends. She was of Scottish origin and had a slight and attractive Edinburgh accent. She was big and rather untidy especially about the hair. She had a frank open face with amused blue eyes. Her tongue was sharp and witty enough to make her disliked and feared by anyone pompous or pretentious enough to provoke her ridicule. Among other activities she was responsible for the words of an anthropomorphic cartoon strip in the *Liverpool Echo* called 'Curly Wee and Gussy Goose'. Unlike most strips this didn't rely on balloons, but unfolded its story in a series of quatrains printed below each picture. They were always neatly turned and often very funny. 'Maud Budden is a fool,' said my mother as she read them aloud to me each night before turning to the children's crossword. She meant of course the exact opposite.

73

The strip was drawn by another club member, an artist known only by his surname, Clibbon. He was obsessed by large busts, and the hens or ewes who were among the supporting cast of 'Curly Wee and Gussy Goose' were in consequence generously over-endowed. Clibbon carried this fetish into the Sandon cabaret where he insisted on transvestite roles as an excuse to introduce large balloons under a bathing suit which served as his foundation garment. One year he and my mother appeared as gym-slipped girls, Clibbon inevitably precocious about the figure. They had cut two skipping ropes in half and, by swinging these vigorously enough to deceive the eye, presented the illusion of surprising expertise. They sang a song which began:

> We are two little girls
> We are not fond of toys
> We'd rather be smoking cigarettes
> And mucking about with boys.

The more successful and less salacious sketches and songs from the Sandon Cabarets were recycled for three public reviews which were performed during the thirties at either the Royal Court or the Liverpool Empire to raise money for charity. They were based on the formula invented by Charlotte and Cochran and were called Murmurs: Northern Murmurs (1933), Southern Murmurs (1934) and Nursery Murmurs (1935). Although too young to be taken to the Sandon Cabarets, I was allowed to watch my parents perform in the Murmurs despite the fact that the Griff considered some of the sketches unsuitable.

My mother was prominent in Northern Murmurs and stole all the notices in Southern Murmurs. As a result, she claimed, of jealousy among the other performers, she was given comparatively little to do in Nursery Murmurs and much of what material she did get was from another hand than Maud Budden and of inferior quality. When Nursery Murmurs turned out to be a comparative financial and critical flop, she was far from displeased. I remember her most clearly in Southern Murmurs as a Liverpool flower girl in a shawl and cloth cap commenting to an imaginary assistant about her invisible customers in the style perfected by Ruth Draper.

'Here's a wider, Meg. 'and me them whites . . . Flowers, lady? Luke lovely on yer 'usband's grave, lady. Show up beautiful against the hoak and brass 'andles, lady . . . No wonder 'e died. I'd die if I 'ad that face lukein' at me over me fish and chips of a night.'

The music for these reviews was arranged and conducted by Alfred Francis in white tie and tails. In the middle forties, when I had begun to collect jazz records, Tom rushed excitedly into the nursery where I was playing Ellington's 'Rockin' in Rhythm'. He had recognized it as the overture music that Alfred Francis had chosen for *Southern Murmurs*.

Maud tried briefly to break into radio and appeared in a few plays broadcast from the BBC's northern studios in Manchester. I can remember hearing her in the small role of a Liverpool woman deprived of her son in a play about the press gangs in the eighteenth century. It was called *Hawks Abroad*. She didn't make much progress however and soon, easily discouraged if she didn't succeed at anything instantly, relinquished her ambitions. She told us that the doorman at the Manchester studios had said to her, 'You won't get anywhere here, love, if you're not in't click.' But how, I now wonder, did she come to discuss her frustration with the commissionaire?

Her other great woman friend during the thirties was called Sylvia Maxwell-Fyffe, the sister of Rex Harrison. She was married to a Scottish barrister who looked rather like Mussolini and was to become a post-war Conservative Home Secretary with a draconian belief in capital punishment and, more oddly, given Sylvia's many gay friends, a relentless prosecutor of homosexuals. Sylvia was very chic and wore pearls and scarves and little hats with veils. She radiated enjoyment and enthusiasm. She and my mother organized several parties together, usually hiring one of the rooms at the Sandon for the purpose. Sylvia had a rapid rather quacking voice which made everything she said sound amusing.

The other reference point in Maud's 'smart' Liverpool life was David Webster who lived with his parents and his friend Jimmy Bell, in a handsome early Victorian terrace house overlooking Prince's Park. Maud was a little in awe of David whose plump persona and rich Dundee cake diction dominated the arts and whose circle extended far beyond the confines of the city. David, later to become General Manager of Covent Garden, was then General Manager of the Bon Marché, epitome of fashion in

Maud's admittedly provincial experience. There was a restaurant on the top floor where we sometimes had tea. I loved going up in the lift and hearing the lift girls intone like a ritual the various departments in their rather affected voices. ' Going up. Next floor boys' and girls' wear, evening wear, ladies' retiring-room, restaurant.' Sometimes there was a trio playing in the restaurant led by Alfred Francis at the piano, whom I supposed to be playing hookey from his cake shop round the corner. The restaurant was in art-deco pinks and greens. The ice-creams came in metal cups on long stems.

David and Jimmy were always asked to my mother's more interesting dinner parties and usually came, but they didn't often ask her back. This rankled, but David was too much of a catch to allow her to do more than grumble. My father, on the other hand, was quite irritated by his insisting on whisky instead of gin as this meant getting in a special bottle. Yet David was such good value, so full of gossip and name-dropping tales of the world beyond the city limits, that he was always welcome, and his stately arrival eagerly awaited. He was also a member of the Sandon and in one cabaret he was concealed, with the exception of his face, inside a cast of Epstein's neo-primitive Genesis, a marble statue of a pregnant woman which had been exhibited, amidst much moral outrage, at the Blue-coat Chambers to raise money for the building's restoration. His simulation of Genesis's labour pains at the end of the sketch was considered a triumph. It took place in a green spotlight and David's final line was, 'I'm such a very young girl to save such a very old building.' My mother was fond of describing review sketches and when, as in this case, the end was signalled by plunging the stage into darkness, would cry, 'Black out!' with definitive emphasis.

These names: Maud Budden, Alfred Francis, Sylvia Maxwell-Fyfe, David Webster, played as much part in Maud's conversation as her theatrical list. For me they epitomized the exciting life she led. Until I was almost grown up everything Maud did and said seemed remarkable. 'If I'm at home,' she'd say, 'all I have for lunch is Ryvita, cheese and an apple', or 'Keith Winter (a well-known playwright of the period) always says he's seen me breathing over a tomato juice at more cocktail parties than any woman he knows.'

76

My father fitted into her life perfectly well. He was liked by all her friends and never tried to impose any of his. Even when, later in life, she became more difficult and occasionally hysterical, he never criticized her. The only clue he ever gave of mild irritation was to refer to her as 'your mother'. The only one of her friends he actively disliked was a bossy and dwarfish woman journalist called Mary Ventris who wrote a column in the *Liverpool Echo* called 'A Woman's Note'. Tom called her 'Little Runty' and groaned audibly when he spotted her through the window waddling up the path on her bow legs, but then my mother didn't like 'Little Runty' much either. She was just rather intimidated by her, as she was by anyone of forthright opinions. Only once, to my knowledge, did she stand up and be counted and that was when a woman criticized the actress Ena Burrell for having affairs with young men. 'She is not only a great actress,' said Maud, 'but a loyal and true friend'; and with this she left the room. She repeated this curtain line many times in my hearing, by which I deduce that she believed it to be an act of great moral courage reflecting on herself. Indeed, given her placatory and timid temperament, it was exactly that.

The other important aspect of my mother's life was her voluntary work. Part of this, the organization of an annual charity ball at the Adelphi, her presence on appeal committees, her involvement in sales of work and bazaars, tied in with her social life, but most of it was the reverse of glamorous. For at least three days a week she sat behind a desk at The Personal Service visited by 'clients' who were in trouble with bureaucracy or felt they were entitled to grants or supplementary benefits and didn't know how to go about it. The Personal Service, which later amalgamated with the Citizens' Advice Bureau, was Maud's cause. Through it she experienced a sense of purpose and of fulfilment.

Politically she voted Conservative. Not to have done so would have exposed her to criticism, but she always said she felt 'tempted' to vote Labour in local elections, although she believed that it would be to everybody's advantage if politics played no part in municipal affairs. Nevertheless she was appalled by poverty and her instincts, while perhaps occasionally patronizing, were generous and sincere. It's perfectly true that The Personal Service was run on behalf of the working classes by middle-class ladies, a concept now generally suspect. But at the time only middle-class confidence could deal with indifferent bureaucrats and red tape. Maud, so timid in controversy on a personal level, was a tiger on behalf of her clients. She knew their rights backwards and was determined they should get them.

She had become involved in social work during the First World War when she had trained under the formidable feminist Eleanor Rathbone, a cousin of the Mellys, working for the Soldiers and Sailors Family Association, much of whose activities were devoted to ensuring that widowed common-law wives received their pensions. Maud was not without an awareness of the ambivalence of charitable endeavours. She recalled walking down a slum street to further some enquiry and hearing one elderly 'Mary Ellen', the Liverpool name for those beshawled old women who were the matriarchs of the slums, remarking sarcastically to a contemporary, 'There goes a bit of charity for someone's back-yard.' There was, however, a tendency to use her clients as a source of mildly snobbish anecdote, to relate how a child opening the door told her that she'd 'see if the lady was in' and then shouted up the stairs, 'Eh Mam, there's a woman 'ere from der Pairsonal Sairvice.'

She also claimed to 'respect the Conservative working man'. 'Why?' I asked her in my angry teens. 'Because he votes against his interests?' As always, when criticized, she coloured and changed the conversation. It was just one of those remarks which, she'd discovered, pleased most of her acquaintances and which she'd never actually thought through. Sometimes also there was a failure of empathy. As a non-smoker she was always indignant whenever a woman, deserted, beset by debt, another child on the way, chain-smoked through an interview. On balance though, Maud did a great deal of good and was frequently asked for by name by those in recurrent difficulties. Occasionally she was genuinely surprised. 'My husband', one woman told her, 'does it up me be'ind not to have no more kids. He empties the chamber-pot down the sink, when me mother's in the 'ouse, and he calls me a Roman Catholic bastard – now that's not nice is it?' Of course she didn't tell me about this until much later, when I was almost grown up. She saw that what made it funny was the incongruous and even restraint of the woman's reaction to this catalogue of various marital failings, but I've no doubt the advice she offered was constructive, or at any rate uncensorious.

Although her work over the years gave her more awareness of working-class life and more than most of her set, she had no working-class friends, although she once admitted rather coyly to being kissed by a one-armed liftman during the 1914–18 War. Years later, during the early days of the jazz revival, I brought home a piano player I had met at a concert. 'He must be the most Liverpool person we've ever had in the house,' she said, before adding, 'as a guest.'

On a more personal level she called on several old women, most of whom had been 'in service' and now lived in the small dark over-furnished houses off Aigburth Road with a canary for company. There was something of the Lady Bountiful about those expeditions and they always made me uncomfortable even before I was able to understand why. The old women were ever impressed by Maud's condescension. She basked a little too easily in the sycophancy. Still less did I enjoy the visits to the Home for Incurables, a charitable nursing home where 'worthy' cases were admitted to die. I hated the sweet sickly smell of the rooms, the scared old faces, the yellow hands fumbling with the bedspread. Even then I found the name intimidating, grotesquely Victorian in its determined refusal to conceal its function. It was however slightly less brutally identified than the Catholic equivalent (all the 'Incurables' were Church of England). The Catholic institution was called The Hospice for the Dying.

Maud was of course a woman of her time. It is pointless to apply today's standards to her social assumptions. Certainly she derived satisfaction from being admired for her 'selfless' dedication, but she achieved certain positive results, relieved some hardship. She didn't only visit the poor. There was also an American millionairess who lived permanently in a suite at the Adelphi. Her name was Mrs Beere and she was a tiny little woman whose amiably bemused son René, a friend of Uncle Alan's, was to die of alcoholism towards the end of the thirties. Mrs Beere was pathologically mean and expected my mother to bring her own sandwiches while she herself tucked into smoked salmon and crême caramel sent up from the French restaurant on an elaborate trolley and served by an obsequious waiter. Once, when I was about nine Mrs Beere sent me out to buy some medical preparation from a nearby chemist. She gave me the approximate money and on returning I offered her the penny change. 'You can keep it,' she told me with an air of great magnamity. She was very proud of her '*petite*' appearance and once asked a Jewish acquaintance what nationality he would imagine her to be if he didn't know she were an American. She hoped that the answer would be French, but it wasn't. 'Jewish, Mrs Beere,' he told her with firm realism. I didn't mind visiting Mrs Beere because I was fascinated by the idea that anybody should live in a hotel, especially one so grand as the Adelphi with its 1930 Louis Quinze décor and rosy silk wall-hangings.

There was also an old plump myopic woman on Maudie's list. She had been the mistress of a famous actor, but had later become a devout Roman Catholic. She was badly off and her flat was both dusty and depressing, but the décor was pure Ballet-Russe with tasselled light shades and an ottoman covered with huge cushions and grubby pierrot dolls. The cheap crucifixes and madonnas looked out of place in such louche, if dilapidated, surroundings.

From an early age I enjoyed going out with my mother even when our destination was not all I could wish. I was impressed by her knowledge of Liverpool, her sudden purposeful dives into side streets, her ascent up the linoleumed stairs of scruffy buildings full of small wholesalers to an upper floor, where there was a man who mended watches or a 'little woman' who made hats. Her dressmaker was the fattest woman I've ever seen outside a fair booth. She worked in the tiny front room of a decayed Georgian house, her mouth bristling with pins. She smelt of rancid fat. She would copy, rather approximately, photographs of clothes Maud had torn out of *Vogue*. My mother spent very little on herself. While some of her richer or vainer friends wore mink or sable she made do with a 'pony' coat bought in a sale or a rather beady-eyed, moth-eaten fox fur that bit its own groin with a clip. Tom, given his careful nature, did nothing to encourage her to build up her wardrobe. When I was about seven I decided to remedy this. At my request she released me at the entrance to the Bon Marché and I went to ask if it were possible to buy a fur coat for about five shillings, the amount she had 'lent' me to get her a birthday present. They told me it was not possible, but Maud pretended to be just as pleased with the ugly 'slightly shopworn' fake crocodile handbag which was within my budget.

My father's life – golf on Saturdays, snooker at The Albert on Fridays, occasional invitations to shoot or fish – naturally involved me far less during my childhood. Even my mother's interests impinged only occasionally although, as I grew older, she began to spend more time with me, to include me in many of her activities largely perhaps because I showed such a precocious and enthusiastic interest in everything she said or did. Even so the nursery remained the centre of my life, the afternoon walk the principal event of the day. Gradually things assumed a pattern. The seasons established themselves. Christmas, Easter, the summer holidays became fixed rather than unplaced occurrences.

In 1932, when I was six and Bill was three, something extraordinary happened. My mother, then forty, had become pregnant again and my sister Andrée was born. I can't imagine that this, given my mother's age, was deliberate, but the birth was without complications and its outcome enchanting. Andrée had huge slightly slanting eyes and a snub nose. We all adored her and I felt none of the sibling rivalry which made my relationship with Bill so difficult to sustain. Nevertheless, when Andrée was at the crawling stage and we were all three playing in the nursery, she put a bead into her mouth and it became lodged in her throat. I noticed this, but was playing with some plasticine and totally absorbed. Andrée began to turn purple and it was Bill who thought to toddle on to the landing and shout down, 'There's something the matter with Andrée.' Our nanny, who had been fetching tea, ran up the stairs, up-ended her and smacked her on the back until the bead was dislodged. Everybody was rightly appalled at my indifference and so, once I had taken it in, was I. Even now the heavy smell and oily consistency of plasticine triggers off a sense of guilt.

Andrée arrived at the height of the Depression. Maud used to say that when I was born my father gave her a diamond ring, when Bill was born a platinum ring, but that when Andrée was born all he could afford to do was shave off his recently cultivated moustache. She was very touched by this gesture as she could 'never be doing with facial hair'.

81

Number 90 Chatham Street, first occupied by my great-grandfather, George Melly MP, in the late 1850s, was an austere Georgian corner house of some size. Many of its windows had been bricked up at the time of the window tax. Although the front door was indeed in Chatham Street, the main façade overlooked Abercromby Square with its small residents' garden.

Chatham Street and Abercromby Square had once been fashionable but the merchant princes had long since departed. Most of the houses had become seamen's lodgings, and Number 90 alone, like a Victorian whale stranded on a polluted beach, retained its original identity. The Mellys, with their passion for appropriation, referred to this one house as 'Chatham Street' or 'Chatty' for short, as though the lodging houses didn't exist.

When I was born, there were still three members of the family living there: my Great-Uncle Willy or Bill (the names were interchangeable), and his sisters Eva and Florence. Their brother George had moved out after his marriage in 1917 to a lady called Lydia Elizabeth Edwards. Four years later she went mad, or as Willie Bert Rawdon Smith put it rather more tactfully in his notes on the family, 'became a complete invalid'. Great-Uncle George died in 1927, but his wife lived on until 1932. I never met her, and am unaware what form her madness took although the Griff, rather surprisingly, let slip that she had once been invited to play bridge with her, and that 'Mrs Melly dealt all the cards to herself'. Great-Aunt Florence died in 1928 when I was two. By the time I was conscious of Chatham Street only Aunt Eva and Uncle Willy remained *in situ*.

A visit to 'Chatty', most commonly for Sunday lunch, was an intimidating experience for a child. The short walk from the 33 tram stop outside the Women's Hospital through those decaying once-handsome streets and squares accompanied by the distant sound of a Salvation Army band, helped to build up a certain dreamlike anticipation. Standing on the porch step in front of the forbidding shiny black door, hearing the bell peel in the distant kitchen basement, Bill and I, and later Andrée, were sometimes overcome with giggles, sometimes unnaturally grave, at any rate very aware that we were on the threshold of a different world, as remote from everyday reality as Alice's Wonderland. Maud, still in awe of the older Mellys' initial disapproval, was in part responsible for our tension, but even Tom never seemed entirely at ease. Here no doubt his shortcomings as a schoolboy and business man had been made clear to him, the opposition to his marriage formulated. His defence took the form of affectionate mockery. It was the most common reaction amongst his generation of the family, a kind of nervous frivolity.

The door was eventually opened by Davis, curiously described as 'the head waitress', who had been at Chatham Street since 1914. Dressed in a severe black uniform with white cap and apron she nevertheless gave an impression of White-Queen-like dishevellment and calm panic. Like Gangie's Marjorie, she identified members of the family by trusting the surname as taken for granted. She addressed my parents as Mr and Mrs Tom, Gangie and Gampa were Mr and Mrs Heywood, her employers Mr Willy and Miss Eva. Davis had a rapid, very slight Liverpool accent. I never knew her Christian name or, at the time, imagined that she even had one.

Despite its Georgian exterior, 'Chatty' was completely Victorian inside. The only concessions to the twentieth century were a telephone, a wireless set and, on the piano in the library, an anachronistic little nest of art-deco ashtrays in 'jazz' colours with aluminium rims. Otherwise it was as though by stepping into the hall one simultaneously mislaid at least thirty years and, in some rooms, fifty.

Just inside the front door, crammed into quite a small vestibule, was a huge glass case of stuffed animals largely engaged in carnage: a fox looked up from dismembering a rabbit; a stoat was in the act of pouncing on a fieldmouse; a squirrel, frozen in terror, recoiled at the descent of a swooping hawk suspended from a wire. There was also a large cupboard, carved with Melly crests, and containing several boxed grey toppers, and facing it a substantial table, flanked by two of those uncomfortable little high-backed armorial chairs, and on it a silver tray for visiting cards.

All the corridors at Chatty were painted a deep shiny orange-brown. When I was very young I was terrified by a picture hanging opposite the curve of the staircase. It was probably a copy of some detail from a seventeenth-century mannerist and showed the face of a bearded old man screaming in pain or terror. The fine curve of the staircase was broken by a series of small inch-worms of metal screwed at regular intervals down the handrail to discourage young Mellys, now old or dead, from sliding down the bannisters.

I knew little of the upper floors. The nursery and schoolroom were long closed up. My grandfather and his brothers and sisters were the last generation to have grown up in the house. All I knew of the nursery was derived from a late nineteenth-century water-colour at The Grange; a fire glowing behind a high fender, a dappled rocking-horse, a Noah's Ark on the floor. It's true that the drawing-room was on the first floor, a high Victorian symphony of faded gold, rose and royal blue, but by the thirties it was only used for the grandest family occasions. Its chandelier, stripped of its branches and pendant drops, was wrapped in a pendulous sheet like a great bag of cottage cheese. As those who lived at Chatty grew fewer and older, the number of rooms in general use contracted. Uncle Bill and Aunt Eva slept upstairs of course and there were guest-rooms when anyone came to stay. Davis and the servants climbed up the back stairs to the attics late at night and crept down again at dawn to black the grates, light the fires and dust and polish, but in my childhood the life of the house was effectively confined to three rooms on the ground floor: the library, the dining-room and the little morning-room, with their handsome mahogany doors.

The library was furthest away from the front door at the end of the shiny orange passage with its screaming old man. It was a room almost without colours – brown, sage-green, dusty blacks – and smelt of old leather. The only window to have escaped the window tax looked out on to Chatham Street, but there were some small French doors leading out on to a dark little garden yard with a tree in it. The light in the library was always subterranean. The nest of 'jazz' ashtrays on the piano were as incongruous as a clown at a funeral.

Although quite large, the room was cluttered. There were plants on stands and two marble statues on columns: a bust of an idealized woman with sightless eyes and a cherub with an intricately-carved swag of lace draped strategically across its presumably minuscule privates. The furniture was unmemorable and uncomfortable. Only Uncle Bill's chair with its stuffed armrests and curved legs had a certain distinction. It was set to the side of a steel grate next to a small table for his silver cigarette box and table lighter. It was never moved an inch. It was the library, rather than the drawing-room, which was used for family parties.

Directly opposite was a lavatory with a porcelain bowl decorated with blue irises and set into a rectangle of mahogany with a brass plug let into an oval indentation on its surface and pulled upwards to flush the cistern. There was also a small stand-up lavatory basin for gentlemen attached to the opposite wall, and in the bottom of this lay several small pebbles. I couldn't, I still cannot, imagine the function of those pebbles. Later, when I first heard about people 'passing' gallstones I wondered if that was what they were. The walls of this room were hung with old sepia photographs of my great-aunts in their youth, mostly seated in boats in the Lake District. As I knew that their generation never mentioned natural functions I found it odd and a little unnerving to encounter their fixed expressions gazing at me as I sat on the mahogany seat or stood at the little basin. This lavatory was only used by men and boys. The ladies were directed somewhere upstairs.

The morning-room, to the left of the front door, was small and undistinguished with wooden transom screens covering the lower half of the two windows to stop people in Chatham Street looking in and in consequence keeping half the light out. Aunt Eva did her accounts here and wrote her letters, but it was important to us in that one of the cupboards contained toys and books, the remnants of the abandoned nursery, with which we were allowed to play after lunch.

These were mostly Victorian and in many cases extremely ingenious. There was a twisted metal snake which crawled rapidly up or down a long flat rod held perpendicularly and pierced by evenly-spaced holes. There was a monkey which performed acrobatics on a trapeze and was set in motion by squeezing the narrow base of the forked stick between which it hung. There were diabolos, spinning tops with whips, bagatelle and spillikins, but our favourite toy was a more recent addition, probably Edwardian, possibly dating from the Great War. It consisted of two wooden ships, a dreadnought and a submarine. The submarine was loaded with a torpedo, spring-activated by pressing a button. The body of the dreadnought concealed a mousetrap-like mechanism and, after setting this, one replaced the top deck cautiously and built up the superstructure on top. The torpedo was fired across the carpet from some feet away and, if it hit the target painted on the side of the dreadnought it set off the mousetrap, and top deck and superstructure were flung into the air with astonishing range and velocity. It took only a second to destroy the dreadnought and several minutes to put it back together, but it was extremely satisfactory to operate and Bill and I would frequently quarrel as to whose turn it was.

The books were rather dull on the whole, improving and pious works in very small print. But there were some splendidly engraved, hand-coloured volumes of fierce beasts and one fascinating book full of sadistic tales about naughty children getting their come-uppance, which even I was able to read as it deployed no word of more than three letters, a restraint which must have meant considerable circumlocution.

'Ned,' one story began, 'why did you get the cat and put the cat in a bag, and put the bag in the sea?'

'For fun.'

'It is not fun for you and no fun at all for the cat.'

Needless to say this homily had no effect on Ned, but he was eventually bitten on the leg by a mad dog and lay in terrible agony, the jeering of the creatures he had tormented ringing in his ears.

'Do you say it is for fun now?' asks a fly he had partially dismembered or, to revert to the monosyllabic style of the original, 'did get the fly and did get the leg off the fly'.

While we played or read, the grown-ups dozed in the library in the gap between lunch and tea. Everybody ate far too much at Chatty and most of the men drank too much. The liverish, rather disgruntled state to which this reduced them between the enormous meals was known as Chatty fever.

It was in fact the dining-room I remember most clearly. We

usually went straight in on our arrival. Uncle Bill, especially after Aunt Eva died, frequently spent the whole day there, sitting in a chair which was a pair to the one in the library, chain-smoking Turkish cigarettes through an ivory holder, a glass of brandy and soda on the little table at his side. When he had finished a cigarette he would lean forward and blow through the holder accurately projecting the dog-end into the fire. It was a completely traditional Victorian dining-room: the walls were crimson, the furniture mahogany, the pictures – a copy of a Murillo, a huge riverscape, still-lives with fruit or lobsters – all heavily framed. The dining table was enormous and would easily sit twenty people. There were huge sideboards at each end. On the other side of the fireplace there was a false door balancing the real one, with a cupboard behind it for glass and china. On the back of this door it was the custom for young Mellys to be measured at various ages; their height, name and the date pencilled in alongside the mark. I found it very strange to see my father's name next to the figures three feet six inches, and the date, 12 October 1905, or my grandfather's in 1876 when he was only three feet two inches tall.

There was seldom just us for lunch. Gangie and Gampa were often there, sometimes the Leathers, frequently several Rawdon Smiths. The volume of sound, a family characteristic, was constantly *fortissimo*.

Eva, while short and plump, was a formidable figure. Her clothes made no concession to the century. She dressed entirely in black and her voluminous dress reached the ground. She wore a locket with a coil of hair in it, a memento of someone close to her who had died. Her white hair was worn up. Her face was ruddy and plump and her slightly protruding rather luminous brown eyes and flat features gave her a distinctly pug-like look. Like her late sister Florence, she had a passion for education and, to my apprehensive terror, insisted on seeing our school reports and on setting us mathematical problems or asking us to read to her. Her comments on our shortcomings were scathing and as painful to Maud as to us. She was, however, basically kind and once our inquisition was over, adept at amusing us. Eva did a considerable amount of charitable work, but her main occupation was running Chatham Street. Her hobbies were water-colour sketching and completing enormous jigsaws. Her paintings were not up to much but everybody was expected to admire them. She usually submitted several to the annual exhibition at the Walker Art Gallery, the Liverpool equivalent of the Royal Academy Summer Show, and they were most often hung. One year, however, her contribution was rejected and, to make matters worse, a painting of a bluebell wood by Dorothy Leather, my Auntie Golly, was accepted and hung 'on the line'. Aunt Eva didn't take this at all well and Uncle Bill, never noted for tact, attempted to reassure her, in front of Dorothy, by saying that the judges obviously didn't know what they were talking about.

Eva's jigsaws came from a club and were properly made of quite thick wood. She was a complete purist. No picture or title was provided by the club, but even this was not enough for her. She would most often turn the pieces face down so that there was no help from areas of colour, and only when it was completed, would she place a large board over the surface on which she had worked and turn it over to reveal 'The Changing of the Guard' or 'Deerstalking in the Highlands'. This abstract activity took up a fair amount of her time. Her jigsaw was laid out on a huge baize-covered tray on a rather rickety little table in the morning room, and one dreadful afternoon Bill and I, in our excitement over a direct hit on the dreadnought, knocked it over when it was three-quarters done.

Eva had a pocket in her throat and as, like most of the family, she ate far too fast, food would frequently lodge in it and have to be coughed up again and reswallowed. This was a noisy and prolonged operation and the convention was that nobody paid any attention, simply shouting even louder than usual to be heard. Shortly after my parents' marriage they were invited to dinner at Chatham Street and my mother, unused to Eva's retching and gasping, felt and showed her dismay. Eva drew breath for a moment to say that if Maud were upset she had permission to leave the table. Maud, who was trying hard to ingratiate herself, went crimson with embarrassment and shame.

Eva died in 1937, but her brother Bill lived on alone at Chatham Street until 1944. Willie Bert's description of Uncle Bill seems to me so succinct and plaintive that I'm going to reprint it in full, and then to relate those facts which impinge on my own memory or which I learnt from my father, about the almost silent figure sitting in front of the steel grate in the dining-room on Sunday mornings.

Willie Bert wrote:

William Rathbone, George and Sarah Melly's 7th child and third son, was born at 90 Chatham Street on March 30th 1867. Known to every one as Willy, he was always rather delicate, and was educated at the Royal Institution, Liverpool. In 1883 his health broke down and he was sent for 15 months to live with Lord Dalhousie's head keeper at Panmure, which laid the foundation of his great interest and knowledge of natural history and shooting.

In 1891 he spent three months in Naples studying sponges, but had to come home as he was ill. He then spent a year in South America as Supercargo in Lamport and Holt's ships; after which he was in their London office for a year or so before joining his father's firm of George Melly and Co. in Liverpool, in January 1894, and becoming a partner in October after his father's death.

His interest in life was never business but always birds and shooting. In 1894 his uncle, George Holt, took a shooting at Llwyn Ynn near Ruthin, always referred to as The Farm, for the entertainment of his nephews (and nieces) and put William in charge. This went on till the estate was sold in 1913, William assuming more and more of the financial responsibility. It was a good general shoot producing over 1,000 head most years. All the members of the family went there year after year, his sister Florence acting as hostess.

In 1914 he took a grouse moor at Farndale in Yorkshire, but gave it up on the outbreak of war. From then until the death of his brother George, he had no shooting of his own but spent many weeks each year at Rosedale Abbey. After George's death in 1927, he became tenant of the Rosedale shoot and carried it on in the same lavish way as it had been in the past, but spending some weeks there in the spring and summer bird-watching and photographing. He was a very keen photographer and left hundreds of prints all in books duly annotated. For some years he used to prepare magic lantern slides from some of his photographs which he showed at the family Christmas party.

In March, 1932, it was decided to close the firm of George Melly and Co., and he retired from business, but at Rosedale on October 4th that year he had some sort of stroke which left him a completely different man, very silent and taking very little interest in what went on around him. Up till then he had been a very talkative man and although so handicapped by ill health, was tremendously energetic and lived life to the full. He would walk all day after grouse or partridges and then stay up half the night talking or playing cards. He was always more than generous to his nephews and nieces.

Shooting and photography were by no means his only interests. He fished, played golf and croquet whenever the opportunity offered. He said he had taken part at some time in his life in every sport except hunting.

He never married. From the time he came home from South America he suffered terribly from psoriasis. He died on 9th March, aged 76. A greater age than any of his brothers.

I was only six when Uncle Bill had 'some sort of stroke' and have therefore little recollection of the 'tremendously energetic', 'very talkative man' of earlier days. In fact I can only remember him once outside his own front door and that was when he took me, aged about five, to visit the Liverpool Zoo. This was a rather seedy and ill-stocked institution on Mossley Hill which nevertheless, in lieu of anything better, played an important role in my life, as I was and remain fascinated by zoos and had at that time some aspirations to become a keeper when I grew up.

For this expedition Willy wore pepper-and-salt tweeds and brown boots, while on his head was a large, rather shapeless tweed cap which my mother said 'looked like a sponge-bag'. We wandered together for an hour or so examining the mangy lions and tigers in their cramped quarters, the solitary elephant in its sweet-smelling shed, the few snakes, the dispirited bears. Willy, peering through his round pince-nez over his bedraggled nicotine-stained moustache, offered few observations until it was time to go. Then he said to me, 'I like this better than the London Zoo.' I turned to him in appalled amazement. Although I had not yet visited Regent's Park, it was high on my list of priorities if I should ever be taken to London. I knew there was no comparison. My uncle had said something so perverse, so unreasonable that I demanded an immediate explanation. Why? How? What did he mean?

'Not so many damned animals to look at,' he mumbled.

My father told me something of Uncle Willy before his stroke. He had been a great organizer of family outings. One summer in the early twenties there had been a circus pitched on a field off Aigburth Road. It included a lion tamer one of whose beasts, whose name was Nero, was of such ferocity that it was seldom allowed into the ring. Uncle Bill had attended the opening night and was so impressed by Nero's dangerous intransigence that he returned most evenings with as many of the family as could be persuaded to accompany him. As the circus was not doing too well and he had booked the front row for the entire run of the show, he was treated like a Roman Emperor and, like a Roman Emperor, it was the lion act which particularly interested him. Whenever he was present and if, as was most often the case, the lion tamer had decided that Nero was in too uncertain a temper to join his companions in the ring, Willy would demand his presence. 'Let Nero out!' he'd bellow, and it was done. I couldn't help wondering how Uncle Willy would have felt if a fatal accident had taken place as a result of his whim.

There was indeed an element of sadism in him. One of the few ways that we, as children, could arouse him out of his torpor was to ask him to show us the mousetrap he had brought back many years earlier from a visit to Berlin at the turn of the century. This was in the form of a Gothic church and quite large. The top could be removed to show its sinister inner workings. The mouse entered by the church door and proceeded up the nave attracted by the smell of cheese. At the foot of the altar it trod on a board which was sprung in such a way as to slam the door behind it. Having recovered from its panic, it renewed its interest in the cheese and, in pursuit of it, climbed a ladder up the inside of the tower most of which was occupied by a large water tank. At the top of the ladder, and over the tank, was a narrow passage with the cheese at the far end. The mouse excitedly scampered towards it, unaware that halfway across was a trap-door which opened, precipitating the unfortunate creature into the water tank where it swam until it drowned. What was so ingenious about the contraption, as Uncle Willy enthusiastically explained to us, was that the action of the trap, in springing back into the closed position, reopened the church door to be ready to welcome any other passing mouse and, as there was no smell of death, there was no limit to the number of rodents it could dispatch in one mission. I had proof as to its effectiveness. One afternoon Bill and I visited the dark and tortuous kitchens in the basement. In the yard, thrown there by Davis for the nourishment of the Chatham Street cats, were the drowned corpses of four or five mice, the harvest of a single night.

When he had finished explaining the mechanism of this infernal and very Teutonic machine, Uncle Bill would reset it with his constantly shaking hands, replace its religious exterior and ask us to put it back under the sideboard before relapsing into his customary silence.

This withdrawal had marked the end of a more regular family ritual than the release of Nero; the tribal visits to the D'Oyly Carte Opera Company on their biennial appearance in Liverpool, a custom much dreaded by Maudie in the early years of her marriage. This was not only on musical grounds, although no doubt for her Gilbert and Sullivan came under the general heading of 'mini-mini', but also because of Uncle Bill's noisy and extrovert behaviour on these pre-stroke outings. This was due to the fact that, unlike the majority of Savoyards, he considered the overture as a time when chocolates could be ordered and the merits of the Company discussed with members of the family however distantly seated along the row. His competence to pass judgement was founded on his golfing friendship with Sir Henry Lytton and with Miss Bertha Belmore, the two principals. Wishing to make this clear to those around him he would boom out Sir Henry's opinions at second hand. The death of Miss Belmore, far from inhibiting him, added a fresh topic. 'Harry tells me', he'd shout, oblivious to a mounting storm of angry shushing, 'that this woman's not as good as Bertha!' Despite the end of these visits en masse, my father retained his affection for the operas and was delighted that in time I was to share his enthusiasm. His favourite was Ruddigore, which during the thirties had been dropped from the repertoire, so our first visit was to his second preference, The Gondoliers. I enjoyed it so much that he later took me to see The Mikado, The Yeomen of the Guard and the rest of the canon. I learnt many of the songs by heart and would enunciate them in that curiously affected mincing voice favoured by the Company. I tried, at Tom's suggestion, singing them to Uncle Willy, but he showed no more than a flicker of interest. Sir Harry had followed Bertha Belmore into the dark. Gilbert and Sullivan, like everything else except the mousetrap, had lost their savour.

The cause of Uncle Bill's stroke was obscure but there were dark rumours. My father told me eventually that it was believed by some that, as a child, he had been injected for smallpox with a needle, insufficiently sterilized, which had previously been used on a baby infected with syphilis. It is true he never married but this is more probably because of his psoriasis, a flaking of the skin caused by the overproduction of cells, which afflicted his whole body with the exception of his face and hands. This led to terrible irritation especially at night and his only relief was to get up and take a tar bath. There was a limit to the time he was allowed to stay in the water and my father told me that once, staying at Rosedale in a room next to the bathroom, he had been awakened by Uncle Bill murmuring something rhythmically to himself and, on enquiring next morning, he discovered it to be Lewis Carroll's *The Hunting of the Snark*. Apparently the time it took Bill to recite this work coincided exactly with the period he was allowed to submerge himself in the medicated waters.

Apart from his shaking and the psoriasis, Uncle Bill also suffered from a hatred of anything sweet or sugary with the single if inexplicable exception of chocolate peppermint creams, for which indeed he nourished an inordinate passion. In consequence he was given each day his own little dish of Hasty Pudding, a kind of unsweetened soufflé, while everyone else dug into a wide choice of elaborate trifles, tarts and rich rice dishes.

As the head of the household it would normally have been his prerogative to carve the enormous joint which preceded the puddings, but his ague and general disability prevented it. With no apparent irony intended, it fell to him in recompense to ladle out the puddings which were placed in front of him after the removal of the meat course.

'Anyone want any of this muck?' he would enquire. Frequently this was one of the only three times he spoke during our entire visit. The other two sentences were, 'How's yourself?' on our arrival and, 'Look after yourself' on our departure. The contrast for older members of the family who remembered him as 'very talkative' must have been extraordinary.

The great occasion of the year at Chatham Street was the family party held towards the end of the week after Christmas. Almost every Melly and Smith living were present and, in the case of married women, *née* Melly, their husbands and children also. The one notable exception was Willie Bert's mother, Great-Aunt Beatrice, who lived in southern England. After a toast to 'absent friends', Willie Bert always leapt to his feet and proposed

'My Mother' as a codicil. It was more likely her geographical rather than her 'invidious position' as a divorced woman which prevented her presence at the Chatty parties. Not that distance alone kept many members of the family away. My Great-Aunt Nell and her daughter Cousin Nell were assiduous attenders. They both lived together in London in an Edwardian mansion block off the Fulham Road with eau-de-Nil walls and fine Dutch furniture, but stayed a great deal at Chatham Street and indeed lived there during the Hitler war; Aunt Nell looking after Uncle Bill, Cousin Nell driving a Civil Defence ambulance throughout the Blitz. Aunt Nell and her daughter were known as 'Old Nell' and 'Young Nell'.

Old Nell had been the second wife of Hugh Melly, one of Uncle Willy's brothers who had died in 1924, two years before I was born. He was said to have been extremely handsome. His first wife, who was killed in a carriage accident in 1890, had two daughters. She had been a Holt, a member of the shipping family. The older daughter married a Canadian and I never knew her, but the younger, Cousin Joan, married a rather noisy, ferociously right-wing, but personally kindly coalmine owner called Major Arthur Bromilow, and the Bromilows too were very much a presence at the Chatty parties.

Old Nell had three children by Hugh: Pete, who was killed in the 1914–18 war; John, who was a surgeon and took the only British Red Cross unit out to Abyssinia when it was attacked by Mussolini and who was shot on the last day of the conflict by an African rioter who, logically enough I suppose, mistook him for an Italian; and Young Nell herself.

I can remember John who seemed quite extraordinarily charming and sophisticated. He had been a friend of Vivien Leigh's and had written a drawing-room comedy which was almost put on in the West End. He had, like many of his generation during the twenties, a passion for elaborate practical jokes. At the same time, like his mother, he was profoundly religious, and it was the application of his practical evangelical spirit which led to his death in the streets of Addis Ababa in 1936.

Old Nell was, I suppose, plain but with so glowing and saint-like a personality that she seemed to be beautiful. Like Aunt Eva she made no concessions to current fashion but her dresses, while black and floor length, were Edwardian rather than Victorian, and she always wore a tight, boned neck choker in the manner of Queen Alexandra. Unlike Eva and Florence, whose philanthropy was severely practical and objective, Nell's faith insisted on a St Francis-like involvement with those she tried to help. She was preyed on by many petty con-men who came to her with optimistic schemes for self-improvement, and when in London she would visit the embankment night after night with food and money for the down-and-outs. Aunt Eva found this approach intensely irritating, referring rather contemptuously to 'Nell's lame ducks'.

Nell was a great admirer of the Salvation Army. When the film of Shaw's *Major Barbara* came out, she and a like-minded friend staged a planned protest in the Plaza Cinema, Lime Street and were ejected. She was also an animal rights sympathizer long before such a movement existed. She was wracked with guilt at having enjoyed hunting as a girl. It was the ride, she explained, which had been the source of her pleasure, but the ride after all was at the expense of the poor fox and even of his life. To be surrounded by relations who shot and fished with such enthusiasm, staying frequently in a house which contained the fiendish ecclesiastical mousetrap, must have caused her much pain. During the Blitz she took it upon herself to read Uncle Bill the whole of *Gone With the Wind*. Increasingly senile I imagine he made little of it, especially as he was very frightened and confused by the bombing.

Young Nell was a cheerful person, full of fun, obsessed with the Mellys, and given to that vice of all large middle-class English families between the wars of constantly asserting that 'we are just like the Forsytes'. Young Nell never married. She lives in the same eau-de-Nil flat off Fulham Road and is still, at the age of eighty-three, known as Young Nell.

It was at the Chatty party that the remaining Riverslea Mellys surfaced: Cousins Leonard and Fanny, both old and as poor as church mice. Leonard's dinner jacket was green with age. Rotund, bustling Fanny gave us children only half-a-crown each but they were always mint half-crowns which she had drawn especially from the bank.

It was this huge and noisy party then, three generations of them, who assembled yearly for the great family feast. What happened at it was as fixed and immutable as a religious ceremony.

Before dinner the rarely used drawing-room was opened up although the chandelier remained in its shroud. Sherry was on offer. The meal was huge, even by Chatham Street standards. The youngest member of the family had to propose a toast, an obligation which made my sister Andrée almost ill with nerves when it came to her turn. Toasts completed, a long and very boring event followed. The senior member of the family recited this catch to the person on his or her right:

Do you know the muffin man, the muffin man, the muffin man?
Oh, do you know the muffin man who lives in Drury Lane?

To which the person so questioned replied:

Oh, yes, I know the muffin man, the muffin man, the
    muffin man,
Oh, yes, I know the muffin man who lives in Drury Lane.

Then both parties would intone together:

Then we *two* know the muffin man, the muffin man, the
    muffin man,
We *two* know the muffin man who lives in Drury Lane.

Then the person to have answered the question first turned towards whoever was on his or her right and repeated it; was answered in the affirmative and the three acquaintances of the muffin man agreed in unison that they knew him too. Unbelievably, this rigmarole continued until everybody at the table – there must have been well over thirty most years – could shout out the final chorus:

Then we *all* know the muffin man, the muffin man, the
    muffin man,
We *all* know the muffin man who lives in Drury Lane.

Some tried to enliven this incredibly tiresome chore by putting on funny accents but most, with surprising good spirits, simply played it straight. It was never suggested that it might be curtailed or dropped altogether. That would have been considered almost blasphemous.

After everybody agreed that they knew the unnaturally gregarious muffin-man, the ladies went into the library and the gentlemen drank port or brandy and told mildly indecent jokes. Boys were allowed to remain in the dining-room from about the age of twelve for this initiation into masculine mores. Even Uncle Bill became quite animated and told a story about the sexual habits of the Kaiser. He also usually described a 'feller' he had seen on the stage in Paris in the early 1900s who could fart several tunes and blow out a candle at a considerable distance by the same means. Nobody really believed this, but quite recently it was revealed as fact and a book on the gentleman, 'Le Péto-mane', was published proving that Uncle Bill was telling the truth.

The men, whether laughing at the Kaiser's inadequacy or pre-tending to believe in the exploits of 'Le Pétomane', all wore dinner jackets and the same year that I was allowed to remain behind with them in the dining-room, I wore one too. This was not new – the idea of spending money on a dinner jacket for a growing child would have appalled my father – but had been handed down for several generations. Even so I was extremely pleased with myself, despite Tom's joke at my expense earlier in the evening. I'd gone into his dressing-room, ostensibly so that he could tie my bow, in fact to solicit admiration, but all he'd said was, 'Don't annoy the little man. They're very touchy these dwarfs!'

I must have looked rather hurt because he immediately explained the source of this mysterious but unflattering re-action. As a small child in Sefton Park he had seen a dwarf out walking with his 'owner', a showman attached to a travelling fair then in situ. He had scampered curiously towards it, to be met by this informative reproach. Once I'd understood it was only a joke I was completely mollified. I even repeated it on arrival.

When we left the dining-room to 'join the ladies', it was discovered that my brother Bill, jealous that my three years seniority allowed me to stay on, had concealed himself under the table. He told me later that he had understood nothing that had been said and grown extremely bored. In fact my own re-action had been more or less the same, but of course I wasn't letting on. 'You will when you're older,' I assured him dismissively.

The final stage of the Chatty party took place in the library. It was in two parts: 'The Great Divide' and the entertainment. 'The Great Divide' was the name given to the doling out of money in lieu of presents, a rational if somewhat impersonal solution to the problem of how to reward so large a gathering. Uncle Bill would slump in his accustomed chair. Davis would carry in a silver tray piled high with brown envelopes like wage packets. She would stand by her employer and he would pick up the envelopes at random, reading out the name written on each of them: 'Young Nell', 'Gillian Leather', 'Samuel Heywood Melly'. Each of us in turn would go forward, collect our envelope, and kiss him on his cold indifferent cheek. Each knew exactly what to expect: £50 for his generation, £25 for my father's, £10 for those in their twenties, £1 for my contemporaries. It was rather a soulless exercise, the only excitement arising from the order in which we were called and the possibility, never fulfilled, that someone might have been accidentally left out.

The entertainment followed immediately. Gangie and Gampa would offer one of 'Mrs Caudle's Curtain Lectures'; we would perform a carefully rehearsed sketch; others played the piano or recited comic monologues. One year, during Aunt Eva's life-time, a Rawdon Smith girl – I believe it was Hope, one of Willie Bert's daughters – tap-danced to a gramophone record having first changed into shorts. Aunt Eva was visibly put out at this immodesty which must have upset Willie Bert. He was always extremely solicitous towards the old ladies of the family.

As Uncle Bill had already suffered his stroke before I was old enough to attend the Chatty parties, he had relinquished his bird-watching and photography and in consequence no longer 'prepared and showed his magic-lantern slides as part of the entertainment'. I gather that this was no great loss. Young Nell once told me that the performance lasted a long time and that the slides themselves were so blurred and indistinct that the whole enterprise had become known to the more irreverent members of the family as 'Owls in a Fog'.

During the war the Chatty parties became smaller and one year, during the height of the Blitz, there was none at all. Uncle Bill died in 1944 after several days in a coma. Davis, who had looked after him with extreme devotion, told my mother, with initial reluctance, of his end. He had regained consciousness on a cold but bright winter's evening and hauled himself up in his narrow bed to face the setting sun. 'Oh hell!' he'd muttered resignedly and fallen back dead.

I'd been to visit him shortly before this took place. On the chest of drawers was a small glass dome and inside it a stuffed thrush and a golf ball. A brass plaque on the base explained the curious confrontation: 'In 1903 W.R.Melly drove off the 3rd tee at Formby Golf Club. His ball struck a thrush in the air, killing it instantly, and holed in one.'

With Willy's death, Chatham Street was given up and its contents, with the exception of the drawing-room furniture which was left to the museum, sold or divided amongst the family. Uncle Bill left his body for dissection in the hope that 'whatever was wrong with me' might further medical research, but the offer was refused and he was buried in the tiny graveyard of the ancient Unitarian chapel at the Dingle, opposite the Gaumont Cinema. The house itself now belongs to the University. Passing it recently I saw, through a window, the morning-room full of filing cabinets and illuminated by strip-lighting. A girl brought in a plastic cup of tea or coffee and placed it in front of a man sorting out folders on a formica-topped table.

Surrounded by large late nineteenth-century houses, ringed by a sandy ride where middle-class little girls cantered self-consciously past on horses hired from a local riding school, Sefton Park forms a valley bisected by a string of lakes, the largest of which, 'The Big Lake', had boats for hire in summer and, when frozen in the winter, became black with skaters. On the other side of the lakes, dominating the landscape, is the Palm House, a large, circular, domed building of steel and glass in imitation of the Crystal Palace. When it was cold it offered a steamy refuge to expressionless men in bright blue suits and red ties, many of them missing an arm or leg. They were the institutionalized wounded of the 1914–18 war, and would sit all day smoking Woodbines on the fern-patterned Victorian benches. Behind them grew a contained circular jungle, its tropical trees and plants neatly labelled, and here and there, a small marble statue of a coy nymph or simpering maiden with a quotation from a poet carved on her plinth. In summer the men sat outside on similar benches.

Statues ringed the exterior also, life-size and representing historic figures in the arts and sciences. Before I could read, my father invented false identities for those frozen worthies. A Swiss botanist, he assured me, represented the Prince of Wales, while Galileo, holding a globe of the world, he maintained to be Dixie Dean, the celebrated footballer. Beyond the Palm House the park levelled out to form a great plain big enough to accommodate the annual fair; below it a steep hill swept down to one of the little lakes.

At the bottom of this hill were two stone posts aimed to discourage cyclists as there was then only a few yards across a road before the iron railings which ringed the water. I had at one time a small yellow motor car with push pedals and on one of our visits to look at Dixie Dean and the Prince of Wales my father made the following proposition. He would squat behind me on the yellow pedal car, in itself a rather precarious operation, and we would then free-wheel down the hill between the posts, whereupon I would have to turn the wheel abruptly to the right in order to avoid the railings. At five or six, for I can't have been any older, this seemed a perfectly reasonable if exciting thing to do, for I trusted Tom entirely and the danger didn't occur to me. We did it, gathering considerable speed, and shot between the posts missing the railings by a few inches. The mystery is that I cannot imagine what got into my father. It was most unlike him, and either or both of us could have been killed or badly injured. He told me not to tell my mother who 'wouldn't understand' and I never did. Perhaps though, like Maud's driving, it is a false memory.

Most visits to the park were less traumatic. Accompanied by my mother or a nanny we usually carried with us one of those creased and crinkly brown paper bags which are no longer manufactured, full of crusts cut from sandwiches, and any stale bread on the point of claiming Mrs Spilsbury's attention. This was to feed the ducks, and was indeed known as 'the ducks' bread', but very little of it reached the throng of mallards, Canadian geese and the odd swan for whom it was intended. En route, almost before we had reached the bottom of Lark Lane, my brother and I and later my sister had eaten most of it. We wouldn't have looked at it in the ordinary way, of course, but in the open air (and because it was for the ducks) it tasted delicious. The phrase 'the ducks' bread' became in time shorthand for any eating up of stale or rejected food. My mother had a loathing of waste and would finish anything left on a plate or about to be thrown away. Such odds and ends: a spoonful of steak and kidney pie, some congealed custard, a wilting salad, never reached the dustbin. 'Your mother', Tom would say on catching her guiltily but obsessively spooning them up, 'is at the ducks' bread again.'

The Park, like much of Liverpool, paid its reluctant homage to London. The sandy perimeter ride was called 'Rotten Row'. At the end of the 'little lakes' was a cast of Kensington Gardens' Peter Pan. During my childhood, a full-sized replica of Piccadilly's Eros was installed opposite the café at the bottom of the hill which led down from the Lark Lane gates. The café was rebuilt at the same time. The wooden 'Elizabethan' shack was replaced by a more solid art-deco structure. Peter Pan and Eros belong for me in Sefton Park. When later I saw the originals *in situ* I thought of them as 'displaced'.

There was little else of interest: a fine Victorian crescent aviary, an obelisk, two artificial 'caves' stinking of urine, a decaying Wendy House on the sward behind Peter Pan and a flat-bottomed Jolly Roger in the shallow lake below him. There was a Happy Valley and a Fairy Glen, a solemn statue of William Rathbone, after whom Uncle Willy was named, in a marble frock-coat, his hand on a marble book staring in side-whiskered indifference over the Big Lake.

The dangerous swoop down the Palm House hill apart, nothing extraordinary happened to me in Sefton Park. If I were to walk through it with a stranger to Liverpool, they would see a park and nothing else: dirty lakes, replicas of famous statues, a large conservatory, worn grass and undistinguished trees. I cannot explain, even to myself, why no corner of it leaves me unmoved.

If the park formed the 'landscape' of my childhood, the tram was its most potent presence. There are no trams in Liverpool now. They were phased out soon after the war. The point about the tram was that in never deviating from its tracks, the perspective of street and park was always held in exactly the same relation to the eye and gradually, through repeated journeys along the same routes, assumed the clarity of a Canaletto, the definitive view. Rattling along Park Road for example – a street of small shops, innumerable solid pubs and great soot-blackened Catholic churches – the cobbled, hilly streets of two-up two-down houses which led down to the river did so always at the same angle, and the horizon of the Mersey with its shipyard cranes on the other shore and the Welsh mountains beyond them remained fixed, imprinted on the memory with extreme precision. Trams were noisy. I could hear them whining and clanking from my bed in Ivanhoe Road, and occasionally a blue or green flash from some faulty electric contact would illuminate the night sky. The names of their destinations were printed on cloth and rolled into place behind a glass-fronted panel on both the back and front of the vehicle: Garston, the Dingle, Fazackerly, St Domingo's Pit, the Pier Head.

The tram, like 'the push-me-pull-you' in the Dr Dolittle books, was the same at both ends. When it reached its terminus and had to go back the other way, the driver would pull on the thin rope suspended from the sprung pulley which connected it to the electric wire above, and lead it round like a giraffe to face in the opposite direction. Meanwhile the conductor, in his dark blue uniform and peaked cap, would walk from one end to the other of both decks noisily pushing the slatted wooden seatbacks, which were hinged in such a way as to reverse their position so that those who boarded the tram were always facing the way they were going. The controls too, nautical in their elegance and simplicity, were identical and there were two entrances and a set of stairs at each end.

Liverpool people never called a tram a tram. It was either a tram-car or, more commonly, the car. 'I went into town like on the car.' The tram conductors had a certain bravura. They seemed to enjoy pulling on the leather strap, strung down the centre of the lower deck, which went 'ting-ting' in the driver's cabin. They cracked their ticket punches with enthusiasm, and shouted 'I theng yow!' when offered the fare (or 'fur' as most of their customers pronounced it). The late Arthur Askey adopted that 'I theng yow' as his slogan but few outside Liverpool knew where it came from. Tram conductors' fingers were black from handling the change in their big leather satchels. The tickets were very beautiful, rectangular, printed on slightly furry paper in faded colours, pink, pale green, beige, mauve, a washed-out blue. Painter Schwitters would have loved them. Children knew how to fold them in such a way as to construct concertinas.

When I was very young there were still some trams that must have gone back to the turn of the century with outside iron spiral staircases and tin advertisements for medical products, but most of them had been built in the early twenties. They were red and cream outside and had little stained-glass panels, either red or blue and engraved like pub glass, let in to the tops of the windows. On the poorer routes there were sometimes barefoot children in torn jerseys among the customers but most of them wore big boots. There were still a fair number of 'Mary Ellens', old matriarchs of the slums in great crocheted shawls and many layers of petticoats. They wore boots too and some of them male caps. The trams smelt of stale sweat and urine but it was never a smell I disliked. It seemed to suggest to me a dangerous freedom. My mother, who could remember horse-trams, would listen intently to the uninhibited badinage in order to improve the authenticity of her performance of Maud Budden's Liverpudlian sketches. There was one mad woman who rode the number 1 or 45 very frequently. At each stop she would shout out 'The back of the baths'.

Halfway up Park Road there was a junk shop we always looked out for as its owner went in for large handwritten posters of marked originality which were frequently changed. One read, 'My dad was good enough for your dad. Let me be good enough for you.' Another, 'Get off that tram, it'll never be yours. Save your fares to buy a bike.' On the back of a tin bath hanging on a nail, he scrawled in chalk 'Big enough to bath a bobby in'.

Trams featured quite strongly in my mother's inner life. Once, when she was a girl and the upper decks were still open, a man had spat and gob had landed in her hair. She mentioned this frequently and with shivering revulsion which was understandable enough. Spitting was still common in Liverpool in the thirties. All public transport had 'Do not spit' notices on them.

The other facet of her obsession with the tram was more mysterious. When I was in late adolescence and our conversations, frequently on the subject of sex, had become extremely open and intimate, I had explained to her, with all the smug assurance of one whose knowledge was extremely sketchy, the theories of Freud. She found them far-fetched initially, but then confessed to the following fixation. She was excited sexually by the following image: a small working-class child runs out into the road almost under the wheels of a tram. Its mother grabs it just in time, curses at it and slaps it vigorously. 'What', my mother asked me, 'would your friend Mr Freud make of that?' She had this habit of referring to people I was enthusiastic about in this way. (Among my 'friends' at this period were 'Mr Picasso', 'Mr Joyce' and 'Mr Eliot'.) I offered what I thought might be the explanation: unidentified early sexual feelings coinciding with witnessing such a scene in reality was my general conclusion. She didn't really listen to my theory. It was too abstract to appeal to her rather literal view of life. I, on the other hand, was fascinated by so clear a 'case'. I thought about it a lot. 'Did you', I asked her later, 'think about this scenario on the night I was conceived?' 'Yes', she said, quite openly, 'I always thought about it when Tom . . .' I found it very odd to think that at the moment when my future existence was assured, my mother was thinking of a child pulled from under a tram, cursed at and slapped.

In the late thirties the old red and cream trams were replaced by green streamlined models with seat upholstery, springing and more silent machinery. They were called 'the Green Goddesses' and were considered an enormous improvement. They continued to run for some time after the war and were then scrapped in favour of buses. I never took to them. It's the old red bone-shakers which sway and clang through the Liverpool streets of my memory.

At the far end of Sefton Park, past the Big Lake with its skaters or rowers depending on the season, and across two roads was the bottom of Mossley Hill, the grandest enclave in Liverpool. The ascent started inauspiciously with a few semi-detached houses and a tin tabernacle painted a rusty dark green, but then the great Victorian houses began, set in large grounds; many with lodges at their gates, and protected by high sandstone walls. There were three reasons for our visiting Mossley Hill: Riverslea, the Liverpool Zoo, and Cousin Emma Holt.

Riverslea was the house which the suicidally depressive, fountain-loving Charles Melly had bought for his mother and family after the death in Egypt of André Melly and their return to Liverpool. Charles Melly had eight children, but with two exceptions they had either married or moved away from Riverslea by the time I came to know it. Of these emigrés the most powerful and richest was Charles's second son, Edward Ferdinand Melly.

Edward was a coal owner and lived at Nuneaton where he was twice Mayor. According to my father he had both a tyrannical will and a ferocious temper. At the beginning of the 1914 war, driving his gig through the streets of Nuneaton his path was blocked by a long column of volunteers under the command of a young lieutenant. Cousin Edward bellowed for the ranks to be broken so that he could continue on his way, and, on being refused, threatened to drive through them at a gallop. The young lieutenant drew his sword and said that if he tried he would run him through. My father considered this a brave and commendable action.

Tom was in some awe of his elderly cousin, having once suffered his serious if collective displeasure. In the early twenties Edward had taken a house on the coast of Scotland and invited several of the younger generation to stay. Among them were Tom, Young Nell, and Nell's brother John, then a medical student and very addicted to practical jokes. There was a great storm and next day, among the rocks, were huge and almost solid drifts of spume and spray. At John's instigation Nell and my father had collected some of this and persuaded the cook to serve it as a pudding that evening. It was described, quite accurately, on the individual menu cards as 'Sea Spray'.

Cousin Edward, who, unlike Uncle Bill, had a sweet tooth, helped himself to a large dollop from the cut-glass dish; the storm after his first mouthful was the equal of the night before and those responsible were threatened with a seat on the next available train south. He eventually calmed down but was not, even in retrospect, at all amused.

As a small child on a visit to Riverslea I had, it seems, a brush with Cousin Edward. I disagreed with him on some minor point in the works of Beatrix Potter and obstinately proved I was right by producing the appropriate book. My parents had trembled, but Edward unexpectedly hadn't lost his temper. I can't remember the incident myself, but it had so impressed Maud and Tom that they frequently referred to it. Cousin Edward and his third wife – he had buried her predecessors – were killed by a bomb in 1941.

Cousin Fanny and Cousin Leonard were the only two of Charles's children who still lived at Riverslea. Unlike their brother Edward, they were very badly off and the Gothic house was peeling and crumbling about them. Fanny looked like an improvident farmer's wife and had a large mole sprouting hair, something of a hazard when she embraced us. She kept hens in the overgrown garden and even, it was reported, went puffing down to Aigburth Road to buy potatoes in order to save the minimal additional expense of having them delivered. Leonard was tiny and mouse-like. He wore threadbare grey suits and a wing-collar, and had a small but straggly moustache. He exuded a rather sweet melancholy like a character in Chekhov. Indeed the whole atmosphere at Riverslea, with its decaying grandeur and faded chintz furniture, was what I later recognized to be Chekhovian, especially on a late summer's afternoon when the sun streamed through the French windows of the drawing-room and there was an air of mild regret hovering over the delicate but cracked tea service.

Beyond the windows, the garden was a jungle and very exciting to explore. Only the lawn was kept in order, and that because the Riversleas had a passion for croquet, that most illtempered of games, at which, Tom told me, all the envy and rivalry between the two branches of the family had found an outlet during his childhood visits. On Boxing Days too, in order to recover from the excesses of a Chatham Street Christmas Day, the George Mellys would mount an expedition to Riverslea to challenge their cousins at hockey, a perfect excuse for hacking away viciously at each other's shins. Once, during my own childhood, Leonard and Fanny had two great-nephews to stay with them and the custom was briefly, although on a reduced scale, revived. They were tough and vicious little boys and I could understand why my father had dreaded the 26th of December, a day which also happened to be his birthday. Leonard and Fanny were in themselves gentle and unaggressive. Fanny, while so comparatively poor herself, did voluntary work in the slums of Scotland Road, and was, according to Willie Bert, much loved. I can believe it. She was a most cheerful and uncomplaining old lady.

Leonard and Fanny could, of course, have sold Riverslea with its large grounds and lived the rest of their lives in comfort, but I don't suppose it even occurred to them. As it was, the wallpaper was damp and peeling, the carpets threadbare. In one room was a billiard table piled high with old newspapers. I once suggested to my mother there might be several dead Riverslea Mellys buried and forgotten under them. In one of the disused and empty bedrooms in the Tower hung a trapeze. Leonard was interested only in sport. When my mother was unofficially engaged and already under siege from the disapproving Chatham Street uncles and aunts she happened to be standing behind Leonard at an amateur rugger match in which my father was playing. She was appalled to hear Leonard say to his companion, 'Young Tom's playing very badly. Too many late dances with that damn girl I shouldn't wonder.' To me he would drone on about cricket, a game which, for reasons which will become apparent, I nursed a considerable loathing. He had been the President of the Liverpool Cricket Club for many years and used to arrange the public school tour.

Fanny died in 1942; Leonard in 1951. The house was left to

the University, who sensibly, if unimaginatively, knocked it down. I have the catalogue of the auction of its contents, a truly surreal list of accumulated rubbish: Lot 74: a small bronze depicting monkeys shaving a bear. Lot 113: laundry basket containing linen and sundry photographs. Lot 274: under-bed wardrobe containing model railway lines and preserved lizard.

The Liverpool Zoo marched on Riverslea. It had moved there from Otterspool Park, where I can only just remember it, despite vehement objections from the residents of Mossley Hill. The lions would keep them awake at night. A dangerous animal might escape. It would encourage the *hoi polloi*, some of whom might trespass.

Despite Uncle Bill's seal of approval, the zoo was what Gangie would have called 'a poor do'. Mr Rogers, who had hired my father the monkey with such unfortunate results, was a big jovial pipe-smoking man who looked rather like the late Rab Butler. As I was amongst his most frequent visitors he made me a 'Junior Fellow' (were there any other 'Fellows' I wonder, either Junior or Senior?), and would sometimes show me around himself. In the reptile house there was a large python called Billy. One of my privileges as a Junior Fellow was to be allowed to drape Billy round my shoulders. Recently, outside the Tiger Balm Gardens in Singapore I came upon an Indian gentleman with a snake he was prepared to hire out for a small fee so that tourists could take each other's photographs holding it. I was unable to resist. It was the first time I had handled a python for over fifty years.

The zoo was usually rather empty except on bank holidays. I preferred it that way, resenting the noisy jostling ignorance of the visitors almost as much as did the residents of Mossley Hill. I was delighted one such afternoon when a lioness turned round in her small cage and urinated vigorously over the crowd. The star turn was Mickey, a vicious, fully-grown chimpanzee. Mickey had two tricks. The first was to obey his keeper's command to 'blow 'em a raz, Mick' by passing his lips against the back of his hand and emitting a loud and prolonged fart-like note. His other trick was quite dangerous. On warm days he was to be found in a large paddock surrounded by low railings. He was tethered in the middle of this by a long chain attached to a stout post. He had two footballs and, having blown his 'raz' several times to hysterical applause, would roll one of the footballs gently towards the perimeter and then make frantic signals for someone to return it. Eventually a father, hoping to impress his children, or a young man his girl, would bend over the railings. At this point Mickey would hurl the second football with great force and accuracy at his benefactor's head.

Mickey substantiated another of the local residents' worries by escaping. He headed for Aigburth Vale and broke into an office rented by a charitable organization with which Gampa was connected. Here he had pulled out the files and scattered the papers, and shat all over the desk and into some of the drawers before his recapture. My grandfather was not lucky with monkeys.

Aware of Mickey's trick with the footballs I knew better than to fall for it, but I did have a potentially alarming encounter with the zoo's solitary elephant. I had persuaded the Griff to accompany me on this occasion and we were standing comparatively close to the great beast in its garage-like shed. Suddenly and without warning it wrapped its trunk round me and lifted me high into the air. The Griff gave a little cry of terror and dropped her glove. The elephant put me gently down again, picked up the glove and ate it. The Griff's panic gave way to indignation but the keeper, when we eventually found him, was most unhelpful.

'I could luke for your glove like over the next day or two,' he said, 'but you wouldn't want to wear it would you? Not after whur it's been.'

I for my part pretended that the reason the elephant had picked me up was because I had deliberately given the word of command as used by Toomai in Kipling's *Jungle Book*.

I held my seventh birthday party in the zoo's gimcrack little half-timbered café followed by a conducted tour which included my handling of Billy, a feat which, as I'd anticipated and planned, quite impressed my school-friends.

The zoo was never a success financially. Shortly before the war it went into liquidation and Billy, Mickey and the rest of its rather scruffy exhibits were transferred to other prisons.

Past the zoo and Riverslea, right at the top of Mossley Hill and facing the large sandstone church with its resonant chimes loud enough, if the wind were in the right direction, to be heard in Ivanhoe Road over a mile and a half away, stood Sudley, the house and extensive grounds of Cousin Emma Holt. Cousin Emma's mother had been a Miss Bright whose sister had married my great-grandfather, George Melly. Her father, George Holt, was a partner and co-founder of the shipping firm Lamport & Holt for which Tom had briefly and reluctantly worked. George Holt was also a director of many companies and left what in those days was an enormous fortune, £600,000. A benefactor of the Liverpool University College, later Liverpool University, a collector of important pictures and an ardent Unitarian, he could well stand as the epitome of the benevolent Victorian capitalist.

Emma was his only child and heir. She never married, although the prospect of such a fortune must have offered a challenge to many an ambitious or mercenary young man. She was in fact remarkably plain with a long face, an incipient moustache, and very small eyes. At the same time she was both shrewd and self-aware. It is possible she knew that it was unlikely she would be loved for herself alone and rejected any suitors, but here I am only speculating. Her character on the other hand was original and her generosity, especially to young people, unstinting.

The gates of Sudley were actually around the corner from Mossley Hill. There was a small lodge and a long drive, with street-lamps at intervals, winding up to the house itself. This was large but low, built of sandstone in a restrained Victorian neo-classical style. The front with its Doric porch was comparatively narrow and in part obscured by rhododendrons. The main façade faced south, its tall windows overlooking a steep grass bank and narrow lawn beyond which, enclosed by iron railings, was a big field in which sheep grazed. The estate was ringed by bluebell woods.

There was an ornamental conservatory attached to the house and a walled kitchen garden with a range of greenhouses of ascending temperatures in which grapes were grown and orchids cultivated. At the back of the house was an enclosed courtyard with disused stables, one of them converted into a garage and, rather mysteriously, a row of occupied pigsties. The whole of this area, including the pigsties, was built of bright red, glazed brick, a startling effect which always induced in me a feeling of pleasurable anxiety.

Visiting Sudley, usually for Sunday lunch, was a formal experience which, like Chatham Street, intimidated my mother into using her 'church voice'. She would implore us to behave even as we yanked on the bell-pull but, being in fact less in awe of kindly Cousin Emma than any of her generation, we usually, much to Maud's anguish, blotted our copy-books. Even Bill, in general more to be trusted than I, suddenly announced one lunch time that we had received a Christmas card of a monkey (presumably Lawson Wood's repulsive 'Grand pop'), which our nanny had said 'looked just like Cousin Emma'. Maud turned crimson.

'No, Bill,' she improvised in panic, 'I'm sure what she said was that Cousin Emma *sent* you the Christmas card of the monkey.'

This was a brave try, if unconvincing. Cousin Emma's cards were inevitably of Beatrix Potter animals, and anyway Bill wasn't going to let her off the hook.

'No,' he said emphatically, 'she said it *looked* like Cousin Emma.'

'What lovely plums!' said my mother on the edge of hysteria.

I was watching Cousin Emma closely during this exchange. I could see she was not at all angry – if anything, she was, almost imperceptibly, amused.

The interior of Sudley was far more impressive than the dark jumble of Chatham Street. Apart from the kitchen area, never visited and concealed behind a green baize door, there were very few ground-floor rooms: a little cloak-room, a library and, *en suite*, a great drawing-room, a small morning-room and the dining-room, all three facing the field with its flock of sheep.

The L-shaped hall was enormous with a parquet floor and a fine staircase curving up under a glass dome. There was a delicious smell of beeswax polish and pot-pourri. The library was dark with mahogany shelves lining every wall, and fine leather-bound books, but the three rooms facing south were brilliantly lit and furnished in restrained high Victorian taste.

There were many objects to intrigue us, notably two stuffed cranes under the well of the staircase. In life these handsome creatures had roamed the grounds, but it was the picture collection which, from an early age, excited my interest. I have been fascinated by painting since I was very small, initially I think by the puzzle of illusionism, and, unlike many children, I was always pleased to be taken to exhibitions and galleries. Nevertheless it was at Sudley, for the Chatham Street pictures were a mixed bag and heavily discoloured with varnish, that I realized the charm and possibility of a private collection.

It was, I suppose, typical of the informed taste of its period. It included a large Turner in the dining-room, several eighteenth-century portraits by Lawrence, Raeburn, Joshua Reynolds, etc., a beautiful little William Dyce and a few Pre-Raphaelites, in particular the smaller version of Holman Hunt's *Christ in the Temple*, a jewel-like picture in which the young Jesus is discovered by His parents lecturing the old rabbis. Once Cousin Emma discovered my potential liking for art she would frequently lead me round the collection and explain its history but it was the Holman Hunt that provided the climax to these little tours.

The picture wasn't hung but mounted on an ornamental easel in the hall. Attached to the easel was a large magnifying-glass suspended on a brass chain. 'You see, George,' explained Cousin Emma, 'Mr Hunt went to endless pains to be true to nature.' She then picked up the magnifying-glass and focussed it on the head of one of the Jews listening to the young Lord Jesus. 'He even', she continued, 'painted in the cataracts on the old man's eyes.' At this she drew back the glass so that an eye increased dramatically in size. I could see the milky translucent skin over the eyeball, a demonstration I never tired of.

Holman Hunt had stayed with Cousin Emma's father and it was his host who had been responsible for the purchase by the Liverpool Corporation of the painter's grotesque masterpiece *The Triumph of the Innocents*, in which the resurrected, recently-slaughtered babes accompany the fleeing Holy Family but are visible only to the Baby Jesus as they sport around him on what looks like a rainbow-tinted water bed.

Cousin Emma went to a lot of trouble to keep us entertained. She would read the *Tales of Beatrix Potter* and the poems of Edward Lear in her clear unpatronising voice with its Lancashire-inflected a's. Most of my elderly female relations had this slight regional intonation, but none of their brothers or male cousins displayed the least trace. I can only suppose it was because the boys were sent away to public schools in the South while their sisters were educated in the school-room by governesses. Cousin Emma pronounced glass to rhyme with 'ass' and would offer us in consequence 'a glas of mealk'.

In a cupboard in the library there was a marvellous collection of Victorian toys which she would show us but prudently refused to allow us to play with except under her supervision. There was an epidiascope, a forerunner of the cinema. It was a circular metal drum which you loaded with a picture-strip of creatures in a sequence of positions. You then spun the drum round on its base and by looking through a series of little slits around the top you could watch horses apparently jumping over fences or clowns tumbling through hoops. There was a kaleidoscope and a three-dimensional stereoscope but above all – and in this case Cousin Emma wouldn't allow us even to touch it, but wound it up herself – there was an incredible musical-box. This was in the shape of a lettuce. When the music started the leaves parted and the head and shoulders of a life-size white rabbit emerged. It twitched its ears and nose, nibbled on the edge of a leaf but then, when the music finished, popped abruptly back into the heart of the lettuce whose leaves closed over it again with a click.

There must have been a large staff at Sudley both inside and out, but I can only remember Aimée, the elderly head parlour-maid, and Stanley, the grumpy old chauffeur. They both exuded tight-mouthed disapproval of everyone except Cousin Emma but especially of children. Aimée would open the front door to us as though we were the first wave of barbarians at the gates of Rome. If Cousin Emma ordered Stanley to drive us home in the sedate Daimler his back would transmit his disapproval and resentment at such a course.

On the other hand Eleanor Dodsworth, Cousin Emma's secretary and eventual paid companion, was a most cheerful person. She was the niece of one of the Brights' personal maids, and had been in the employment of both the Mellys and the Holts for many years. She liked a cigarette on the sly (Cousin Emma would allow no smoking at Sudley except by the men after dinner in the dining-room) and would respond to anything she agreed with by crying 'Eggs-actly!' Bill and I would often amuse ourselves at home by imitating Cousin Emma and Eleanor Dodsworth in conversation.

Bill: 'Eleanor, would you like a glas of mealk?'

Me: 'Eggs-actly.'

Around Easter Cousin Emma in her long dove-grey coat and straw bonnet would climb into the back of her Daimler and, with Stanley at the wheel and Eleanor Dodsworth chattering away beside her, leave Sudley behind and head north at a speed not exceeding forty miles an hour. Her destination was a house on the shores of Coniston Water where she spent the summer. It was called Tent Lodge and faced 'The Old Man', a mountain frequently invisible in mist and drizzle.

Sometimes Aimée would travel in front of the Daimler next to Stanley. More often she would have preceded her mistress by train with the reduced staff necessary to service the smaller but by no means insubstantial house. Fires would certainly have been lit and beds aired to welcome Cousin Emma, but if it was a fine afternoon she would walk down to the lake through a pretty little wood to pay homage to Wordsworth by admiring the daffodils.

Tent Lodge was a pretty Regency box of a house so named, although I never saw the logic of it, because the corners of all the rooms were curved instead of angular. The exterior was of buttermilk stucco, the roof low, the main façade facing the lake over a gently sloping field. Next to the house, separated by a steep road, was Tent Cottage. It had a trellis porch and a monkey-puzzle tree in the garden. Here Aimée and Stanley lodged, but there were also some extra bedrooms used on those occasions when there were too many guests for Tent Lodge to accommodate.

On the hill behind the house was a home farm; at the side a kitchen garden. There were brick paths and cold houses, potting frames, piles of wicker baskets, and soft fruit ripening under nets. In fact it was exactly like the kitchen garden in *Peter Rabbit* and Cousin Emma would sometimes hint that it may well have been the source of the original. But although a great admirer of Beatrix Potter's, and a neighbour, she hadn't got on with her personally. She had once asked her to tea, expecting a stimulating conversation about her work, much of which Cousin

Emma knew by heart, but Mrs Heelis, as she had become after her marriage to a hen-pecked Hindhead solicitor, stumped in wearing dirty boots and would talk about nothing but sheep-breeding. The visit was a disappointment to Cousin Emma and the invitation never extended again.

Although it was a Regency house, Tent Lodge had been furnished by Cousin Emma's father in mid-Victorian style: a very solid dining-room, a rather fussy but charming drawing-room. The many pictures weren't a patch on Sudley – mostly pale watercolours of the Lakes or the Italian alps – but there were some of those little paintings of birds' nests and, on an easel by the dining-room window, an oil of Ruskin writing in his study at Brantwood, the next house along the lake from Tent Lodge. Gampa, staying as a small boy with his Uncle George Holt, had once met Ruskin, and the old gentleman had given him a dedicated book which Gampa had subsequently and rather irritatingly lost.

There was no electricity at Tent Lodge. Oil lamps were brought in at dusk, and on the hall table were candles to take up to the bedrooms with their walls papered with repetitive ribbons of rose buds or honeysuckle.

We stayed occasionally at Coniston either at Easter or for part of the long summer holidays. It rained a lot, but the fine days, or more rarely weeks, were extraordinarily beautiful. There wasn't all that much to do but we were never bored for long. Sometimes we rolled down the steep grass bank in front of the house until we were dizzy or 'charged the shrubberies', a game I'd invented, in which Bill and I, for Andrée was still too young, would run full pelt into the rhododendron bushes which seemed to part before us like the briars in 'The Sleeping Beauty'. We walked to the village the other side of the lake and visited the Ruskin Museum. It was not all that impressive and furthermore cost a penny to go in. There were Ruskin's collections of rather dusty minerals, his walking stick, and a few beautiful water-colours of rock formations or Venetian architectural details, but what we liked best was a xylophone he had constructed from pieces of tuned slate laid across a framework of wood and which we were allowed to play with a little felt-covered hammer.

Mostly though we fished, first collecting minnows in a celluloid trap with bread crumbs on it suspended by a piece of string at the end of Cousin Emma's jetty, and subsequently transferring them to a bucket to use for live bait. We'd row far out on to the lake in a dinghy but all we ever caught were small perch with their bright striped bodies and treacherous erectile spines. We'd carry them proudly up to the house, nevertheless, although nobody was in the least interested except for the piebald farmyard cats. The excitement was to sit in the dinghy with its creaking rowlocks and faint smell of tar and to watch the red and white float bob tentatively once or twice before jerking resolutely under the water while we imagined that *this* time it was going to be a whopper. Indeed just once, out in the boat with my father, I hooked a pike which consented to be reeled up to the surface, looked at us contemptuously with its cold eye, turned, snapped the cast, and swam unhurriedly down towards the bottom again.

I wished there had been trout in Coniston instead of perch and Tom told me that there used to be, but with the coming of the tourists it had been fished dry. When he was a small child he had gone off one misty morning to find his father who was casting from the shore. He thought he recognized him but, on drawing close, discovered it to be another gentleman. A little further on was someone else who he was sure was his father. It was not, but there, in the distance, was yet another angler. He ran towards him, but this was a stranger too. Soon he was miles from Tent Lodge and so exhausted he sat down and burst into tears. A kind man found him and took him back. Gampa had gone the other way along the shore and was within two hundred yards of the house all the time.

If we were at Tent Lodge in the summer there were other major expeditions involving grown-ups. There were picnics on Peel Island at the far end of the lake and at least an hour's row. It was a rocky little island, covered in gorse and pine trees, a marvellous place to play pirates. Sometimes we climbed The Old Man, which was steep but unchallenging, more a stiff walk than a proper climb. At the top was a cairn, a tall irregular mound of pieces of slate. You added a new one on which you'd scratched your name and the date. You could only climb The Old Man on a clear day. There were mountains all around you, cradling the flat green valleys with their lakes and tarns, and in the distance the sea. The roofs of the village lay directly below and across

Coniston Water was Tent Lodge itself, a neat little doll's house. Getting down was harder than climbing up. It was difficult not to slip and slide on the rough shale. There was a slate quarry at the bottom.

Occasionally we'd be driven to a sheep-dog trial, watching the patient dogs circling the stupid, hysterical sheep, now creeping, now running as they did their best to drive them all into the pens, and time after time one sheep would turn aside almost at the gate and belt off up the hill, allowing the rest to disperse again. There were other entertainments at the trials, especially Cumberland wrestling in which huge men, stripped to the waist, would move cautiously and very slowly round each other before encircling each other's bodies with their great arms and attempting, rather ponderously, to force their rivals off-balance. Bill and I would try it when we got back home and Bill, although three years younger, usually won, unless I lost (but concealed that I'd lost) my temper.

Cousin Emma was not always there when we stayed at Tent Lodge although whether she went to visit other elderly ladies or returned temporarily to Sudley I have no idea. Like her parents she would often lend the house to members of the family for both holidays or honeymoons. After their marriage Maud and Tom had stayed there on their way to Scotland where Tom was to fish; an unselfish or masochistic concession on my mother's part as she had no interest in fishing whatsoever. On arrival at Coniston my father developed a quinsy – a very painful boil in the throat for which there is no relief until it bursts. My mother was so distracted she sent for Gangie, who came hurrying north to look after 'poor dear Thomas'. Walking with her mother-in-law in the fields, Maudie had worried that anyone spotting them would imagine their marriage was already on the rocks. The quinsy finally burst and my parents left for Carlisle where they were to spend a night in a hotel. On the notice board was a letter addressed to Thomas Quinsy Esq. Imagining it to be a joke, probably the work of John Melly, my father crossly tore it in two only to discover, to his considerable embarrassment, that there was a real Thomas Quinsy staying there.

Cousin Emma died in 1944. She left Sudley and the pictures to the City of Liverpool, and the house and the collection are open to the public. In one of the rooms the Chatty drawing-room furniture is displayed behind little ropes. She left Tent Cottage to Eleanor Dodsworth, and Tent Lodge to Willie Bert Rawdon Smith; a reward perhaps for his unselfishness in escorting her and Aunt Eva home half-way through the Sandon Cabaret. He lived there for a few years and then sold it and moved, with his wife Daisy, into a bungalow he had built in the outskirts of the village where he stayed put until he too died.

Emma, although so kind and gentle, was not without convictions. One summer she had a running battle with the new vicar of Coniston who wanted to let girl hikers attend the services in headscarves. Cousin Emma was strong for hats. She was also at the forefront of those residents who protested about Sir Malcolm Campbell's decision to try and break the water speed record on Coniston in his boat *Bluebird*. I doubt, however, that she was amongst those who went so far as to booby-trap the route with submerged logs. Nor did she protest when we all got up at five on the morning of the attempt to watch Sir Malcolm roar to noisy victory in the still grey dawn, shattering the reflection of The Old Man. She just felt that Windermere would have been more suitable.

Tent Lodge and Coniston are among the green places of my childhood. There the imaginary world of Beatrix Potter and the reality on which she based it became one. I have always had this dubious need to reinforce life through art or literature, to appreciate it at second-hand, and it was at Coniston, however unconsciously, that I was first aware of this. In the little lanes between dry-stone walls I imagined meeting Mrs Tiggy-Winkle waddling along with her basket of washing, or spotting, emerging from the mound of lawn-clippings in the far right-hand corner of Cousin Emma's kitchen garden, the black-tipped ears of the Flopsy Bunnies sleeping off the soporific effect of lettuces.

When I was four I was sent to school, a kindergarten called Camelot. It was just around the corner from 22 Ivanhoe Road and was run by a short but formidable lady called Miss Katie Yates. She was very erect, had a rather sallow skin but fine aquiline features, and carried pince-nez on a gold chain which rested on her shelf-like bosom. She had kindly but alert brown eyes, wore her hair up and spoke quietly, but with considerable authority. Her sister, although it seemed unlikely, was a great champion of the gypsies, or Romanies as she preferred to call them, had lived amongst them and written several books on the subject.

Miss Yates had started her school thirty years before in a room over a shop in Lark Lane where Uncle Alan had been amongst her first pupils. Success had enabled her to move the hundred yards to Waverley Road where she lived on the top floor in a flat. The rest of the house, which was rather bigger than ours, was devoted to the class-rooms, minimally furnished. Woodwork was taught in the cellar, and the big double-room on the ground floor acted as an assembly hall and as a setting for end of term concerts and the Christmas play. There were no carpets at Camelot, but the floors of stained wooden boards were kept highly polished by a solitary, rather grumpy, elderly maid. There were few pictures, but I was early on both fascinated and frightened by a sepia reproduction of a Roman soldier guarding some prisoners at Pompeii while the molten lava fell from the air about him. It was called *Faithful unto Death* and the life-size original was in the Walker Art Gallery, although oddly enough I found it less terrifying than its smaller replica. I was extremely in awe of any destructive natural phenomena, but especially of tidal waves, earthquakes and volcanoes, none of which were likely to prove much of a hazard in suburban Liverpool. I dreamt once of red-hot lava creeping and bubbling into the hall of Ivanhoe Road and gradually rising in level as I, with great difficulty, climbed the stairs only a step or two ahead of it. As it rose it spoke in a boily-bubbly voice. 'I'm coming,' it said, 'I'm coming, I'm coming *for you!*'

Faithful unto Death was in the assembly room, and I frequently had a chance to examine it. At nine on the dot, while we all stood in makeshift rows under the supervision of one of the mistresses, Miss Yates would make her entrance. 'Good morning, everybody,' she would say briskly, and we in our piping and ragged trebles, but with all the enthusiasm which children experience in fulfilling a ritual, would answer her in unison, 'Good morning, Miss Yates.' What then took place was some form of non-denominational prayers, for several of the pupils were Jewish or Catholic, followed by a hymn, usually 'All Things Bright and Beautiful' accompanied by Miss Gibbons or Miss Edwards at the upright piano.

It was seldom however that this daily scenario went through without a hitch. Most days one of the several children who suffered from either nerves or a bilious digestive system would suddenly throw up on the polished wooden floor. At this, no matter what point we'd reached, Miss Yates would clap her hands and tell everyone else to 'turn away' – further embarrassing, I should have thought, the unfortunate child. On cue, for it was her daily chore to hover outside during assembly, the elderly maid would come into the room and mop up the mess with the dish-cloth and a bucket of water which she kept in the hall at the ready. It was during these interruptions that I had the chance to study in detail the courageous centurion at his terminal post. Miss Yates would also take the opportunity during assembly to admonish, although never by name, any child who had been reported for letting down the tone of her little school. These crimes were not grave. The most heinous I can recall was of someone who had been seen eating sweets on a tram.

Situated as it was in a network of streets whose names evoked the world of medieval chivalry in the works of Sir Walter Scott, Camelot paid homage to an even earlier legend. Although there were only about thirty pupils we were divided into houses: Percival, Tristram, Lancelot and Galahad, each with its coloured badge sewn on the pocket of our blazers. To begin with you were put into the kindergarten under the supervision of a very pretty girl called Kitty Coope. She was the daughter of a Church of

England canon, one of those ecclesiastics sufficiently elevated for Gangie to drop his name into the conversation whenever a suitable opportunity presented itself.

I had been told that 'Kindergarten' meant 'Children's Garden'. I found it confusing that the whole school was called a 'Kindergarten', and yet we were in a class which was called 'the kindergarten', a children's garden within a children's garden. I was equally puzzled as to why Camelot was called a kindergarten at all. It was a house, its garden a scruffy little patch of grass with a few straggly laurel bushes.

Although everyone went home for lunch, when you were still in the kindergarten you didn't come back in the afternoon. The only refreshment provided by the school was a choice of hot milk or water at the mid-morning break. The milk always had a nasty skin on it and the water was served in thick mugs which somehow, although I was perfectly fond of water, made it taste brackish. You had to have one or the other and Miss Edwards made sure you drank it all up. I still can't abide water in a cup or mug.

Life in the kindergarten class was very pleasant. You crayoned in pictures in a colouring book (it was long before the days of free expression), moulded plasticine, played with a sand-pit, watched tadpoles turn into frogs in their season (what happened to the mature frogs? Were they released into one of the lakes in Sefton Park?), and did raffia work. Tom, who was very amused by anything I had to tell him about Camelot, was extremely sarcastic about the little raffia purses or place-mats that I brought proudly home. 'Miss Coope is very good at raffia,' he'd say with some accuracy, for I was very clumsy with my hands and needed a lot of 'help'. The fact that it was true made his teasing no more bearable and I would protest with increasing vehemence that I'd done it all by myself. Maud naturally and ostentatiously used the nasty little purses and set the tatty place-mats until she felt I'd forgotten about them.

Once I'd left the kindergarten, however, I began to feel less at ease. I discovered you were meant to learn, not just what interested you – I had no objection to that – but things which didn't, like adding up and dividing, French, geography and reading. The latter I finally mastered (in memory practically overnight) and I quite enjoyed history – we used a little book entirely composed of myths: Alfred and the cakes, King Canute, the Princes in the Tower – but for the rest I refused to pay any attention at all. This both worried and puzzled Miss Yates and the staff. I was clearly quite bright, in some respects almost precocious, so why couldn't or wouldn't I learn anything? Miss Yates gave me several stiff talkings-to, but although I promised to try they had no effect at all. Severe and witty Miss Gibbons tried sarcasm; broad-beamed Miss Edwards scorn; pretty Miss Dobson persuasion, but I continued to acquire very little knowledge from these conscientious ladies.

I could, on the other hand, memorize poetry easily and recite it with dramatic if rather hammy facility. The day of the school concert at the end of each term was my apotheosis, the moment when the ugly duckling turned temporarily into a swan. Miss Yates very much dominated these occasions: 'Shall I compare thee to a summer's day', a breathless and nervous child would announce. Then it would continue, 'Shall I compare thee . . .' only to be interrupted by Miss Yates. 'Who's it by, dear?' 'William Shakespeare,' the by now thoroughly rattled child would concede before beginning again, all memory and concentration shattered.

One term, encouraged by Miss Gibbons, who had a streak of mischief behind her severe horn-rimmed glasses, I recited *Albert and the Lion*, the humorous monologue I had learnt by heart from a gramophone record and which, with my talent for mimicry, I could deliver fairly convincingly in the strong Lancashire accent of Stanley Holloway's original. All the mistresses, with the exception of Miss Yates, were delighted by this deviation from 'Fear no more the heat o' the sun' or 'I once had a dear little doll, dears', and my contemporaries, too, enjoyed the rather bloodthirsty and callous couplets. Miss Yates, although clearly unhappy, didn't interrupt, but when I'd finished she clapped her hands for attention and told the school that although George had been clever 'in his way', she would be most displeased if she heard any child trying to imitate the accent. Having an accent at Camelot, not 'speaking properly', was certainly on the level of being detected eating sweets on a tram.

The Christmas play was a far more ambitious project than the end of term concert. We played it twice; a 'dress rehearsal' in front of our nannies and an 'opening night' the following afternoon for parents and relations. The play, which was always a fairy story, was written by one of the staff and the costumes were ingeniously constructed by Miss Coope from coloured crepe paper and safety pins. One year I was a jester in blue and yellow motley and genuinely thought that at the 'dress rehearsal' I had given a pretty impressive performance. I was therefore all the more hurt and shocked when Miss Yates stopped me in the corridor next morning and hoped I'd do better in front of the parents. Did I give a bad performance or did Miss Yates feel that I needed deflating? Perhaps both.

Miss Yates was also responsible for one of the few serious tickings-off I ever received from my mother. I'd fallen down a flight of stairs at Camelot and, probably because there was no carpet, had hurt myself quite badly. Children seem to fall downstairs frequently; I'd done it many times before but always without injury. In a panic-stricken way I'd even quite enjoyed it: the world suddenly fragmented, gravity set at odds, bits of stair, bannister, skirting-board, wall and ceiling jumbled up together at speed. This time however it was not at all pleasurable and, with a bruised knee and a bump on the head, I was so shaken that I'd been sent home early. Maud, full of concern and sympathy, had asked me if I'd cried. 'Oh, no,' I told her airily, 'not a bit.' 'Brave little man!' she said. 'Brave little soldier!'

A couple of nights later, coming down into the lounge after tea, looking forward to the American Colonel spitting into the fire or another chapter from *The Jungle Book*, I was confronted by a mother I didn't recognize, cold and grim. 'I met Miss Yates in Lark Lane', she said, 'and we talked about you falling down the stairs. I said, "Wasn't George brave not to cry?" and she told me you'd quite naturally howled and screamed. You must never tell lies, George! There'll be no reading tonight. You must go to bed now!'

I was frightfully upset, but at the same time couldn't see what all the fuss was about. No doubt I'd cried after my fall but, by the time I denied it later I'd convinced myself I hadn't. I could 'see' myself hurt certainly but courageously dry-eyed, making light of my injuries. I was not only upset by Maud's reproaches, I was also put out. Of course she came upstairs later and 'made it all right' but I'm still puzzled by what got into her. With her need to be liked at all times, especially by her children, her moral reproach, while perfectly justified, was completely out of character.

Jester and stairs apart, I wasn't at all unhappy at Camelot. I'd enjoyed quite a lot of it – joining the Wolf Cubs for example and prancing round the carved wolf's head in the assembly room chanting 'We'll dib dib dib. We'll dob dob dob.' During wolf cubs we had to call Miss Dobson 'Akela' and, although I could see little resemblance between her and the Father Wolf in the Mowgli stories, I'd liked the connection between life at school and the magic world in the dark red book with Kipling's mysterious swastika on the cover.

Bill overlapped me at Camelot by several terms, and it was irritating that he should be so much quicker than me at learning things. Although three years younger, he was reading before I could and did well at everything else too. By the time I left I'd learnt one useful if dangerous lesson: that if you could make people laugh you could get away with almost anything. Miss Gibbons, for instance, was frequently exasperated with my lack of concentration, but I seemed able to amuse even her, and she was seldom cross for very long. Only Miss Yates was impervious to jokes. When I left at the age of seven she told me seriously and rather sadly that she was sure I could do better if I tried, that archetypal reproach of a teacher confronted by a bright but idle child.

10

At Camelot I developed the ability to separate areas of life one from the other, a trick for which I was to be increasingly grateful. As soon as I was home or during the holidays Camelot ceased to exist except as a source of anecdotes to amuse Tom. However, even at home things were less happy, because the nursery had become a torture-chamber. Firm but kind Bella, although she was to return later, had gone and her place was taken by a handsome fiend, a sister of the Leathers' nanny, called Hilda Cadwallader.

Hilda was a savage and chilly disciplinarian particularly at meal-times, implementing her rigid injunctions with the aid of a thin green garden cane which she flicked with great accuracy under the table to catch me, and more rarely Bill, across the calves or thighs. Her principal obsession was that if we took anything at tea we must put it on our plate before transferring it to our mouths. As forgetting to do so was to court instant and painful retribution I soon, like one of Pavlov's dogs, learnt this lesson and to this day on taking a sandwich or a biscuit automatically, however rapidly, touch my plate with it. 'Eating everything up' was another of Hilda's strict rules, a common one I know. My mother, who much to our relief would sometimes join us for lunch or tea in the nursery, would wait until Hilda had left the room to get the pudding and then rapidly gobble up whatever we didn't want off our plates. This I found, while welcome, very confusing. Was Maud on our side and if so why didn't she tell Hilda we needn't finish things we didn't like? Did she know of the existence of the thin green cane? We probably hadn't told her about it; children just don't. But if she did know, why didn't she forbid its use? I now realize that the reason was Maud's terror of a confrontation with someone of strong character and Hilda was certainly that. Andrée, still in her high-chair, was spared the rod but not a certain amount of force feeding and a slap on the leg if she persistently threw her spoon and pusher on the floor.

Our walks, too, became less interesting because on many afternoons, ignoring Sefton or even Prince's Park, Hilda would head down Aigburth Road to meet her sister, the Leathers' nanny, and spend the afternoon chatting and looking in the shops. This was very boring for Bill, my cousin Gillian and me (Andrée was still in her pram, John already at school all day) but at least it reduced Hilda's attention and left us free to scamper ahead or hide round corners. Once I stole an egg from a mound displayed on the sloping marble slab of a fishmonger's in Aigburth Vale. I don't know why I did it and was instantly so frightened that I threw it into a bush in someone's front garden. My crime preyed on me to such an extent that several months later I imagined I overheard the woman in the fishmonger's say to a customer as we passed, 'A bad little boy pinched an egg from this shop when I wasn't looking and I've told the police.'

I don't know how long Hilda was with us, certainly long enough for Andrée to be talking and sitting up at the table. But eventually she left, a day of celebration for me, and her place was taken by her other sister, May. This was, on the face of it, good news. May had been house parlour-maid before her elevation to the nursery and seemed to be a cheerful girl with a plain, friendly face and big glasses. My optimism turned out to be misplaced however. Somehow the flight of stairs from kitchen to nursery transformed May into a tyrant like her sister. The gardening cane remained in use, the rules as strictly enforced. She didn't stay too long, however, and her place was taken by a sweet-natured girl called Minnie Shearer and eventually by the return of Bella, but by that time I was beyond the jurisdiction of nannies anyway.

The kitchen, both before and after May's metamorphosis, remained a refuge and a place of comfort. Following May's promotion, Edna, Auntie Min's successor as cook, was joined by a very jolly girl called Ethel. In Liverpool every year there was a fancy dress dance at St George's Hall called 'The Servants' Ball'. Such a concept, such a name for such a concept, appears absolutely grotesque now but it didn't then. The Servants' Ball was a very popular function and comparatively valuable prizes were offered for the best costumes in several categories: single, couples, most comic, most artistic, etc. Edna and Ethel won the couples prize two years running: one year as Laurel and Hardy (Edna was big and plump, Ethel small and thin) and the next year as 'The Bisto Kids'. I hadn't seen Laurel and Hardy on the screen then – I hadn't been allowed to go to the pictures – but I knew what they looked like from *Film Fun*, my favourite comic.

My comfort during the regime of the Cadwallader sisters, and indeed at all times of stress, was a small bear I'd had ever since I could remember. Its name was 'Little Ted' and over the years it had gradually lost arms, legs and eyes until hardly any of the original remained. It was repaired by my mother, no great hand with the needle, and as it also shed all its fur, it was eventually quite a repulsive object. Nevertheless Little Ted was a powerful fetish, so much so that I even took him to Stowe and later on into the navy where it was eventually lost, creating in me considerable, although suppressed, anxiety. How did I avoid teasing by school boys and seamen for having a Teddy bear? By pretending, like Sebastian Flyte, that it was a bit of camp, although in fact it was nothing of the kind but an important psychological prop. Little Ted was far more of a help in adversity than God or his son, 'GentleJesusmeekandmild'. I said my prayers because I was told to, but I gabbled through them at a fair lick especially on the cold linoleum of winter. My real solace lay on the pillow, its button eyes hanging on threads, its limbs and old woollen glove fingers lumpily stuffed with cotton wool, one ear gone, its body held together by a pair of grubby but remedial pyjamas knitted by the Griff.

God and Jesus were something of a puzzle. They lived in Christ Church, Linnet Lane, a quarter of a mile away, round the corner at the Sefton Park end of Ivanhoe Road. It was a big, rather simple Victorian church with stained-glass windows with a lot of purple and red in them. There was a stone pulpit and the Bible was on a lectern which was a fierce brass eagle. The clergyman's name was Goodeliffe. He was also rather fierce but not very old. Maud 'didn't care for him', but she went to the eleven o'clock service every Sunday and often to Holy Communion as well. Tom only went to church on Christmas Day.

When we were small we didn't go to the eleven o'clock service but to the children's service at half-past ten. Only middle-class children went to the children's service. Working-class children went to Sunday School in the afternoon. Mr Goodeliffe seems to have subscribed to the verse in 'All Things Bright and Beautiful' in which it is firmly maintained that God 'made them high and lowly and gave them their estate'.

There was a 'Children's Corner' in Christ Church, Linnet Lane. You had to say a prayer there if you went into the church when there wasn't a service on. It had Margaret Tarrant pictures in it. One of them, which we also had at home in the night nursery, was a illustration of 'All Things Bright and Beautiful' and was a bit like a coloured version of the Peter Pan statue in Sefton Park with rabbits and butterflies and a faun, but with Jesus instead of Peter Pan. Another was called 'Suffer the little children to come unto me'. Nobody told me that 'suffer' in this context meant 'allow'. I was puzzled and a little alarmed by the title, but then a lot of religion was like that. 'Our father,' I prayed, 'witch art in Heaven.' I knew witches were meant to be wicked. What were they doing practising their art in Heaven where everybody was meant to be good? In 'Suffer the little children to come unto me' Jesus was surrounded by children 'of many lands', but only one of each: a black boy, an Indian girl, a Red Indian, a Chinese boy, a Japanese girl, an Arab boy, and by far the biggest, a rather stern British boy scout. Jesus was in a white robe. He had very long hair and a beard and a light round his head. Most of the people in the stained-glass windows had lights round their heads too, but enclosed by black lines. In Margaret Tarrant's picture of Jesus it was more like a glow, as if He were an electric light bulb.

The theology at the Children's Service was naturally enough rather simple: stories mostly, which I enjoyed, especially the blood-thirsty ones from the Old Testament; a few hymns and simple prayers. Mr Goodeliffe's principal message was that if we were good we'd go to Heaven, that God loved us and saw every-thing we did, and that Jesus died on the cross for our sins. He told us it was the Jews who killed Jesus. This worried me a bit. I couldn't imagine the Griff or Uncle Alan and Uncle Fred doing something cruel like that, even if Fred did murder people in the Masons.

My main problem, though, was to imagine what God looked like. The best I could do was a kind of smile in the air, but if I imagined it for long the smile got fainter like Alice's Cheshire cat. Jesus of course was easier because of the pictures, but I thought he'd look very odd walking down Ivanhoe Road or shopping in Lark Lane. Perhaps he dressed differently now, at any rate when he wasn't in his house. Mr Goodeliffe dressed differently after all. In church he wore a long black dress with a white one over the top and a pretty coloured flat scarf hanging down the front, but if you met him in the street he was dressed in a suit like everyone else, and the only way you could tell he was a clergyman was by his black shirt with a stiff white collar turned back to front. Even so Jesus' hair and beard would have made him look peculiar. Tom told me that when he was younger if you saw a man with a beard you shouted 'Beaver'. Would people have shouted 'Beaver' at Jesus? Perhaps that's what they did when they mocked him before he was nailed to the cross.

Later on we had to go to the grown-up service. That was very long and boring, but it was almost worth it when you came out afterwards knowing that once Tom got back from The Albert there'd be roast beef, roast potatoes and Brussels sprouts in the dining-room or at the Griff's. We always had Sunday lunch downstairs and then Tom wound the grandfather clock.

Once, when I was about seven, I had a vision of God which was very different from the smile in the air. I had to have a tooth out and was given gas. Mr Williams, the dentist, faded away before I'd counted to six, and I found myself at the centre of the universe with all the stars round me and a kind, gentle voice saying, 'I am God. I am God.' But then the cosy universe I was enclosed in was shattered into thousands of pieces and I was faced by a limitless and terrifying void. Furthermore another, deafening voice took over, bellowing and thundering, 'No you're not. I AM GOD! I AM GOD!' Yet despite this apocalyptic vision which even at the time, like my subsequent headache and vomiting, I put down to the effect of the gas, I wasn't so much worried by religion as simply puzzled. I just accepted it as something you had to do, like going to school.

I discovered later that my mother's theology was almost as simple as my own. When Tom died in the early sixties she believed, and it was a great comfort to her, that she'd meet him again but couldn't make up her mind if he'd be wearing his pyjamas or his old mackintosh. Tom himself was not at all religious. He still said his prayers when I was a child, but in later life got straight into bed. He always got very angry with Mr Goodeliffe on Christmas Day because he took the opportunity, given a full house, to tick off those of the congregation, of whom my father was one, who usually went to The Albert instead. In revenge, Tom would sing funny versions of the carols: 'When Shepherds washed their socks by night' and, in the year of Edward VIII's abdication, 'Hark the Herald Angels sing; Mrs Simpson's pinched our King'.

Although it was very long, I didn't mind the Christmas service so much. The carols had better tunes than the usual hymns and, from our pew, I could see in the Children's Corner a lit-up crib with the Holy Family, the shepherds, the kings and an ox and ass carved from wood. I didn't mind the Harvest Festival either. It seemed so odd to see potatoes, cabbages and other vegetables and fruit of all kinds piled up all over the church like the trestle tables outside Waterworths, the greengrocer's in Aigburth Road.

Eventually Mr Goodeliffe left to tell off other fathers who only went to church on Christmas Day and his place was taken by a big man with tiny but kind eyes and a very red nose. He was called Mr Thompson. Maud liked him much better than Mr Goodeliffe and he was sometimes asked to tea. He made jokes too, something Mr Goodeliffe never did.

Tom didn't like Christmas much anyway. He hated the paper-chains and holly they put up in The Albert. He called it 'Christmas crap'. When eventually they took it down he'd come home looking very pleased. 'They've taken down the Christmas crap in The Bertie,' he'd tell us to explain his good humour. He loathed carol singers ringing the bell and would tell them, right up to Christmas Eve, that they were too early. Some of his resentment of the season may have been because his birthday was on the 26th. As a child, and indeed for the whole of his life, people tended to give him one present instead of two.

I myself had mixed feelings about Christmas Day, based I imagine on too great expectations. I quite liked helping to put up the Christmas crap in the nursery (the rest of the year it was kept in a cardboard box in the cupboard under the stairs) and especially the big green paper bells which lay flat in the box but opened up to become round and honeycombed. I also derived pleasure from the coloured glass balls we hung from the branches of the small tree we'd bought at Waterworths, although it was very annoying when they came adrift from their little silver collars and the two thin metal prongs which held them on their hooks. It was also a bonus that Hilda and later May were less strict. But nevertheless Christmas Day itself was always somehow a disappointment. It was not that we believed in Father Christmas (although I did, certainly until I left Camelot, firmly subscribe to the tooth fairy and her compensatory sixpence for a milk tooth placed under the pillow); rather it was to do with waking too early, opening stockings in the dark, going into our parents and being told to go away and go back to sleep. Everything turned into an act. We were expected, except by Tom, to enjoy ourselves too much, to be 'wide-eyed with wonder'. There was too much to eat at the Griff's. The Christmas cake was too rich and too soon after lunch. At the end of the day I went – willingly for once – to bed, tired, bilious and obscurely disappointed. I still mistrust Christmas and understand perfectly why Tom was so pleased when they took down the Christmas crap in The Albert. I was twice, as a child, ill on Christmas Day.

Nevertheless the Christmas holidays as a whole were full of treats. One morning, for example, my parents would take us to 'do' the grottos in the big stores. These varied a great deal depending how up-market the shop was. The Bon Marché was too grand to bother. George Henry Lee's was the most elaborate with Father Christmas reached only after a trip in a moon-rocket or a sledge-ride to the North Pole, and he wore proper baggy red trousers and boots. Lewis's was average. You walked into the grotto past animated 'Nursery Land' figures and Father Christmas allowed you to spend a bit less time on his knee before giving you your 'present', wrapped in blue paper for a boy and pink for a girl. The boys' presents at Lewis's were always rather large wind-up cars 'made in Japan'. They had nasty sharp edges and soon broke. The girls got cheap dolls resembling Shirley Temple. But my father's favourite grotto, and the one we rated least, was Blackler's, a cut-price emporium in the centre of

Liverpool. Here Father Christmas, assisted by a pert fairy in a tutu, sat amongst no more than a few papier mâché rocks and the presents were the sort of things you got from crackers. Father Christmas himself had a beard which clipped on over the ears instead of a proper one stuck on with spirit gum, and he wore ordinary grey trousers under his red robe. He also had a strong Liverpool accent and smelt of beer. ''Ave you been a good lad?' he'd ask. 'What yer want for Chrissie den?' One year, Tom told me later, the Blackler's Father Christmas was sacked when the under-manager found him screwing the Fairy behind the papier mâché rocks. When I was very small and the grottos were the only reason I was taken to the big stores, I believed that the lifts didn't go up and down, but from shop to shop, from grotto to grotto.

The other, and indeed greater, highlights of the Christmas holidays were the pantomimes. Like the grottos, these could be graded. The Royal Court was considered the most 'artistic' with a proper transformation scene and a ballet, but we found it the dullest. Cousin Emma took a huge party of children to this, followed by a tea at George Henry Lee's. The Court Pantomime sometimes engaged Douglas Byng as its dame, a considerable bonus for me who knew his records so well and had met him personally – a fact I made quite sure all the Holt cousins appreciated. In keeping with the refinement of the entertainment and indeed his own persona, his dames were upgraded, never the nurse, always the governess, not a cook, but a housekeeper. Given that it was a family entertainment he didn't, to my regret, recite any of his discreetly obscene monologues, but he was even so very funny, something of a relief in contrast to the gentility of the rest of the entertainment. In *The Sleeping Beauty* when the Court, covered in cobwebs, awoke after the interval, Douggie's reaction to the Fairy Queen's announcement that they'd been asleep for a hundred years reduced Bill and me to helpless, if knowing, laughter and earned us a censorious look from Cousin Emma. 'A hundred years!' said the appalled Douglas Byng, 'and I forgot to put the cat out!' Like Maud and Tom, Bill and I were very much amused by scatological humour.

We were taken to the Empire, the huge Palace of Varieties opposite St George's Hall, by Gangie and Gampa. This was a big brash show-biz panto with stars like George Formby and Arthur

Askey, and lots of catchphrases from popular radio shows and advertising slogans. It was very long but always very enjoyable, and by the time the 'entire company' came on for their final bow, dressed in elaborate finery, and swanning down a high bank of glittering steps to acknowledge their applause, we had been seduced into exhausted complicity by the slapstick, community singing and exuberant vigour.

Pantomime, despite the 'I theng yous' and the references to Bovril stopping 'that sinking feeling', was still comparatively traditional. The Principal Boy was always a girl, and the demon king shot up in a puff of green smoke through a trap door, and spoke, like his opponent the Fairy Queen, in rhymed couplets. Even so my father, while always very interested in the Principal Boy's legs, complained that when he was young they didn't limit themselves to the same few traditional stories: *Cinderella*, *Babes in the Wood*, *Mother Goose*, *Humpty Dumpty*, *Robinson Crusoe*, *The Sleeping Beauty*, *Little Red Riding Hood*, *Dick Whittington* and *Aladdin*, but drew freely from a wider field. 'They did things like *The Yellow Dwarf*,' he'd tell us. He never mentioned any of the other things they did, nor indeed what had impressed him so much about *The Yellow Dwarf*, but he'd bring it out each year as a stick to beat the unimaginative limitations of the modern pantomime. Nevertheless he was always pleased when it was *Cinderella*, then as now the most hackneyed story of all, but this was entirely because of the moment when the crystal carriage emerged from the wings to take Cinders to the ball. It was drawn by Shetland ponies and what interested Tom was the possibility, surprisingly frequently fulfilled, that one or more of them might shit on the stage.

My parents themselves took us to the Christmas play at the Playhouse and the panto at the Pavilion, a seedy theatre in Lodge Lane, a rather run-down area not far from Sefton Park. Here, all memories of *The Yellow Dwarf* obliterated, Tom's relish for the tatty and the meretricious was allowed full play. There were lashings of vulgarity and in the second half the plot was more or less abandoned and everyone just performed their speciality acts. To call them pantomimes at all was really a misnomer. They were basically music-hall bills with a cursory nod towards the panto in acknowledgement of the season. We often went to see Old Mother Riley as the dame and 'her beautiful

daughter Kitty' as the principal girl. Old Mother Riley's real
name was Arthur Lucan. His 'daughter' was, in fact, his wife.
Never beautiful and, with the passage of the years increasingly
less so, she was apparently a drunken termagant who made
Lucan's life a hell. On stage, though, they were in the great
tradition: Old Mother Riley in her bonnet and shawl, writhing
and banging her elbows together in paroxysms of anxiety as to
where Kitty was and what she'd been getting up to. Then going
at her hammer and tongs on her eventual return. 'You went to a
museum,' she'd shriek. 'You went to a museum to see the antiques! Why did you 'ave to go to a museum to see antiques?
Why couldn't you come 'ome and see your mother!'

We didn't only go to the Pavilion at Christmas. My parents
loved the music hall and would take us quite often during the
rest of the year. It was there we saw 'The Uncle Ronnies' and, for
the first time, Frank Randle, my favourite comedian of all.
Dressed as an old hiker, glasses awry, sparse hair sticking up in
tufts, his absurdly skinny legs emerging from baggy shorts,
belching, burping and frequently removing his teeth, he presented a hideously ludicrous spectacle. 'Eeeee', he'd start off,
holding onto his huge phallic stick for support, 'ah've supped
some ale toneet!' 'A disgusting old man!' said Tom admiringly.

Some years it was *Peter Pan* at the Empire instead of a pantomime, and it was always a children's play at the Playhouse. One
of these plays so impressed me that when we got back to Ivanhoe
Road I reconstructed it with Bill and even Andrée, although she
was only two and a half and needed a lot of direction, and we
performed it for our parents. They were so amused that the
following Sunday they asked the original cast to tea and we acted
it out in front of them. It was a great success and the following
years we repeated it. It became known as 'The Melly Version'. As I
grew older 'The Melly Version' became more ambitious, with
scenery and some old candle footlights from Chatham Street.
School friends too were recruited and I suspect that what had
once been rather charming and droll grew to be a considerable
bore for the poor actors and actresses on their one day off. This
never occurred to me of course, and I very much doubt if it
occurred to Maud either. Mary Ventris, alias 'Little Runty', the
Louella Parsons of Liverpool, was also invited and wrote it up
several times in her 'Woman's Note' in the *Liverpool Echo*.

11

Although I'd been taken to the theatre from an early age, I wasn't allowed to go to the cinema until I was almost seven. Maudie had never cared much for the 'pictures' and had rationalized her dislike into believing them to be bad for children, a potential drug. I'd been chipping away at her resolve for some time before I succeeded. It was my enthusiasm for wild beasts that eventually won the day. Walking rebelliously down Aigburth Road with Hilda en route to meet her sister, I spotted a large poster outside the Rivoli, at that time the district's only cinema. It was to advertise a film called *Trader Horn*, about a man who collected animals for zoos and circuses. The poster was in full colour. The hero with a gun glared with desperate courage from the edge of a swamp. Behind him an immaculate girl in an open-necked shirt and jodhpurs recoiled in some alarm. His desperation, her alarm were fully justified: a crocodile glided purposefully towards them, a giant boa-constrictor lowered itself from the branches of a tree, a lion and a leopard, crouching in the long grass that edged the swamp, showed more than a passing interest, while a bull elephant trumpeted its displeasure in the background. With all this at stake, I went down from the nursery after tea determined to use whatever means I could to break her injunction, and went up to bed triumphant. The very next afternoon we were to go to the matinée of *Trader Horn* at the Rivoli, Aigburth Road.

The Rivoli had been built in the early twenties. Like the Rialto a mile and a half away, but on a more modest scale, its inspiration was Moorish, the low façade covered in creamy ceramic tiles. The inside was fairly scruffy, many of the seats broken, the carpets full of holes, a stale smell of bodies masked by strong disinfectant. The matinée was sparsely attended; a few little gangs of noisy children and isolated old age pensioners. Nevertheless there was nowhere on earth I would rather have been. I was 'at the pictures'.

In the event, although I was not so stupid as to let on, I found *Trader Horn* something of a disappointment. It had lots of good bits – lions caught in nets, natives digging concealed pits for elephants, a charging rhino, a lovable chimp – but what confused me was that at no point was there a scene which in any way resembled the multiple and highly coloured confrontation promised by the poster. Nevertheless I walked home with Maud as if I had successfully passed some initiation test, and boasted so much at tea that Bill became hysterical with envy and burst into angry and prolonged tears. As a result, and to my ill-repressed fury, he was taken to see *Trader Horn* the very next day! I felt I'd done all the spade-work only to allow Bill, three years younger than I was, to blub his way into reaping the benefits. Nevertheless I'd been to the pictures and there was no way now of stopping me going whenever I wanted to.

The only practical difficulty was getting people to take me, but here I discovered that most members of the family enjoyed the excuse, and also preferred this or that genre of film, so that after a certain amount of research I was soon able to cover the whole spectrum. My father, with his curiously narrow but intense tastes, liked *Mutiny on The Bounty*, which he was prepared to visit any number of times and even put up with my imitations of Charles Laughton for several hours afterwards, and gangster pictures. Maud hated gangster pictures, but quite liked Fred Astaire and Ginger Rogers and indeed all musicals. Gangie liked Douglas Fairbanks Junior pictures and costume drama in general with plenty of sword fights, but she hated the concomitant torture-chamber scenes for which I had a morbid passion. The Griff would take me to anything I wanted provided one answered in the affirmative a question dating from her youth: 'Do they speak well of it?' I didn't really enjoy going to the pictures with the Griff though, because she fell instantly asleep and I would be forced, as I thought for her own enjoyment, to keep nudging her. Sometimes Bill and I – for I had soon become reconciled to his profiting at my expense in exchange for having someone to discuss every sequence in detail – would tease her by asking if she'd enjoyed scenes which weren't in the film at all. Uncle Fred would always take me to Chaplin or the

Marx Brothers. My only sadness was being barred from films which in those days had an 'H' (for Horror) certificate. I longed for Frankenstein and Dracula, for the Wolf Man and The Mummy, but the only time I could see them on the screen was when they appeared in spoofs, most often to the discomfiture of Old Mother Riley.

The cinemas themselves for me were almost as magical as the films they showed. The Rivoli, my first, held a special place in my affection, but I was tremendously excited by the 'modernistic' splendours of the big Picture Palaces in the centre of Liverpool. The commissionaires in their para-military uniforms, the thick carpets, the chrome bannisters, the framed photographs of the stars lining the stuccoed walls, the ice-cream girls in their twin spotlights during the intermission. There were also, as a special treat, the cinema cafés with their 'dainty teas': fish and chips with very thin bread and butter, the scalding chrome tea pots, knickerbocker glories, fancy cakes. In the film and the cinema I had found my faith and my cathedral.

At some point in the thirties, and within a year of each other, two huge cinemas were built in Aigburth Road, both within a quarter of a mile of where we lived. This, once I had learnt of it, was a source of great pride and anticipation. The Gaumont opened first. It was at the Dingle, opposite the Corporation tramshed and the Ancient Unitarian chapel. It was built of special pale brick in 'streamlined' art-deco, like a modern liner. Inside too it was luxurious but not flashy, restrained in detail, comfortably functional. The Mayfair, despite a flat façade, and being a little farther away down Aigburth Road – almost next door to the Rivoli which must have suffered in consequence – was much more what I'd hoped for. In particular it had a sensational curtain, ruched in many folds which were lit from both above and below in a wide spectrum of slowly changing colours: yellow with purple shadows, red with green, pink with blue. I thought it the most glamorous effect I'd ever seen. The cinema organ too (although as an instrument it bored me and I longed for its grimacing practitioner to sink back into the pit so that the programme could start) was bigger, brasher and with more effects, both musical and visual, than its nearby rival. In the end however, despite my aesthetic prejudice in favour of the Mayfair, it was what they were showing which decided whether I dragged my companion up or down Aigburth Road. The Gaumont, the Mayfair and the Rivoli are all bingo halls now.

Although films were shorter then – ninety minutes was the average – they gave you full value for your one and ninepence: the main film, a support feature, a comedy short or two (I was finally able to check up on the accuracy of Edna and Ethel's appearance and demeanor as Laurel and Hardy at the Servants' Ball), the news and a travelogue. I liked everything but the last two. I was very bored by a much-imitated man called James Fitzpatrick who seemed to end every travelogue with the sentence '. . . and so, as the sun sinks in the west, we say farewell to . . .' But my obsession was the cartoons and especially the early Silly Symphonies of Walter (as he was known at that time) Disney.

They still revive and show on television the formative years of Mickey Mouse and Donald Duck and even, occasionally, The Three Little Pigs, the most celebrated of the Silly Symphonies, but most of them are never to be seen and yet rank, I believe, amongst the Disney Studios' most original works. The opening of the Tatler, Liverpool's first news theatre, was an important date for me because it was there, despite having to sit through many tiresome features, that the new Silly Symphonies had their premières: The Pied Piper, King Midas (The Golden Touch), Rock a bye Baby (with its bogeymen, a run-up for Dumbo's pink elephants), Peculiar Penguins, The Robber Kitten, Noah's Ark, The Grasshopper and the Ant and many more.

The fat, jostling, red letters announcing a Silly Symphony stood out against a background like a quilted yellow eiderdown. Then the screen went dark and an iris lens opened from the centre to reveal a country where the flowers had flat black centres and simple petals the colours of sweets and the trees were as plump as pillows. Certain images still haunt me: the rats in the Pied Piper covering a chicken carcass like a fur-coat and then retreating a second later to reveal only the bones, like a mounted prehistoric monster in a museum; the obscenely hairy and skinny wolf disguised as a mermaid, wearing lipstick and a gold wig, and strumming a harp in midstream in an attempt to seduce the wise little pig in The Lie Detector; the passing of the storm in Trees and Flowers. I loved Mickey too; I was never as fond of the bad-tempered duck, but have always regretted the phasing out of the supporting cast. When was the last time Minnie fluttered her long eyelashes? What became of Horace Horsecollar, Clarabelle Cow, Peg Leg Pete, and the Mae-West-shaped diva, Clara Cluck, the farmyard nightingale? I shared this passion for early Disney with Gampa who was always prepared to take me to the Tatler until I was old enough to go by myself.

All these characters appeared in strip form in *Mickey Mouse Weekly*, a comic published around 1935. In the first issue, anticipated by me since its announcement some months earlier, I discovered you could join the Mickey Mouse Weekly Club and receive a badge, the password, how to give a secret handshake and a diploma. I had included a page of rather stilted drawings of Mickey, Minnie, Clarabelle Cow *et al.* with my application. I spent a great deal of my spare time learning to draw them by heart and was absolutely delighted to receive a personal letter back from the editor. 'Mickey and the gang sure thank you for their portraits,' it said.

I would have spent all my time at the pictures if I could but there were other activities in which I was expected to take part. Dancing lessons, for example, first at Miss Jones's studio in the centre of Liverpool. It was a proper studio with a barre and wall-length mirrors. Miss Jones was very old – she had even taught Maud as a child – and she wore a long black dress and held herself very erect. The forefinger of her left hand was in a fat bandage and according to my mother always had been. Apparently she had 'a whitlow'. I absorbed this explanation, but had no idea what a whitlow was; indeed I hadn't until a few moments ago when I looked it up in the dictionary:

Whitlow (-o), n. Inflammatory tumour on finger esp. about the nail. [Earliest form *whitflaw*, app. = WHITE + FLAW]

It makes perfectly good sense.

Miss Jones taught very formal dancing: gavottes, quadrilles, reels and the schottische. We were expected to wear black, patent-leather shoes with buckles. We danced to an equally old lady at the piano.

I didn't go to Miss Jones's for long. Perhaps she retired or Maud felt she was too old-fashioned or expensive. We moved to a School of Dancing in the suburb of Allerton beyond Mossley Hill whose proprietor was a Miss Saul, obviously a professional name as her husband, who had the kind of hairline moustache Maud 'didn't care for', also taught us. 'Ballet, Modern, Tap' it said on the board outside the semi-detached house. The studio here was the empty front-room and we danced to a wind-up gramophone. It was less boring and intimidating than Miss Jones's, but I never got to be any good and as soon as I was allowed to gave up.

We learnt to swim at the noisy Cornwallis Street baths which stank of chlorine and where Maud was always worried we'd 'pick up a verruca', and we were taught tennis by a professional at the Racket Club, the smartest club in Liverpool, on a wooden court where, under an echoing glass roof, the balls made an incredible noise like guns going off. I quite enjoyed playing tennis.

We went ice skating at a rink which had been one of the centres of Maud's flirtatious social life before the Great War. I didn't like ice skating as it made my ankles ache. I much preferred roller-skating but that, somehow an inferior activity, I had to learn for myself. On Saturday mornings we were taken into town where, in the restaurant of the Bon Marché, a Miss Eyenet ran what she called her 'Fun Club'. I hated the Fun Club! Most of the time we spent doing Swedish gymnastics – one and two and three and four – but at the end of the two hours there was a bran-tub which you dug into and pulled out a present. One Saturday I won a tennis ball which had a very strong camphorated smell. I began to sniff at it on the way home on the tram, and continued to do so all day until I was violently sick on the nursery floor. It must have contained an intoxicant of some kind and what I was doing was the equivalent of glue-sniffing. I still sniff surreptitiously at tennis balls but they are always scentless.

I didn't learn riding in Sefton Park although I could have, and in the winter I did my best to avoid tobogganing and snowball fights. I loved watching the snow fall from inside the warm nursery and the way it made the houses in Ivanhoe Road glow a specially intense shade of sooty-red, but I hated 'winter fun' and, unlike Bill who was lethal, I couldn't throw a snowball. I have never seen the pleasure of being wet, cold, uncomfortable and possibly hurt.

One morning, when I was about seven and a half and in my last term at Camelot, I went into my parents' bedroom and found them looking at glossy 'curricula' for Liverpool's preparatory day schools. They'd rejected St Christopher's although it was just round the corner, and the junior wing of Liverpool College, and decided on a school called Parkfield in Parkfield Road only a few hundred yards away. 'Your cousin John was there', Tom explained, 'and Ronnie was quite satisfied. The headmaster, who's called Twyne, is a pompous ass, but most schoolmasters are. No, we think it's probably the best choice.'

That holiday I went with my mother to George Henry Lee's and bought the school uniform: grey flannel shorts and blazer, football shorts and two sweaters, one white, one black, cricket shirts and flannels, black shoes and house-slippers, a belt with a snake buckle, a cap and tie in alternate stripes of Oxford and Cambridge blue. I wasn't especially apprehensive. I'd be home every night and all day on Sundays. It was only round the corner. I could tease Bill for still being at a kindergarten . . .

I didn't know it then, but I was soon to be very, very grateful for my ability to keep the different areas of my life in separate compartments. Even the prospect of writing about Parkfield, evoking Mr Twyne, induces a mood combining gleeful rage and retrospective terror.

12

W.W.Twyne, the headmaster and proprietor of Parkfield, was a big man. Of course to children everyone looks big but he seemed so in relation to other grown-ups. He was burly but not fat, and smouldered with malevolent energy. Bald with a ruddy-brown complexion, his features were in themselves handsome, but his expression was usually one of petulant and disappointed frustration and his rages, which were frequent, distorted his face into a hideous and terrifying mask like a Japanese warrior in a print. When he was in a rare good mood, he could be surprisingly gentle and amiable. We basked in his good humour, fawned like puppies in the hope of sustaining it; but we watched him warily, knowing only too well that it wouldn't last for long.

He was a very physical man with a large store of what would now be called body language. During his rages he would pace rapidly up and down as though in a cage, turning heavily on his heel every four paces. Simultaneously and continuously he would shoot his cuff, insert the digit finger of his right hand into his collar to loosen it and then shoot his frayed cuff again. We sat frozen during this performance, wondering on whom or on how many his retribution would fall. He would accompany this ritual with a series of oaths, mild enough, even comic in themselves, but delivered with such explosive venom that we felt no urge to smile. 'My Godfathers!' he would shout, 'Ye Gods and little fishes! You people really are the limit!' and always in conclusion, 'It's the pestilential day-school system!' When we were alone together, as a form of exorcism, we frequently imitated this performance. Mr Twyne's absurd nickname, 'Twimbo', was another way we hoped to reduce him in our minds to less intimidating proportions.

The forms his physical retribution took escalated from pulling you up to your feet by grasping either the short hair over the ears or

143

the fatty part of the cheek between thumb and forefinger and then shaking you like a rat, through knocking you rapidly and repeatedly across the side of the skull with his knuckles or the bowl of his pipe, to slippering you with your own house-slipper. Little did I think, when casually trying on a pair of those house-slippers in George Henry Lee's with Maud, that such apparently innocuous objects were to become the instruments of pain and humiliation.

'Give me your slipper!' Twyne would shout to the offender, 'Bend over!' Anything between one and six heavy blows with the heel of the slipper might be anticipated depending, not on the seriousness of the offence, but on the rage of the executant. There was nothing, and I am unable to decide if it was better or worse, premeditated in Mr Twyne's assaults. You were never sent for and beaten in cold blood for a specific crime. Nemesis was instant and completely unpredictable. Sometimes he would slipper the entire school (about forty in number), explaining to each boy, as the blow descended, the individual shortcoming which justified his inclusion in this holocaust. 'You don't do enough work.' 'You talk too much.' 'You've got a cold,' etc. This last may appear especially unfair, but it was Twyne's belief that catching a cold was a matter of choice and indicated some kind of moral failure. It was just one element in an eccentric mental system of quite extraordinary rigidity.

Twimbo was not well dressed. His wardrobe seemed to be confined to one rather shiny brown suit, although I suppose there may have been a second or even a third of identical cut and shade. He wore heavy brown shoes, a little down at heel and, in the street, a greasy trilby hat. His only tie, thin, crumpled and stained, confirmed the fact, frequently referred to in conversation, that he had been educated at Clifton College. He was rather dirty in his habits. In the winter, having blown his nose vigorously, he would bend down to dry the steaming greyish handkerchief at the gas fire, and in doing so revealed that the crotch of his trousers had worn through, allowing us the doubtful pleasure of staring in some awe at his pendulous testicles.

In one of the class-rooms, every morning at about nine fifteen, we could hear outside a loud and puzzling splash. One day, the master or mistress having left us alone 'on our honour', one of the bolder boys decided to solve this conundrum and cautiously put his head outside the window. Twyne's quarters were at the same height and on the same side of the school and, to the minute, his hand emerged from his bedroom window grasping a full chamber-pot which he emptied precipitately into the ivy below. The mystery was solved. This rather eighteenth-century gesture, while the subject of prolonged ribaldry, seemed to us out of character, but I realize now it was probably to do with his almost Swiftian disgust at bodily functions. If we needed more lavatory paper we had to approach him and, after handing it over, he would order us to carry it under our coat 'in case the Matron might see it'. One of his many aphorisms ran as follows: 'Anyone who uses a public lavatory except in a case of dire necessity is a filthy pig!'

His emptying of the chamber-pot into the ivy was presumably because it would have embarrassed him to allow the maid to do it, although at that time this was considered perfectly acceptable practice, and if he'd gone to the bathroom to do it himself there was the possibility of meeting her en route. His statement as to the only justifiable use of a public lavatory illustrates his curiously formal and indeed memorable use of language. No great lover of literature – his revealed taste was for 'rattling good yarns' (*Treasure Island*, Sabatini, Ballantyne, John Buchan, A.E.W. Mason, Rider Haggard were all he advised us to read in our leisure hours) – he nevertheless, even in his rages, relished an ornate phrase. His favourite quotation, which he ascribed to Dr Johnson, was, 'Sir, you are intoxicated by the exuberance of your own verbosity.' His own verbal reactions to a given situation were almost equally elaborate.

His voice was slightly rasping, becoming more so as his temper rose. His accent was received middle-class of the period, clipped rather than drawling but with a southern bias which sounded alien to our northern ears. All his 'a' sounds came out as 'e's'. He pronounced 'back' as 'beck', and he shortened his double 'o's' while lengthening his single 'o's'. 'Afternun', he'd say, and, for 'often', 'orfen'. Today it is only by listening to British films of the thirties and forties that you can hear this accent in its prime, but there is a distinct echo of it in the voices of the more elderly tennis and cricket commentators on TV.

He was no highbrow. Musically, while detesting what he called 'jazz', by which he implied any form of modern dance music, he expressed enthusiasm for nothing beyond Gilbert and Sullivan and 'the old-fashioned waltz'. In his relaxed moments he admitted, with revealing candour, to a delight in the character of Dickens's Wackford Squeers and, less culpably, a liking for the work of Will Hay, a contemporary comedian who usually appeared in the role of a blustering but ineffectual schoolmaster. Indeed, although very infrequently and only at his most expansive, Mr Twyne would admit, 'despite its deplorable vulgarity', to a weakness for the music-hall.

It may seem perverse that while there were no borders at Parkfield, he should have insisted that everything that enraged him was the result of 'the pestilential day-school system', but his school and its geographical situation were, in his eyes, far from ideal. He detested the North of England, making an exception only for the village of Kirkby Lonsdale on the edge of the Lake District, and ideally he would have chosen to be the headmaster of an all-boarding preparatory school in Somerset or Wiltshire, not too far from his beloved Clifton. Why and how he had landed up in Liverpool was one of the several mysteries surrounding him. We knew nothing of his family, although there were rumours of two sisters. Of his previous career all he told us was that for a time he had been an assistant master at Terra Nova, a prep school for which he admitted warm admiration despite the fact that it was situated near Southport, a rather grand resort ringed by golf clubs, but only thirty miles away.

Given that Parkfield was a day school, Mr Twyne did all he could to control his pupils even after we returned each evening to 'the softening influence of home'. We worked on Saturdays. We were forbidden to go to the theatre or cinema or even into a shop, or to associate with children from other schools, not only during the term, but for a week before the end of the holidays. For a time he even made us assemble at Parkfield on Sunday mornings to attend the eleven o'clock service at Christ Church, Linnet Lane *en masse*, thereby adding to the boredom of the ceremony the fear of earning retribution for giggling or not paying enough attention. Some parents, however, objected to this practice, either because they wanted their children to go to their own local church or because, if they attended Christ Church anyway, they preferred to go *en famille*, and eventually Twyne reluctantly agreed to abandon the church parade.

Why did I put up with it? Why didn't I complain to Maud and Tom who would certainly have taken me away from Parkfield and sent me to a gentler establishment? In part I suppose, as in the case of May and Hilda, I had too much pride to whine, but largely it was because Twyne stressed frequently and menacingly that anyone who left had to give a term's notice and in the case of several boys who did, he offered the rest of us a practical demonstration of just what to expect. Never missing an opportunity to enlarge our knowledge of Latin, he would accompany their increased ration of hair-pulling, cheek-pinching, knuckle-bashing, pipe-welding and slippering by intoning rhythmically the while, 'Proditor, Proditoris, masculine, a traitor'.

'We'd have paid the term and you wouldn't have had to go,' Maud said to me later when, Parkfield behind me, I told her about the extent of Twyne's physical violence, but I didn't know that at the time and wonder, even if I had, whether I'd have taken advantage of it. I have always been very obstinate and perhaps my hatred of the man had a certain ambivalence. I half-cherished his dislike of me. If I couldn't seduce him I would make quite sure I stood for everything he disapproved of.

Twyne had no degree and, so far as I know, had not attended a university, but there was no question of his knowledge and love of Latin, the only subject he taught. Any boy with a facility for the language or who worked hard at it, while not exempt from assault, tended to attract less of it. If he were also 'promising' at rugger or cricket or even better, at both, he was in an even stronger position. Bill, arriving three years in my wake, fulfilled all these qualifications. He had in consequence a much easier ride.

'Rugger and Latin prose are all a gentleman needs,' Twyne told us – inappropriate advice I would have thought for the sons of business men and prosperous tradesmen who were his pupils. He would certainly have added cricket if it wouldn't have spoilt the rhythm of the sentence. I had immediately decided that Latin was one of those subjects in which I had no interest and was not prepared to do a hand's turn; I hated the mud and potential for injury on the rugger field and feared the speed and hardness of the cricket ball. I was a 'duffer' in the classroom and a 'rebbit' at games. These, however, were negative failings. I would quite often go out of my way to needle him.

My method was never direct. The lad I admired most in the

147

whole school, a rather stupid and unimaginative boy called Frazer, on one occasion, during a full-scale assault from Twyne, broke loose and shouted 'Lay off!' in a loud defiant tone. I'd never have dared do that. My strategy was to prattle on in apparent innocence about what I knew was calculated to enrage him – my mother's friends in the ballet, for example. He had a profound and just conceivably suspect hatred of any activity he considered effeminate, and the ballet ranked high. I knew that Twyne would be unable to criticize my mother directly, but of course I didn't win. 'Melly Major,' he asked me, 'would you rather go to the ballet or watch a good game of rugger?' I could see the trap, but was at this point unable to recant. 'I'd rather go to the ballet, sir,' I told him. 'Give me your slipper, Melly Major!' he bellowed.

Sometimes I enraged him by accident. One teatime he heard me commiserating with a boy because his birthday always fell during termtime. Twyne beat the wooden trestle-table for silence, told the school what I'd said, and then asked every one of the forty boys whether they would sooner have their birthdays during the holidays. Each of them replied, some a little shame-facedly, in the negative. I was then hauled to my feet and beaten, my punishment confirmed by this cowed consensus.

Yet, even towards me, he would sometimes, however rarely, extend a moment of favour. '*Mel, Mellis,*' he would always decline on these occasions, 'neuter – honey'. While this lasted, and it was never for long, I would feel more than relief, almost love.

Parkfield School occupied a large Victorian stone house with a red-brick extension housing the class-rooms and dining hall. At the front there was only a short curved drive and a bed of gloomy, overgrown laurels masking the building and Twyne's piss-pot emptying from the road, but behind there was a large yard, cemented over, with an outside lavatory and a shooting gallery along one side and across the yard, through an opening in the high wall, the playing-field.

What Twyne always called 'the carriculum' was quite elaborate. Rugger and cricket of course, but also rifle-shooting in the long shed where we lay full length on our elbows on prickly mats, 'squeezing not pulling the trigger', and boxing in the basement, a hideously painful business of bleeding noses and cut lips which he always referred to as 'the noble art of self-defence'. In the summer we went swimming once a week in a hired indoor pool the other side of Sefton Park. This wasn't too bad as it involved a long Noah's Ark-like walk during which you were allowed to talk to your partner, and just to get out of the building at all was a relief, similar in impact I should have thought to that experienced by a long-term convict on changing prisons and thereby catching a glimpse of the outside world going about its normal business.

At the baths Twyne's method of teaching those who couldn't swim was, predictably, to throw them in at the deep end, only hauling them out if they were in real difficulties, and I was extremely grateful I had already mastered, at the Cornwallis Street baths, an adequate if stilted breast-stroke. If it was raining hard on the day we went swimming Twyne, rather than write off what he had paid in advance for the pool, would order a fleet of taxis 'with terrible trouble and at horrible expense' as he put it. I learnt later that the school was always on the verge of financial collapse so it was indeed an inexplicable extravagance.

Parkfield's stated object was 'to coach boys up to the standard of the Common Entrance Examination for the Public Schools' and to this end, apart from Latin, we were taught English, French, History, Geography, Mathematics and Scripture. In addition there was Music, Art and Carpentry once a week. For these 'extra' subjects teachers came in, but for the others there was a permanent and presumably hideously underpaid staff.

Two of them, Miss White (Maths) and Miss Maclean (French), are little more than names now, although I can remember that Miss White, while small and elderly, was an effortless disciplinarian and that Miss Maclean smoked a great deal and possessed a leopard-skin coat. The rest of the permanent staff remain in much sharper focus: Mr Taylor and Mr Oliver because they liked me; Miss Chesterton because I irritated her so much. Mr Taylor and Mr Oliver were both, I suppose, in their early twenties, and Mr Oliver, unlike Mr Twyne, was actually a BA, a fact heavily emphasized in 'the carriculum'. They were both keen territorial officers and amateur rugger players, and you wouldn't have expected them to take to me at all, but they did.

Mr Oliver was rather good-looking in a clean-limbed kind of way. Mr Taylor on the other hand was prematurely bald with a ginger moustache and owlish spectacles, and I liked him even better than Mr Oliver. They both taught English and History at different levels of the school, and it was true that these two subjects were the only ones I was any good at. I don't think, however, that this is why they were on my side. It was more to do with the fact that they were both very bored, loathed Twyne, admired my refusal to submit to his will and, above all, that I made them laugh.

When I was still in the bottom class and, except in English and History, bottom of it, Mr Taylor discovered to his surprise that I could recite Shakespeare and, with Mr Twyne's reluctant permission, loaned me to Mr Oliver to take the principal role whenever the top class was stumbling its way through one of the plays. That I could read blank verse fairly convincingly didn't mean that I could understand much of it – it was more to do with my imitative facility. Tom had taken me to see *Macbeth* when I was still at Camelot, and Maud would sometimes, as a change from 'Naughty Little Briar Rose' and 'Burglar Bill', recite me some of the famous speeches in which she had triumphed at The Green Room before the Great War. I had been thrilled by *Macbeth* and moved by Maud's rendering of 'Build me a willow cabin' and 'The quality of mercy'. As a result I had caught the rhythm of Shakespeare and, provided I understood the gist of the speech, could turn in a creditable performance for a boy of eight.

Later, however, whenever I said anything which amused either of them, or recited a new monologue by Stanley Holloway, or imitated the Western Brothers – popular comedians of the time who dressed in tails, wore monocles, and drawled their way through satirical songs of aristocratic fatuity – I would be sent to repeat it in the other's class-room. If I were to meet Mr Twyne *en route*, they told me, I was to explain that I was needed to read a speech by Shylock or Othello. But as Twyne was always in his own class-room, stressing perhaps that while *nubio* meant 'to marry' it only applied to women, I never had to resort to this excuse. Naturally I was delighted at these expeditions, not only because I adored showing off, but also because I was in league with grown-ups in the deliberate deception of Mr Twyne himself.

Sometimes Mr Oliver became irritated at my continuous need to divert, at my untidiness or lack of concentration, but Mr Taylor never did, which was why I preferred him. The only time he spoke harshly to me was not because of anything I'd done, but he was irritated by Gampa's admittedly rather dubious insistence on being addressed as 'Colonel'. 'He has no right to the title,' said Mr Taylor, quite red with passion. 'He was only a Colonel in the Territorial army. He would have to have been in the regular army to earn the right to be called Colonel! I would refuse, yes refuse, to address him as "Colonel". I would call him "Sir". As he is an older man I would naturally call him "Sir", but Colonel – never!' I couldn't understand why Mr Taylor, although I'm quite sure he was technically correct, became so heated on the subject, but I somehow felt it was better not to question Gampa or even Tom. It would be betraying Mr Taylor.

One afternoon at tea (doorsteps of brown bread thinly smeared with margarine and jam which came out of huge tins and tasted of onions) Mr Taylor and Mr Twyne had a row. We were all, of course, riveted but were unable to work out from what they said to each other what the row was about. They were perfectly civil on the surface and both finished off every sentence with a 'sir'. But their voices were quivering with suppressed rage and Twyne's finger, always a bad sign, was constantly easing his collar. Whether as a direct result of the row, or because of a more general antipathy from which it arose, Mr Taylor left in the middle of the summer term. I cried when he said goodbye to me. I cried on the way home, and I howled and sobbed to Maud and Tom that evening.

'He was my friend,' I explained to them repeatedly as they tried, rather worriedly, to calm and comfort me, 'he was my friend!'

Bill, who was in the room, suddenly realized that he did not like all the attention I was receiving, and decided to get in on the act.

'He was my friend too!' he wailed loudly and somehow managed to burst into tears as convincing and copious as my own.

I stopped crying at once. Bill had only arrived at Parkfield that term whereas I'd been there for three years. He hardly even knew Mr Taylor! I was absolutely furious with him. It was like *Trader Horn* all over again.

Miss Chesterton, who taught Geography and Scripture, was quite young, handsome rather than pretty, and clearly very nice.

Her dislike of me rankled and was based, I've come to the conclusion, on my preciousness and tendency to pronounce confident value judgements. Two examples will suffice, both of which took place at tea. Sir Henry Newbolt – Twyne's favourite poet as it happened – had just been created Poet Laureate. I pronounced magisterially that this was ridiculous. It should obviously have been Kipling. Miss Chesterton snapped that I was in no position to judge. I was very hurt.

The second confrontation was over a joke. 'Did you know', I asked the boy sitting next to me shortly after the coronation of George vi, 'that the King has been going around with Mrs Simpson's sister-in-law?' He looked very surprised until I explained that Mrs Simpson's sister-in-law was (ha-ha) the Queen. Miss Chesterton overheard me, as she was intended to. I wasn't going to waste a joke like that on one dim boy, especially as it was the kind of joke that Mr Taylor would have sent me to tell Mr Oliver. Miss Chesterton, however, was not at all amused. She said it was disgusting and an insult to the Royal Family. I told her that I had heard it from my Uncle Fred. It was my customary ploy to retreat behind a grown-up if challenged, and this time anyway it was true. 'That doesn't make any difference,' said Miss Chesterton. 'It's unsuitable here!'

Twyne was at the head of the next table but luckily did not pick up this exchange although, unexpectedly, he wasn't a passionate monarchist. The Empire, yes. The public schools, certainly; but his enthusiasm for the Royal Family was never more than luke-warm. Of course he never admitted to this directly but several times he repeated something which struck me later as significant. 'When I was inspected by the Prince of Wales during the war,' he told us, 'I could see that he was wearing make-up. The Royal Family wear make-up!' It was clear that he found this extremely suspect. For a man, whether Royal or not, to wear make-up was almost on the level of being a ballet dancer.

The temporary staff consisted of a carpenter, a lugubrious Liverpudlian who was passionate about dove-tailing. I was as bad at carpentry as I'd been at raffia. He used to pick up whatever I was trying to make, hold it up to the bare bulb of the basement, and squint along it with one eye. 'Luke at dat,' he'd say gloomily. 'It's all cock-eyed.'

Music took place in Twimbo's sitting-room, a dusty and

masculine apartment with leather furniture and an upright piano, on the ground floor of the older part of the house. We didn't learn to play instruments, just to sing, either in unison or two-part harmony, a selection of sea shanties or folksongs. We were taught by a small, cheerful and somehow pathetic lady called Miss Nangle who also accompanied us on the upright. It was all perfectly agreeable and the songs: 'What shall we do with the drunken sailor?', 'As I was going to strawberry fair', rather jolly. The only time there was a near disaster was when we were learning a new folksong allegedly written by Henry VIII. It was called 'The Carrion Crow' and the first verse went:

> Oh wife, oh wife bring out my bow
> Heigh ho, the carrion crow.
> Oh wife, oh wife bring out my bow,
> For I mean to shoot that carrion crow.
> Twiggle Twiggle Twig Dum Twee!

The trouble was the absurd last line. Every time we sang it through, I became more and more hysterical and hysteria is catching. Miss Nangle was very patient. 'Boys! Boys! It's not *that* funny! Now calm down! Let's start again, shall we? One, two . . .' It was no good. Eventually we could hardly get through the first line before the thought struck us that only four lines on we would have to deal with 'Twiggle Twiggle Twig Dum Twee', and we would dissolve into giggles.

It was a hot summer's day and the sash window was wide open. We stood in a semi-circle round the piano and I was facing the window. I looked up, wiping away my tears, and saw that Mr Twyne, who could always move remarkably quietly for so large a man, was leaning on the window-sill thoughtfully smoking his pipe. How long had he been there? Did he realize I had started the whole thing off? His expression was enigmatic, but that didn't mean anything. The fact that I had stopped laughing so suddenly had an instant effect even on those with their backs to the window. We froze like a herd of deer scenting danger. Miss Nangle, facing the piano, had no notion as to why the atmosphere had changed so rapidly. We sang through the first verse, including the refrain, as if it were a dirge. When I looked up, Mr Twyne had vanished like a ghost.

'That's better!' said Miss Nangle. 'But now it's *too* serious. It's meant to be fun! We'll try it again next week, turn to "Bobbie Shafto".'

Miss Nangle also taught me the piano at home.

Art was my favourite subject. We were taught it on Saturday morning by a man called Captain Banks or, as Twyne pronounced it 'Ceptin Benks'. He was short and rather dapper and quite old. He was very bald and freckled with many grave marks on his hands. He smelt strongly of scent. His method of teaching was to demonstrate on the blackboard with coloured chalks. He taught us about perspective, shading, highlights, the ideal proportions of the face and body. He would run at the blackboard, make a mark with the chalk giving it a little twist at the end, a little flourish, and then retreat backwards equally fast to examine the effect with his head on one side and a look of total self-satisfaction.

Sometimes he gave us his own small watercolours to copy. They were poor things, very wishy-washy, usually of boats pulled up on a shore. They were framed in *passe partout*. He didn't tell us much about the history of art, but spent a long time attacking the modernists whom he felt had robbed him of recognition. In particular he raged against 'the Sandon Studio artists', many of whom I knew. 'They paint purple women with green hair,' he shouted, working himself up into a paroxysm of rage.

One Saturday, instead of copying the boats, we went to Sudley with Captain Banks to look at Cousin Emma's pictures. He'd asked me to arrange this expedition and I had. I was in fact rather proud that he should have considered that a relation of mine had a collection worth visiting, especially as Captain Banks had never taken us to the Walker Art Gallery. Perhaps, though, that was because Twyne wouldn't allow it. As it was open to the public, it may have come under the same taboo as cinemas, theatres or shops.

Cousin Emma, having greeted me personally and affectionately, much to my satisfaction, asked me to introduce her to the Captain and then showed us round herself. Captain Banks bobbed and smarmed about her in the oiliest fashion; confirming her judgement, leaping back from the pictures as if he had just completed them himself, stressing constantly how privileged we were to be there. As we were putting on our coats and caps in the hall, under Aimée's suspicious eye, he took her aside and engaged her in earnest conversation. 'No thank you, Captain Banks,' I heard her say firmly, 'I'm afraid I don't feel able to take up your kind offer to paint either the house or myself.'

She told Maud later that she believed Captain Banks had arranged the whole outing in the hope of netting this commission. I was sorry for him – even at nine I could recognize pathos – but equally I was rather embarrassed.

13

The rest of the personnel at Parkfield was made up of a cook
whom we never saw, a maid-of-all-work who did everything
except empty Twyne's chamber-pot, and a 'groundsman' who
mowed the playing field and rolled the cricket pitch. There was
also a matron called Miss McClaren. It was surely unnecessary
in 'a pestilential day school' to employ a matron but I suppose
she could have been responsible for the catering. She was
dressed, however, as a proper matron in a kind of hospital
uniform with a cap, and I think she was hired to bolster up
Twimbo's dream of running a real boarding school in the West
Country. She was very kind-hearted, and when Twyne knocked
anyone about, a look of distress and anger crossed her open
Scottish features. One term she was not there any more, nor was
she replaced, but Mr Twyne, when we asked him what had
become of her, dismissed her, with great bitterness and in defi-
ance of her gender, as a '*proditor, proditoris*, masculine, a traitor'. What had she done, we wondered? Had she perhaps
threatened to report him to the NSPCC?

A term or two later we acquired an even less necessary addition to the staff – a staff sergeant. His name was Rutter and he had
been in the Mozambique Rifles. Thinking back on his appearance I believe he may have had some black blood: his nostrils
were very wide, his mouth generous, and he had crinkly hair.
His head was large, his body broad and compact, but what was
perfectly obvious to anyone with even an inkling of such things,
was that he was a screaming queen. Didn't Twyne, with his
phobia about effeminacy, recognize this? Is it just conceivable
that he was Twyne's lover? Certainly his duties were light
enough. He took PT in the concrete yard. He taught us shooting
in the long wooden shed. On very wet days he would lecture,
with slides, on life in the African bush. He helped out

Twimbo on the playing-field or during boxing in the basement. He also cut our hair. A barber had always come in to do this during term-time, but now Sergeant Rutter took his place. His haircuts were drastic. 'Oh no!' cried my mother in only partially mock anguish when Bill and I came gooseberrying home after the Sergeant's radical application of the clippers.

He was a kind man though, and stopped Mr Twyne from throwing boys into the swimming bath by insisting on teaching them himself at the shallow end. While patently gay, he was not – and boys always know even if they don't know what they know – at all paederastic. My parents could not believe it. Sensing Maud's fascination and liking for homosexuals, he used to rush up to her on sports days or on meeting her in the street shrieking 'Bless you, Mrs Melly,' a sentiment Twyne, who both mistrusted and disliked her, would never have endorsed. My father, on his return from the office, would sometimes imitate this greeting, and he always referred to Sergeant Rutter, although naturally never to his face, as 'Pansy' Rutter. After a couple of years he left and we were sorry to see him go. Whether for the reason I have tentatively and with no positive evidence suggested, 'Pansy' Rutter had acted as a restraining influence on the excesses of W.W.Twyne.

Much as I dreaded Twyne in the class-room I was at least in part protected there by others, some of them 'promising' athletes who were as unenthusiastic and idle when it came to mastering 'Letin prose' as I was myself. It was on the playing-field that some of our worst confrontations took place and it was cricket especially that brought out what he called the 'bolshie' in me.

During rugger matches, by running about a lot and making sure, as discreetly as possible, that I was in the wrong place, I could at least present the illusion of involvement. What I hated about rugger was not so much the games, which at any rate lasted a specific time, but the scrum practices on Saturday afternoons. These, when I was longing to get home, went on and on, well into the dusk, and were made all the more frustrating by Twimbo's reiterated and mendacious promise that each successive scrimmage was to be 'the last scrum of the day'. 'Show some guts, you little forwards,' he would bellow as an excuse for prolonging the muddy tedium another ten minutes. 'Guts' was the strongest language I ever heard him use, and even here he would qualify it later at tea by telling us that it was a word 'justifiable on the rugger field but not in the drawing-room' even though 'these days duchesses swear like bargees'.

His attitude to women was, I suspect, deeply hostile, and he covered this by excessively formal politeness which some mothers, but not Maud, found charming. Sometimes he would instruct us on how to greet a lady in the street. He would borrow one of our caps, which on his large bald head was already a dangerously risible spectacle, and would then pretend to walk in a somewhat military fashion for some paces before recognizing an imaginary aunt or 'another boy's mother'. He would stop, smile rather savagely, and raise the cap into the air with his right hand. 'Good afternun, Mrs Clutterbuck,' he'd enunciate clearly before replacing the cap and resuming his even pacing. We were then expected, either individually or collectively, to repeat this absurd exercise, 'Mrs Clutterbuck' and all.

It was, however, in relation to sport that his misogynism became nakedly manifest. He told us that women were, by temperament, totally unsuited to playing anything, illustrating his thesis by citing the behaviour of a certain M'mselle Suzanne Lenglen, a French tennis champion of the twenties, who several times at Wimbledon had 'thrown down her reckit in pure rege'. He also told us that we must never play any game with a girl, 'not even tennis, not even with your own sister' because of the unacceptable possibility of being beaten.

Cricket, however, was a male preserve and he took it for granted that any man who had no interest in it was totally beyond the pale. Had I been more circumspect or less obstinate I could have faked it, expressed some enthusiasm if no aptitude, learnt at least the positions on the field, but I made no such concessions. If, when arranging the fielding, he directed me to silly mid-off or square-leg I made it patently obvious that I had no idea in which direction to aim. During test matches, when we were expected to sit through lunch or tea in rapt silence, listening to the commentary on the wireless, I emanated boredom and, if questioned, total ignorance as to the state of play. He could slipper me as often as he liked, but my rejection of the mystique of 'King Willow' remained absolute, the centre of my integrity.

Once, when batting, I scored a four, but was relieved, although also rather hurt, when he dismissed it contemptuously as 'a cow shot'. 'There are only two strokes in betting, Melly Major,' he remonstrated, 'Forward and beck!' He demonstrated these alternatives with an invisible bat, 'Forward and beck!'

I still know nothing about cricket, but retain and cherish a single sentence of his on the subject, not because of its content, but because of the way it was expressed – Twyne at his most baroque. 'When Jessop was betting,' he used to say, 'nursemaids would leave their charges.'

The boys who assembled under Twyne's threatening shadow came from a fairly wide social spectrum. Some were the sons of professional men: doctors, lawyers, architects. The majority of us were the children of business men. A few had fathers who had succeeded in trade: fishmongers, market gardeners, coal merchants, who had decided they could afford to turn their sons into gentlemen. Twyne was not in a position to be selective. He needed a full school to keep his shaky financial position from collapsing.

None of us was actually what he would have chosen; even the doctors and lawyers were Liverpudlians. Ideally his pupils would have been the sons of small Wessex landowners, military men and colonial administrators. He had no dreams of running a fashionable school; in fact he despised 'Society', foul-mouthed duchesses and all. He had no ambitions to boast that his boys went on to Eton or Harrow. The public schools he favoured were those modelled on Dr Arnold's Rugby: Marlborough, Repton, and of course Clifton. His ideal boy 'worked hard and played hard'. The quality he most valued was *esprit de corps.*

Naturally he became apoplectic at the idea of progressive education, reserving his especial venom and verbal exuberance for the Montessori System. This he described as 'a pimply youth in a velvet suit doing crochet in a deckchair'.

159

He made no secret, either, of his dislike of the industrial working classes. '*Sperno profanum vulgus*' (I hate the common people), a Latin tag ascribed to Coriolanus, was frequently on his lips. Nevertheless he believed that they, or at any rate their children, were useful in offering us a practical opportunity to apply the lessons we had learnt in 'the noble art of self-defence' in the school basement.

It was the custom of gangs of small and ragged boys from the back streets of Lark Lane and Aigburth Road to lie in wait in the driveways of the big houses near Parkfield in order to duff us up on the way home. Twyne referred to these children collectively as 'oiks', and indoctrinated us with the idea that if we took them on one at a time and applied the Queensberry Rules, we would automatically establish our superiority. Unfortunately the 'oiks' appeared to be unaware of the Queensberry Rules. They used elbows, their heads and boots, and were not prepared to take us on man to man. Their intention was never to hurt us badly. What they hoped to do, and frequently succeeded in doing, was to humiliate what I heard one of them describe as 'dem posh kids wid dair daft caps and dair toffee noses in de ur'. It was Twyne who lusted for reports of broken noses and smashed teeth.

Despite the legendary exploits of an old boy called Barlow Major who, according to Twyne, had left three large 'oiks' unconscious and stacked neatly around a lamppost like a picture in a comic strip, most of us preferred to rely less on our pugilistic expertise than on safety in numbers. The 'oiks' were usually in gangs of three or four at most and so if we walked home in groups of five or six they usually left us alone. One evening in 1935, however, I set off by myself because I had obtained special permission to meet my father on his way home from the office and, although it was termtime, go with him into a shop in Lark Lane to buy my first bike. Twyne was standing outside the gates of Parkfield smoking his pipe, something he frequently did in the summer to make sure that we neither dawdled nor ran, at any rate until we were out of sight, and Tom, I could see, was waiting on the corner of Ivanhoe Road, some two hundred yards away. When I was approximately equidistant between them, three minute 'oiks' rushed out of a driveway and set about me. Aware of the proximity of Twyne I assumed the classic prize-fighter's stance: right fist guarding the face, left arm extended, while they ran rings round me, kicking my shins and elbowing me in the ribs. There was a bellow from Twyne as he became aware of the fracas. He ran down Parkfield Road, an intimidating if absurd spectacle, yelling 'Keep a straight left, Melly Major!' Seeing and indeed hearing him coming, the 'oiks' scampered off, passing within a few feet of my father, towards the safety of Lark Lane. One of them was triumphantly waving my cap. Tom was convulsed with laughter, Twyne out of his mind with rage. 'Why didn't you stop them, Mr Melly!' demanded the furious Twimbo.

'Because I was laughing too much,' said my father. Twyne turned silently on his heel and strode off back to Parkfield. Despite the fact that Tom had been educated at Marlborough, Mr Twyne obviously believed that he was wanting in *esprit de corps*.

Although I didn't like being duffed up, I envied the 'oiks' their freedom, their torn jerseys, the fact that they could stay up as late as they liked and roam the streets. I know this incident took place in 1935 because that night, lying in bed, my beautiful new bike in the little shed in the back-yard, I could hear some of them, possibly even the same gang, singing profane words to a Salvation Army hymn as they swaggered back down Parkfield Road.

> Will you come to Abyssinia will you come,
> Bring your own ammunition and your gun,
> Mussolini will be there
> Popping bullets in the air.
> Will you come to Abyssinia, will you come.

14

I forget which boy it was that, when I was about nine, suggested that he put his hand up my trouser leg and 'rubbed up my dick'. I resisted his invitation initially, it seemed both meaningless and 'rude'; but when he promised me I'd like it, and furthermore I somehow began to feel curiously excited at the idea, I let him do it. As soon as he started to tickle and rub my privates I could feel my 'dick', small as it was, grow hard, and a minute or two later a delicious sensation, starting at the base of my spine, flooded through my whole body. I had experienced, although I'd no idea what it was, my first induced orgasm, but naturally, as I was still several years from puberty, there was no sperm. I felt no hesitation therefore in gratefully doing him the same service. I watched with interest how his eyelids fluttered and he gave a little moan when he achieved what he called 'the funny feeling'. Although temporarily incapable, I couldn't wait to do it again.

I soon discovered that this habit was widespread throughout Parkfield, especially among the older boys. It had, I learnt subsequently, been imported by a boy called Warren, the school's best cricketer, as it happens, and big for his years. He had learnt about it from an older brother who was at public school. There were a few boys in the school who would have no part of it, but most of us were at it all the time – in the outside lavatory, in the changing-rooms, even during class behind the high tip-up desks. It didn't take very long, and we'd no idea of its significance beyond the pleasure involved, but we never stopped. It was like a comforting secret to set against the harsh and spartan world of Twyne.

That it should remain a secret we knew instinctively. A certain guilt about our privates had been inculcated since we were toddlers, although without any explanation as to what we were meant to feel guilty about. Even my mother, with her advanced views on nudity within the family, would tell me and Bill not to touch 'our obies' if she saw us doing so. I've no idea why she called the penis an 'obie' but she did. Alternatively it was known as a 'dumbelow' although this, she told me, derived from a misunderstanding of Uncle Fred's when he was a little boy. The Griff, while giving him his bath, would tell him, having herself washed everything else, to soap himself 'down below', and he misheard it as 'dumbelow' which he concluded to be a name for his 'arrangements'. Of course this demystification of the privates by the use of whimsical names was not confined to the thirties and persists even today. You hear even the most progressive mothers refer to their child's 'willy'.

I soon discovered, although I found it less exciting, that I could 'rub up' myself, and this explained to me why my mother sometimes rushed into my bedroom and whisked back the sheets and blankets with a cry of, 'Where are those handymits?' The myth of the evils and dangers of masturbation was universal then.

An orgasm, while the means to achieve it was new, was an experience I remembered from a dream I had when I was only five or six. I found myself as a pig in a dirty sty at Uncle Percy's farm and derived enormous satisfaction from rolling and wallowing in my own dung. I awoke to what I now recognized as the same feeling I got from 'rubbing up'. I'd also been very interested in my privates. I once dreamed, but believed it for many years to be factual, that I was sitting in the nursery and had discovered a way to remove from my testicles the two hard little balls I could feel under the skin. These turned out to be brightly coloured beads of a curiously electric puce, and I spent a happy time rolling them about the green cork floor before realizing, in a panic, that I'd no idea how to put them back. The beads at least were real, part of a game in the nursery cupboard, and it was one of them that Andrée had swallowed and on which she had nearly choked to death.

At Parkfield we were entirely unromantic about our sexual partners, that was to come later at our public schools, but we did develop purely physical crushes. These led to curious liaisons across the usual lines of interest. Warren himself, for instance, captain of cricket and a brilliant 'all-rounder', became a close friend through this shared interest whereas before it would never have occurred to him to spend his time with 'a rabbit' who couldn't throw overarm. There was a certain amount of selective rejection too. There was one boy I liked very much but refused to engage in sexual activities with because he had plump, wet hands, was overweight, and wore pebble glasses. Equally it took me a long time to persuade a very randy and in truth rather neolithic-looking boy, the son of a timber merchant, to have anything to do with me. Another mystery: why did I find him attractive? He had a low forehead, small eyes and a heavy jaw. All I knew was that I did.

Taking a leaf from the 'oiks' book, I invented a parody of the title song of a film in which George Formby played the gormless lead. Both the song and the film were called *It's in the Air*. Holding an imaginary ukelele and assuming Formby's innocent grin and Lancashire accent I sang:

> It's in the dick
> That funny feeling that's so quick
> to tickle like the heck
> At the back of the neck,
> It's in the dick.

This became something of an anthem to the rubbing-up brigade and we would hum or whistle the tune publicly about the school with looks of knowing complicity.

With all this going on, it was only a question of time before Twyne found out, and when this eventually happened I was a witness. At the back of the school was a small quad, a patch of grass with a conservatory along one side. Overlooking this area was a basement which formed the lower changing-room, whereas the conservatory was used as the upper changing-room.

I was in the lower changing-room, usually a hive of sexual activity, and while changing into my hated flannels I happened to glance out of the window only to spot Twyne tiptoeing across the grass. He stopped outside the conservatory and peered in. There was a moment's delay before he jumped in the air, banged on the window, and rushed into the body of the school yelling, 'Ring up the school doctor!'

I guessed, of course, what had happened, and it was confirmed during the game. Warren, who was in the upper changing-room and, as I'd expected, involved, was fielding opposite me. At each over, as we crossed on the pitch, he managed to tell me the story in single sentences. Apart from his request for the school doctor, an instantaneous reaction which he had not followed up, Twyne had done nothing: no hairpulling, no slippering, simply the order to get changed at once delivered in a neutral if icy tone.

After tea the staff left the dining-hall in a rather self-consciously casual way, and the whole of the lower changing-room were ordered to take the few very small boys who went home half-an-hour earlier, to wash. Later I asked Warren what Twimbo had said. 'Oh, that we'd go blind, and loose a vital fluid out of our backbones and stop being able to play games well,' he told me. Nobody believed this, and quite soon we started 'rub-bing up' again only with rather more circumspection. The only thing which puzzled me was why Mr Twyne imagined that vice was the sole prerogative of the upper changing-room.

For a surprisingly long time, until I suppose I was about ten, I made no connection between 'rubbing up' and procreation. My knowledge of sex was non-existent. Maud, when I'd asked her about how babies were born – for Tom played no part in answering any of our more serious questions – didn't try to fob me off with storks or gooseberry bushes, but her answers were the reverse of graphic. 'The Daddy', she said, 'loves the Mummy so much that a baby starts to grow in her tummy. It's there for nine months and then it's born.' Perfectly correct as far as it went, but I believed in consequence that all that was involved was an act of will. My ignorance was eventually dispelled, not at home but at school, by a very serious boy called Rice. He was as hopeless as I was at cricket and Twyne, in exasperation, had told us to go to the nets at the far end of the playing-field and practise batting and bowling. Ever the proselytizer, I was questioning him as to why he took no part in our sexual activities. 'Because', he said, bowling a wide which would have brained the umpire, 'I believe sex should be used for its true ends – the making of children.' He could see from my face that I hadn't the faintest idea what he was talking about, and he proceeded, with admir-able scientific detachment, to enlighten me. Frankly I couldn't believe him. Had Tom done *that* to Maud? Had all the Parkfield mothers and fathers done it? Had the Griff done it, and Gangie and Gampa? No, it was impossible. It was my turn to be censorious.

When I got home I asked Maud outright and she, who had read or been told that you must answer such questions honestly as they came up, confirmed everything he'd said, only stressing that what was important was the presence of love.

'Is it nice though?' I asked.

'Yes,' she said, rather wistfully. 'It's also very nice.'

I went to bed in such a mental turmoil that I didn't even bother to rub up.

It didn't take me long to make the various connections. Men and women did it because it gave them 'the funny feeling', but you didn't have to do it with a girl to get that although it must be best if you could. I also discovered that most of the boys whom I hastened to enlighten already knew about it, and the various jokes they told, which I'd laughed at but hadn't understood, suddenly made sense. Having broached the subject, I questioned Maud endlessly, and gradually extended my sexual knowledge into quite esoteric byways. She told me about gays and lesbians, why some of her men friends lived together, and so on. She preached tolerance and understanding and revealed, although involuntarily, her own largely unfulfilled sexuality. A lot of things began to fall into place: what Douglas Byng was actually singing about, many of the references at the music-hall. Of these areas the boys at Parkfield knew nothing. I was in a position to enlighten them and, always delighted to be the centre of attention, didn't hesitate to do so. It was even more satisfactory than going on about Maud and Tom letting us see them with nothing on.

15

As a result of all this rapidly acquired and mostly ill-digested knowledge, I began to have crushes on girls. Most of them I recognized to be fantasy figures: film stars, actresses, lady acrobats, whom I would never meet but who could be thought about when 'rubbing up' – for by now this was no longer sufficient unto itself. I had to have a scenario. Much more frustrating were the girls I knew who were in their late teens or early twenties, for I had no interest in my giggling or snooty contemporaries. I became obsessed with several of them, but realized at the same time that they were unlikely to be remotely interested in a boy of nine or ten.

Of these perhaps the one who gave me the most anguish was a tall twenty-year-old Irish beauty with very white skin, jet black hair and huge blue eyes. Her name was Miss Simpson and she had come to teach at Parkfield as a replacement for Mr Taylor. She didn't stay very long, perhaps only a year, but during that time, whatever perils the day might hold, I actually hurried to school with an eager heart. Nor was it only at Parkfield that I saw her. She would sometimes come to the house. My mother collected pretty girls, whom she called collectively 'the young lovelies', to 'fill up' her straight dinner parties. She had met Miss Simpson at a school sports day and my father, whom Maud always liked to please, admitted to finding her 'decorative'. She was asked once and, having 'scored a hit', joined 'the young lovelies' on a permanent basis. Tom called her 'the Duchess', pinning down her employment at Parkfield to 1936, the year of the Abdication, which would mean that I was ten years old.

For me a side benefit of the Duchess's success as a 'young lovely' was the rage and anguish it caused Twyne. He mistrusted and disliked my parents and for one of his staff to be invited to their dinner parties seemed to him an outrage. I made sure he knew of it, too. Maud would ask me to see if Miss Simpson was free the following Wednesday, and I deliberately invited her in Twimbo's hearing. 'Sure,' said the Duchess in her soft brogue, 'wouldn't I be delighted.' Twyne could do nothing. His staff were free to spend their evenings as they wished, but he could later be heard muttering that 'nobody could be expected to do their jobs properly if they spent their nights in dissipation.'

Miss Simpson accepted my worship with tact and charm. Once I tried to declare myself. We were sitting in adjoining deckchairs watching a school match with Bishops Court, a Catholic establishment from Blundellsands. (I never minded school matches because I was not in the team and there were special buns for tea coated with sticky white or pink icing.)

'Miss Simpson,' I said in a fake blasé voice, 'perhaps you don't realize this but boys my age, not all boys perhaps but some, have strong sexual feelings.'

'Is that so now?' said Miss Simpson without displaying either excessive interest or dismissive indifference. 'Well, it's unfortunate for them, but then haven't they got their lives ahead of them?' She gave me a sweet and understanding smile which didn't help much. 'Hadn't we better pretend to take an interest in the game, boring as it is. Twimbo's got his eye on us, and we'll both be in his bad books.'

I ate a lot of sticky buns for tea and was fascinated, as always, by the way boys from Bishops Court crossed themselves before sitting down.

It wasn't all Wackford Squeers or Wedekind at Parkfield. There was also friendship and enmity, the discussion of films seen in the holidays, hobbies, games in their season, smuggled comics, the usual traffic of small boys everywhere. Comics, or 'penny dreadfuls' as Twyne, with typical archaism, chose to call them, were banned and I usually read mine at home. Defiant in spirit, I was very cautious when it came to breaking rules. Unlike some boys, I never went to the pictures during the term, but then I did live very close to the school. I doubt if I would have done so no matter where I lived, because I believed that, like God, Twimbo would find me out.

Leaving aside my own personal obsession with *Mickey Mouse Weekly*, the most generally popular comics were the *Beano*, the *Dandy* and *Film Fun*. Fond as I was of Big Eggo (a greedy ostrich), Keyhole Kate, Desperate Dan (who ate whole cow-pies with the hooves and horns sticking out), Lord Snooty and his Pals, and Pansy Potter, the strong man's daughter, all of whom appeared in either the *Beano* or the *Dandy*, my favourite was definitely *Film Fun*. Apart from its link with the pictures, it gave double value in that it was possible to follow the stories by racing through the balloons issuing from the characters' mouths over breakfast, reserving the more expansive text printed under each frame until I returned home. Then I could read at leisure and with a clear conscience for there was one great advantage about Parkfield: although we came out later than most schools, Twyne did not believe in homework.

Laurel and Hardy took up the front and back page of *Film Fun*. Inside were other single-page adventures featuring, among others, Schnozzle Durante and, more esoterically I would have thought, as their films were generally only released in the North of England, George Formby, Old Mother Riley (and her beautiful daughter Kitty), and even Frank Randle.

The stories were more often than not concerned with what the text described, with almost Twyne-like elaboration, as 'temporary pecuniary embarrassment', solved, after several vicissitudes, by a rich uncle handing over a five-pound note with '£5' printed boldly on it. This was inevitably spent at either 'The Hotel de Posh' or 'The Hotel Stuffem', two establishments where the cuisine appeared to be limited to a turkey (or was it a very large chicken?), a huge dish of mash with sausages sticking out of it, and a bowl of fruit with a prominent pineapple. Laurel and Hardy usually shared their good fortune with two identical girls dressed, unfashionably, in the 'flapper' style of the twenties. Nobody ever 'said' anything in *Film Fun*. They 'chortled' or 'guffawed', 'growled' or 'yelled'. The background detail was also worth studying. When the characters were still 'broke', there was usually a thin cat somewhere in the picture gnawing ravenously at a fish reduced to its head and skeleton.

Apart from comics there were conkers in the winter term

which were allowed at Parkfield and, for a time, the renaissance of that craze of the twenties, the yoyo, which was banned. Tom surprised me by his expertise with the yoyo, a skill he had acquired in his youth. He could even do 'round the world' whereas all I could manage was to make it go up and down on its string and even then with ever-decreasing momentum.

My two best friends at Parkfield were both the sons of doctors. One was called David Hurter who was rather small and very serious. Tom called him 'Mr Penny' after a character in the popular radio programme 'Monday Night at Seven'. Hurter – for although we were close Twimbo's embargo on first names tended to apply even during the holidays – had a jolly mother who adored him. Their mutual passion was catching moths and I accompanied them on several expeditions to the heaths around Southport or the woods and fields of the Wirral. I enjoyed catching the moths in a net and dreamed of discovering a new species, but found it difficult to remember the names and distinguishing characteristics of those we came across and although a dab hand with the killing bottle, I was useless when it came to mounting the specimens once I'd got them home. Still for Hurter's sake I persisted for several years.

Desmond Julian's father was a homeopath, at that time considered an eccentric if not positively harmful form of medicine. Desmond had an older brother called Adrian who seemed to me the epitome of knowledgeable sophistication, and a charming sister called Pauline. His mother was warm and loving and they were indeed a most attractive family. I went on summer holiday with them once in Anglesey and Adrian explained to me, quite without prurience, why Pauline couldn't swim that day; another fact to add to my growing store of sexual knowledge.

Twyne didn't like the Julians any more than he did us, not in their case because of any theatrical connection, but because he thought the Doctor to be dangerously left-wing. In fact Dr Julian subscribed to Sir Richard Acland's Commonwealth Party, but anything less than a total commitment to the extreme right of the Conservatives was, for Twyne, tantamount to carrying a Communist party card.

Hurter, Julian and I formed a dissecting club. Both of them wanted to become doctors like their fathers, and it was the period when I, who couldn't even mount a moth without the wings coming off, saw myself as a famous surgeon. Part of the reason for founding the dissecting club was in opposition to a boy called Nicholas who had started a model aeroplane club. Hurter, Julian and I all detested model aeroplanes, and we also thought Nicholas far too bumptious in general. I approached my father's first cousin, Dr George Rawdon Smith, to ask for his help and he gave us the small dissecting table he had used as a student and a set of rather rusty surgical knives.

We met at our house on Sunday afternoons and went upstairs in procession accompanied by Hurter playing his recorder. There we cut up (in my case hacked up) a rabbit or pigeon purchased from Glendennings, high-class fishmongers and poulterers, of Lark Lane, preserving the organs in jars of formaldehyde, before marching down the stairs again for a large tea. Among the rabbits' brains and pigeons' hearts was our prize specimen, Bill's appendix, which following prolonged haggling I had bought from him after his emergency operation for one shilling and sixpence.

Maud didn't mind us cutting up pigeons and rabbits, but she drew the line when she discovered that I had been to see a vet and reserved a dog he was about to put down. She made me ring up the vet, much against my will, and cancel it. The dissecting club, like the model aeroplane club, gradually petered out, but both Julian and Hurter eventually became doctors.

Julian, who was a little older than I, left Parkfield just before the war. Shortly afterwards Twyne, reading in the *Daily Telegraph* of the Russian non-aggression pact with the Germans, jumped to his feet, threw the paper on the floor and shouted, 'The Julians ought to be shot!'

16

At some point in the mid-1930s Maud and Tom decided that, with Andrée beginning to grow up, 33 Ivanhoe Road was becoming too cramped and that they should move. They first considered buying a very beautiful old house at the entrance to Fullwood Park, a private residential drive curving down from the bottom of Aigburth Road to the river. The house had been built in 1666 and was in bad repair, and Tom, ever cautious financially, decided against it. I was very disappointed as I was sure it must have had at least a couple of secret panels, one of my fixed obsessions. It was eventually bought by a prosperous doctor who immediately knocked it down and built a hideous villa faced in yellowish-brown pebble-dash. He even put a plaque up on the side reading 'Built 1666. Rebuilt 1936', to advertise his crime.

It was surprising that Tom agreed to buy a house at all. He had always maintained that he preferred to rent so that the landlords and not he were responsible for any repairs. I've no idea why he was so nervous about money – he knew that he would eventually inherit a substantial amount – but nervous he was. He even got quite cross if he felt we were using too much lavatory paper. 'Quite unnecessary,' he'd remonstrate; 'all you ever need is two up, two down and a polisher.'

Eventually they settled on a very ugly but large late-Victorian house in Sandringham Drive, next door to York Mansions where the Griff had her flat. About forty years old and very solidly built, it was structurally sound and cost only a thousand pounds freehold, reasonable even in those days as there was almost half an acre of ground at the back. Faced with sandstone, it had bay windows and awkwardly pointed eaves. There was a large porch at the side leading through to a decrepit conservatory mounted on tall brick foundations with wooden steps down to the garden.

The front, whilst badly proportioned, was at least symmetrical, but the back was a mess with haphazardly placed windows and naked drainpipes. It was, however, an undeniably solid property and inside, the rooms, as in so many Victorian houses, were large and well-lit.

Maud decided the way to deal with it was to 'modernize' it. She had most of the walls papered in cream and the woodwork painted shiny black. She replaced the elephantine newel post by a straight elongated cube and boxed in the ornate heavily carved bannisters with plywood. She did the same for the doors, changing their large round china handles for angled chrome or bakelite. She also boxed in the elaborate plaster friezes and ripped out most of the fireplaces, replacing them with gas fires. In the lounge she installed a modern grate with geometrical cream and brown tiles. She carpeted the hall and staircase in 'apple' green and had the outsides of the doors and the boxed-in staircase painted to match. For the main rooms she had curtains made which went down to the ground and had square pelmets covered in matching material. She made two bathrooms: hers and Tom's was called 'the green bathroom' because not only were the walls green but so were the bath, washbasin and lava- tory – the *dernier cri* in 1935 – and the cistern of the lavatory was not high up the wall but behind the basin itself, another novelty at that time. The adjacent 'blue bathroom' for the maids and children was far less grand. It had ordinary white fittings, and only justified its name because the walls were painted a rather raw blue. The top floor, which we didn't use, she blocked off with a cheap door and more hardboard, in case one of us ever needed a flat. It was in one of those empty, undecorated rooms that the dissecting club held its weekly sessions.

With the exception of a large divan for the lounge and some furniture for Andrée's pink, sprig-muslined room, she had to buy very little. What had seemed cluttered in Ivanhoe Road proved quite adequate here. When I used to stay at home during the fifties it seemed shabby and dated but, freshly decorated inside and out, the effect for suburban Liverpool was quite 'daring'. This was confirmed by Aunt Eva's state visit. Looking very out of context in her floor-length black bombazine dress and jet jewellery, she went 'over the house' without comment, only to pronounce magisterially on leaving that it was 'far too modern'. Maud had aimed at modernity and should have taken it as a backhanded compliment, but given her insecurity in relation to the older Mellys she was quite upset. Most people, however, found it 'very exciting', if, in some cases, 'a little extreme'.

In the basement, running along the whole of the back of the house, was 'the big room'. It had a fairly low ceiling, two central columns taking the weight of the building, eight windows and a door into the garden. Maud did no more than paint it cream, build a wooden wall-seat right round it, and put in a gas fire at each end. She knew very well what she would use it for. She would hold a series of huge parties.

Meanwhile it was a marvellous room for us. We had a full-length ping-pong table which, when stood on its side and drawn on with coloured chalk, doubled as the scenery for the later 'Melly Versions', while the space between the two columns formed an ideal proscenium arch. There was of course no secret panel, but in compensation there was a trap-door in a corner of 'the big room' with a steep little ladder leading down into the foundations and, at the front of the house, extensive cellars. In one of these was a large boiler and a pile of coke, for there was an antiquated but perfectly efficient central heating system, in itself a rarity in pre-war Britain where frost patterns on the windows and chilblains on toes and fingers were accepted as the norm in winter. It had to be very cold, however, before Tom felt there was sufficient justification for lighting it.

The garden consisted of a long narrow 'top lawn' which ran parallel to the garden of York Mansions. At the end, flanked by two ugly Victorian urns, were some steps leading down to 'the big lawn' with a herbaceous border along one side and a kitchen garden beyond. Across 'the big lawn' some more steps led up to a garage on a cement plateau and, for access, there was a sandy lane running up the other side of the Griff's, with a double gate at the top leading out again into Sandringham Drive. Tom took over the garden and became quite keen on it. It was a bit too big for him and he wasn't very interested in vegetables, which anyway grew badly in the sour Liverpool soil. In consequence the kitchen garden behind its 'rustic' trellis of rambler roses looked, with its little wooden hut, like an ill-tended allotment, but he mowed the lawns and took a lot of trouble with the herbaceous border. Maud raided this a great deal for the house, but it caused little friction as what she was after in the main was a tall plant called Golden Rod which he considered to be a weed and would like to have up-rooted, but which she thought looked 'very dramatic' in a big beige jug on the square piano in front of the burnt-orange curtains. There was a little wooden gate leading into the Griff's so we could play there too and, when we got a bit older, some neighbours, the Brocklehursts, had a door made in their fence on the conservatory side of 'the top lawn' so that we could use their hard tennis court. From a small terrace house with a back-yard and an 'entry' we suddenly had all this. How we could afford it remains a mystery. Had Tom come into some money from an uncle? Had Gampa advanced him some? Or was it that, with the Depression over, he was doing much better in the buying and selling of wool futures?

Yet despite enjoying our new-found grandeur, and because I was already nine or ten when we moved, it was Ivanhoe Road which remained for me 'the house'. Many of the incidents and conversations with my mother which must have taken place at Sandringham Drive I remember as happening in Ivanhoe Road. I was convinced, for example, that Gampa died when we were still there, but reading in Willie Bert's pamphlet that this took place in 1937 I realized that it must have been after we'd moved. Andrée confirmed this. Although not told about Gampa's death at the time, she remembers going into the spare room at Sandringham Drive and finding Gangie praying at the foot of one of the twin beds with their shot-silk covers. It remained fixed in her mind, although she was barely five, because she found it so strange that Gangie should be saying her prayers in the afternoon. But then Andrée can hardly remember Ivanhoe Road at all. Just the pram room, she says, and mostly only its rubbery smell. A further factor in my confusion perhaps was that both houses had the same furniture arranged in much the same way.

Where was it, for instance, that I gave up listening to Northern Children's Hour in favour of Henry Hall and his orchestra? I'd loved Children's Hour especially Toy Town and a programme called Out With Romany in which 'Auntie' Doris and 'Auntie' Muriel pretended, in a Manchester Studio, to be out on a nature ramble with a rather posh gypsy and his extremely well-trained dog, Rack. Fooled by a convincing recorded background of bird song, Bill and I firmly believed that they were really in the country, although we were surprised and impressed by the number of creatures – hedgehog, fox, badger, otter, woodpecker, stoat, etc. – that Romany, in his stage whisper, managed to bring to the attention of the two 'Aunties' in only half an hour. Quite suddenly, though, I abandoned Rack and his master, Larry the Lamb and Mr Growser, for the suave bespectacled Hall. At first I only liked the comedy or novelty numbers like 'The Teddy Bears' Picnic' and 'Hush, Hush, Hush, Here Comes the Bogey-Man!', but soon developed a taste for ballads: 'The Isle of Capri', 'Red Sails in the Sunset', 'The Story of Love', and particularly 'Pennies from Heaven'.

Miss Nangle, whom Tom had nick-named 'Niddy Noddy', had taught me the piano at Ivanhoe Road and continued to do so for a time at Sandringham Drive. I showed no aptitude for it and hated the simple classics I was expected to learn. Finally I delivered an ultimatum. I would only carry on if I could learn to play dance music. Niddy Noddy reluctantly conceded and I bought, from the music shop in Lark Lane, a song copy of 'Pennies' with a pale blue art-deco cover and a round inset photograph of the young Bing Crosby in the bottom right-hand corner. I thought I'd be able to play dance music at once but found out it was just as difficult as 'The Merry Peasant' or Brahms' 'Cradle Song'. Eventually I was allowed to give up music altogether, although I prevaricated about this for several weeks because Maud had often said that 'poor Miss Nangle is very badly off.' Finally, in defensive tears, I told her, and it was perfectly all right. She said she'd hated having to teach me dance music anyway, and that as I'd no talent even for that, it was really a waste of time for both of us. From then on I saw Niddy Noddy only at Parkfield and, as a bonus, the duets with the Griff came to an end too. Mrs Oochamacootch was no longer in a position to reprimand her partner Mr Umpty Plum, now that he had retired from the concert platform.

I kept the song copy though and bought others when I wanted to learn the words. For some reason I can 'see' the cover of 'Pennies from Heaven' superimposed, like a pop collage, on the sky above a road that led up from Aigburth Vale to the bottom of Mossley Hill. Perhaps one day I noticed that the sky was exactly the same shade of blue.

The wireless played an increasingly important role in Bill's and my life after we'd moved to Sandringham Drive. We wouldn't have missed *In Town Tonight* ('Once again we stop London's busy traffic to bring you some of the interesting people who are IN TOWN TONIGHT'); *The Palace of Varieties*, with its signature tune, 'The Spice of Life', and especially *Bandwaggon* with 'Stinker' Murdoch and Arthur Askey. Big-hearted Arthur and Stinker lived in a flat on the top of Broadcasting House. They kept a goat and two pigeons up there, and their char's daughter was called 'Nausea Bagwash'. On each programme Arthur would sing one of his 'silly songs', the most famous of which began like this:

> Oh what a wonderful thing to be
> A healthy grown-up busy, busy bee . . .

In the last programme of the series Arthur and Stinker had to move out of their flat and, despite the fact that I must have been at least eleven, I burst into tears.

Maud and Tom held a huge house-warming party in the Big Room; Tom never seemed to mind lashing out on entertaining. *Tout* Liverpool was there as well as many visiting theatricals. Ronald Frankau came and did a free cabaret with 'Monty Crick at the piano', although Maud, while grateful, really felt he went too far. 'I like a bit of spice,' she said, 'but he sang a song about balls in front of all those young girls!' Nevertheless the party was favourably reported at length, not only by Mary Ventris in *The Echo*, but by her friendly rival Kitty Russell, who wrote a column called 'Rumour' in the *Liverpool Evening Post*. Cousin Emma sent over a van-load of potted plants from her greenhouses so, for the only time in all the years we were there, the conservatory looked like a conservatory rather than a dumping ground for the detritus of the house and garden. There were so many cars parked in Sandringham Drive that the police came to find out what was going on. They told Maud they thought it must be a Fascist meeting.

One of the uses to which the conservatory was put after the van had collected Cousin Emma's potted plants, was as a place for me to keep my lizards. I'd always wanted to own reptiles but there just hadn't been room at Ivanhoe Road. Now I bought a vivarium, built a little rockery in it and turned one of the dissecting club's kidney bowls into a pool, and it was done. The lizards, bright green and about ten inches long, came from a pet shop in Park Road, and were fed on meal worms from the same source. They became very affectionate. I used to walk around the house with them sitting on my shoulders, a habit which once gave a nasty shock to René Beere, friend of Uncle Alan and son of Mrs Beere, the stingy millionairess who lived at the Adelphi. René Beere, while extremely amiable and no trouble, was a bad alcoholic. He had come to dinner and was just knocking back his third gin and tonic with my father when I came into the room with the lizards about my person. Poor René did a double-take and the ice began to rattle and crash against the sides of his glass. 'It's all right, René,' said Tom, recognizing the cause of his panic; 'they're real.'

Unfortunately, possibly because the conservatory was too cold for them, the lizards died and, although I replaced them once or twice, they continued to die and in the end the vivarium was left untenanted. We weren't lucky with cold-blooded pets. Our succession of tortoises, always called Ptolemy after Jeremy Fisher's guest, never survived a winter. With the death of the last lizard the cast of my bed-time prayer, both quick and dead, was complete and remained unaltered until I lost any semblance of faith. It went:

> God bless Mummy and Daddy,
> Dear little Bill, dear little Andrée,
> Gangie, Gampa and Gaga,
> Uncle Fred and Uncle Alan,
> Jock, Zip, Ptolemy and the lizards,
> All kind friends and relations,
> And make me a good little boy.
> Amen.

The fact that I continued, until the age of about sixteen, to refer to myself as 'a good little boy' would seem to suggest either that I was a moron, or that I wasn't really thinking much about what I was saying before joining Little Ted between the sheets.

More successful was my career as a breeder of budgerigars. I started with two in a small cage in the nursery and graduated to a proper aviary in the garden with nesting boxes and lots of perches. We bought the aviary by mail order from an advertisement in the *Radio Times*. Tom and I tried to put it up ourselves with the help of the enclosed plan but we had to give up and send for the carpenter, Mr Hughes, whom we called 'Good 'eavens' because that's what he always said, in his light Lancashire accent, whenever we asked him to do anything. He said it now when he saw what a muddle we'd got into trying to erect the aviary, but he had it up in no time, and the budgies bred like mad – various blues, green, yellow and even white. I sold them through the pet shop where I'd bought the lizards and made quite a lot of pocket money.

Later, during the war, my father got rid of the budgies, added a rather untidy wire-netting extension to the aviary, and bought some hens which he called 'The White Sisters', not only on account of their colour but also because they reminded him of some nuns of that order who had bought the house next door from the Brocklehursts and turned it into a Convent. The feathered White Sisters weren't anything like as successful as the budgies. They laid very few eggs and what they did lay were extremely small and the shells, despite enormous quantities of grit, were disastrously thin.

Shortly after we'd moved into Sandringham Drive we had to put down Joey, our enormous, much-loved, neuter tabby cat, who had become almost blind and more or less incontinent. He was replaced by a ginger kitten not especially prepossessing, even at an age when most kittens are fairly irresistible. He was called 'Ginger', the lack of imagination in a choice of name indicating the low regard in which he was held. Ginger grew up to be a truly unattractive cat. He was ravenous but scrawny, slightly cross-eyed and, as his teeth didn't fit properly, he dribbled continuously. Needless to say he was exceptionally and obtrusively affectionate, being especially fond of Maud who would occasionally feel obliged to stroke him once or twice with the same expression on her face as if he were a very large black widow spider.

Ginger had the habit of pacing from room to room with his tail stuck perpendicularly up into the air as though determined to display his sphincter muscle, admittedly clean and neat, but of an unpleasing pink which clashed badly with the surrounding ginger fur. Maud was particularly dismayed by this spectacle, but one day, when there was something she desperately wanted to happen, or alternatively not to happen, said that, if she knew for certain her wish would be granted, she would be willing 'to kiss Ginger's arse hole'.

She could never, so far as I know, bring herself to put this to the test. If she had, and her sacrifice had proved worthwhile, it would have meant, among other benefits, that the Second World War wouldn't have taken place. Later on Ginger was partially run over by a tram when he was crossing Aigburth Road. He recovered more or less, apart from a slight Byronic limp, but his tail was completely paralysed and now trailed behind him as he dribbled from room to room in search of affection. This would have made Maud's task even less enviable. She would have had to lift this limp and useless appendage first before attempting to influence the course of history.

For each of us, except for Andrée, Sandringham Drive had both advantages and disadvantages in relation to Ivanhoe Road. For Maud it was too close to her mother, although she must have known this when they bought it, and the Griff was therefore in an easier position to exert her imperious will. On the other hand the size of the house at last allowed her to become a hostess on a scale denied her in Ivanhoe Road.

For Tom it was a bit further from The Albert but closer to Jack and Maisy Forster's so he was more able to slip in there for a gin or two on his way back from the pub. This incidentally was certainly on Maud's list of disadvantages. They didn't row much as far as I know, but when they did it was usually about Tom's boozing. 'That bloody drink!' I heard her shout in pain and rage one evening as I was passing the lounge, and then Tom, equally angry, stormed out of the room and subsequently the house, slamming the front door. I was very upset at this rare explosion and much relieved when, five minutes later, Tom returned and apologized.

Another advantage for my father was that it knocked a good ten minutes off the time he took to get to and from the office. He used to have to walk down to the bottom of Lark Lane or Parkfield Road and catch a tram. Now he could take the overhead railway from the Dingle, a beautiful bit of early twentieth-century engineering, later pulled down, which rattled along above the still prosperous docks and past the great berthed liners.

For Bill and me, it was a slightly longer walk to Parkfield, but in recompense we were less likely to encounter Twyne during the holidays. Frustratingly the bottom of the playing-field with its tall wooden fence faced onto Alexandra Drive and was only a few yards from the entrance to Sandringham Drive. In the winter, when it was dark, we sometimes risked running down the field and vaulting over a low side-wall into the shrubbery of that house which I associated with Monte Carlo. It was an exciting and exhilarating dash, and we were never caught.

For Andrée there were no points of comparison, but she sometimes behaved oddly in relation to the new house. When the builders were still in, we'd gone there for a picnic in the garden, and when it came to be time to go home Andrée, who was about four, refused to move. She just lay curled up on the grass apparently deaf to pleas and threats and in the end Tom, who had become quite worried at her silent embryonic obstinacy, had to pick her up and carry her all the way back. A few years later, when Tom was getting out his key to open the front drive, Andrée suddenly dropped her knickers and deposited a neat turd in the drive. Tom was quite put out and made her pick it up in a laurel leaf and throw it in the shrubbery.

He called it 'untypical' and indeed it was. With her snub nose and enormous slanting eyes she was growing up, like the little girls in the advertisement for Pear's soap, 'to be a beautiful lady'. Very funny and observant, full of affection, at times painfully conscientious, adored but unspoilt, she might have been considered almost too perfect, and perhaps the occasional gratuitous gesture like the turd in the drive was her unconscious revolt against that possibility. Maud, who, as the Griff never failed to point out, didn't bother much about her own appearance, was rather clever about dressing Andrée. She didn't try to make her look winsome and frilly, but bought her rather severe clothes and had her dark hair cut straight, although sometimes she added a huge brown Minnie Mouse bow on one side.

Like everyone else, I loved Andrée, but I wasn't always very nice to her. I sometimes couldn't resist snapping her hat elastic, but my cruellest tease was based on my discovery that, although extremely quick in every other direction, she couldn't understand the mechanism of the joke. She probably would have done so in time, but having realized that the nervous laughter with which she hoped to conceal this fact was entirely spurious, I not only asked her to explain what she was laughing at, but worse, made up 'jokes' with no point at all to trick her into pretending she had got the point. As a result even today if anyone says to her 'Have you heard the one about . . .' she is overcome by panic. Otherwise we became extremely close as she grew older, but although my influence, my Byronic adolescent attempts to mould her as an *alter ego* were dangerously manipulative, Andrée has always been too intelligent, too certain of her own moral position, not to remain her own woman. If anyone it was Maud, with her burning unfulfilled theatrical ambitions, who was a more serious threat to Andrée's identity but here too, at times under considerable pressure, she has always managed to preserve her centre.

Bill had his emergency appendix operation a couple of years after we'd moved to Sandringham Drive. He was rushed off to hospital and for some hours his life was in the balance. I sat up in bed in our twin room talking to Ginny Duckworth who was our 'paying guest' at the time and her fiancé, Larry Rathbone. We told dirty jokes to keep our minds off it, but I was increasingly conscious of Bill's neat and empty bed, and in the end we just sat there more or less silently listening to the hissing gas fire and wondering if no news really did mean good news.

At about four the phone rang. Is there a more sinister sound than a phone ringing when you know why, and that there are only two alternatives? It was Tom to say they thought it was going to be all right. I have questioned Maud's assertion that the long night of tension instantly changed my relationship with Bill, but while we still had rows, and I at least remained very competitive, we certainly began to get on better from about that time. We'd come home from Parkfield together, play ping-pong (the only game at which I have ever developed any skill), listen to the wireless or, on summer evenings, get through a couple of sets of tennis on the Brocklehursts' court with no more than a little mild bickering as to whether a ball was in or out. Every night before we went to sleep, we'd hold what we called 'the daily chat', much of it devoted to the immediate eccentricities of

Mr Twyne or, in the holidays, an analysis, frame by frame, of any film we'd seen. We gradually became friends, even at times conspirators.

Ginny Duckworth, the 'paying guest' who sat up with me the night 'dear little Bill' had his brush with death, was the daughter of Lady Lacon, Maud's friend who 'didn't care for children'. She was a tall girl of about twenty with enormous brown eyes, very long legs, and an interestingly sulky expression and, after the Duchess had left Parkfield, she was the next person I fell in love with.

Despite the fact that he was always perfectly friendly, I hated her boyfriend, Larry Rathbone. He was actually a distant cousin of my father's, but for me, with his loud laugh and swept-back blond hair, he was simply a rival with every advantage on his side. When they had a row – and they had quite noisy rows – I was ecstatic. Despite my calf-eyed devotion and gifts of Black Magic chocolates, Ginny seemed quite fond of me. She would let me sit and talk to her while she wandered round her bedroom in her underwear and pulled on her stockings.

By the time I was twelve I was allowed to stay up for grown-up dinner and, as my parents were out at least three nights a week, Ginny and I often ate alone. She didn't get on all that well with Maud, who thought her 'moody', and Ginny was sometimes quite critical of her. I found this wickedly exciting. No one, except the Griff, had ever found any fault with Maud in my hearing except, by inference, Mr Twyne, and that I took to be in her favour. Ginny, for instance, pointed out that, when my parents weren't there, Maud took a lot less trouble about what we had to eat. In particular the puddings were almost always based on the banana. Sometimes these were mashed with cream, sometimes cut in two with ice-cream down the middle, sometimes chopped up with nuts. I called these puddings 'Sherlock Holmes and Dr Watson' because they were always bananas in different disguises. We had quite a few little shared jokes of this sort at poor Maud's expense, but I would have gone to any lengths, any treachery to please Ginny. Before I went up to bed and the 'daily chat' she let me kiss her a tense goodnight. In the end she married Larry Rathbone and I didn't see her anymore.

I was already at Parkfield when we moved to Sandringham Drive. One night I slept surrounded by rolled up carpets and packing cases at Ivanhoe Road, and the next in the new house. I was quite excited but, several times during the first few weeks, if I wasn't concentrating, I'd find myself crossing Parkfield Road and be halfway down Ivanhoe Road before I realized I was going the wrong way.

17

Once Bill was born we no longer spent the summer holidays in boarding-houses at seaside resorts. From 1933 on, unless invited for a week or two at Tent Lodge, we went for a month to North Wales followed by a month in Trearddur Bay, Anglesey.

The reason we went to North Wales was that following his stroke, Uncle Willy had no further reason for taking a shoot in Yorkshire, but instead rented a series of large houses in the Clwyd Valley with nearby trout and salmon fishing for the benefit of the family. This was very unselfish of him as he no longer fished either, nor indeed ventured out. As far as he was concerned he might as well have stayed at Chatham Street and saved his money. As it was, he just sat in a chair chain-smoking his Turkish cigarettes, drinking his whisky and soda, saying little beyond 'How's yourself' when you got there and 'Look after yourself' when you left, and eating his hasty pudding. It was his sister Eva who ran the place, ordering the enormous meals, supervising the linen, arranging the flowers and, for her own pleasure, painting watercolours and spending hours on end over her great jigsaws.

The older members of the family – Gangie and Gampa and Old Nell – were in residence the whole summer, but the next generation – the Leathers, the Rawdon Smiths and us – were invited to the house for a week or so and then, if we wished to take advantage of the fishing, were expected to rent a farm or cottage in the neighbourhood, although this didn't preclude going over for as many meals as we chose. It was a reasonable and amiable arrangement. The first year Willy took a huge house called Bodrhydden belonging to an Admiral Rowley-Conway. It was so big that the Admiral didn't have to move out, simply confining himself to one wing. He in no way imposed himself, but now and then you would catch a distant glimpse of an erect red-faced

185

figure with two King Charles spaniels at his heel crossing one of the clipped yew walks in the large formal garden.

I was too young to ask about the date of the house but from my memory of mellow red brick and slightly cumbersome renaissance detailing I'd guess it to have been built during the Restoration. Inside there were suits of armour and weapons arranged in patterns on the wall, and great bulbous-legged chairs with either embroidered or worked leather seats and backs. I had high hopes of finding a secret panel, but did not.

What amazed me about staying at Bodrhydden was the breakfasts. I was used to vast lunches at Chatham Street but had never breakfasted there. Coming down that first morning I found porridge and every known form of cereal, boiled eggs on little stands, toast and four sorts of bread, but what really threw me were the long line of silver chafing dishes on the massive sideboard: bacon, fried eggs, poached eggs, scrambled eggs, kippers, breakfast trout, haddock, kidneys, sausages and kedgeree, and, on the table, several kinds of marmalade, honey and quince jelly. I've always been greedy and loved breakfast. The amount I put away even aroused the interest of Uncle Bill. 'You enjoy your food then, young feller,' he said despondently as he shakily buttered a slice of toast.

The presence of Old Nell was a great help to the other grown-ups in keeping the children off their backs. It was her custom to purchase a huge quantity of plain white postcards and, with the help of scissors, stamp hinges and a box of watercolours, build a whole model village with a church, a pub, a wishing well, a manor house and several cottages. We would sit watching her for hours, occasionally encouraged to take over the simpler tasks although most often she had to do them all over again. Another thing that surprised me about Old Nell was that she could make a boiled sweet last for hours.

That year, 1933, I was considered too young to be taken fishing, but Tom used to let me go out shooting with him in the evenings and I was allowed to 'beat' for him, knocking the tree trunks on the far side of a wood to drive the clattering wood pigeons towards him. One day I found a cow's horn in a field on one of these expeditions and fitted it on the end of a stout stick. I called this my 'wandering stick' and would set off by myself into the great park with its red and white chestnut trees to explore the

186

surrounding countryside. I wore white that year and, on my head, a small kepi which I had purchased on a visit to Rhyl. White is not the best colour in which to remain unobserved by shy birds and mammals, but on my return, taking a leaf out of Romany's book, I would pretend to have watched a vixen playing with her cubs at the den's mouth or a badger, untypically abroad in the middle of the afternoon, rooting for grubs. I don't suppose anyone, except Maud, believed me, but no one was so impolite as to call me a liar.

I spent a lot of time, too, exploring the outhouses of Bodrhyd-den. If you opened the stable door quietly when the horses were all out in the fields, there were almost as many rats as in Disney's *Pied Piper*, swarming all over the mangers. I told Tom this and he used to go with me into the stable yard with his shotgun. I'd then fling open the top half of the stable door and he'd fire both barrels, sometimes killing four or five rats at a time. Once I found a beautiful plant growing behind an abandoned pigsty. It had lustrous black berries but I'd been told never to eat anything I wasn't sure of. I took Gampa to look at it, who told me it was deadly night-shade.

Some mornings, very early, Gangie and I would go mushroom picking in the misty fields. They were added to the gargantuan choice at breakfast. When we didn't go picking mushrooms, Bill and I loved to get into bed with Gangie and Gampa when they were drinking their morning tea. Gampa wore a night shirt and they both smelt of warm biscuits.

One Saturday afternoon at Bodrhydden there was a fête. In the yew garden there was a big bush clipped to look like a blackamoor's head. For the fête the gardeners had hung gold hoop ear-rings from its dark green ears and inserted big rolling eyes and white teeth. I'd discovered these objects in a loft and wondered what on earth they could be. I was told they were very old.

Gampa gave me five shillings in pennies. I rolled them down a shute on to a board with different numbers on it. If a penny came to rest on a number and not on one of the squared lines which divided them, you won. I was very lucky and won a pound. I rushed off to tell Gampa and found him chatting to Admiral Rowley-Conway who, for once, wasn't hiding in his wing. Gampa said he was very pleased. Then I went back and lost the lot. When I told Gampa this he gave me a lecture on gambling. 'Always stop when you're on top,' he said quite crossly. I've never been able to do that. That's why I still gamble very little and always for an amount I've decided to lose in advance.

I loved being at Bodrhydden. I think that year we stayed the whole month. The house was so big we didn't have to move out. There was room for any number of Mellys, Rawdon Smiths and Leathers. I told everyone at breakfast on our last morning that I'd decided I 'preferred the country to the seaside'. They all laughed, but I did, and still do.

Uncle Willy didn't take Bodrhydden again. For the next four years he rented a house called Hafod. It was a yellow-washed manor with a stable yard and a tennis court, but it was nowhere near as big. Most years we stayed at a farm nearby, but in 1937 Tom rented a rather 'modernistic' villa called Lount Cottage on the outskirts of Denbigh. Almost every morning Gampa sent the car over to take us into Rhyl or Prestatyn to swim in the big open-air baths. Sometimes Gangie and Gampa came too. Afterwards we usually went back to Hafod for lunch and spent the afternoon there.

Once I went out sketching with Gangie and Aunt Eva and they had a splendid row. Gangie chose to paint part of a barn and a bit of field beyond. It turned out very well. Aunt Eva took on a wide panoramic view with woods and distant hills and it went wrong. She was already gobbling like a turkey-cock with irritation when Gangie, never exactly noted for her tact, said rather smugly that perhaps she'd been 'over-ambitious'. Aunt Eva, mottled with rage, knocked over her spindly little easel and threw her paint-box in a ditch. They didn't speak for two days.

John Leather was at Hafod one year. He had an airgun. We discovered that if you suddenly raised the lid on the corn bin in the harness room there was always a mouse scurrying about on the top of the hard shiny corn. It immediately began to burrow down into it, but if you were quick to aim the muzzle at its fast-vanishing backside and pulled the trigger it more or less disintegrated. We always felt guilty about this afterwards, but it didn't stop us doing it again. We spoke hypocritically of 'keeping down vermin', and I tried to think it was just the same as Tom blasting off at the rats at Bodrhydden, but somehow it wasn't.

In 1935, for the first time Tom and Gampa took me fishing, something I'd begged them to do every year. We drove down a little lane one fine afternoon and Kane had to stop the car when a mother duck and about six babies in her wake emerged from the grass and waddled processionally across. We got to the fishing hut by the River Clwyd and Tom and Gampa put up three rods. They tied on flies for themselves and a big worm for me. I sat on the bank watching my float and listening to them bickering as they fished. Tom was the more impatient. He cast all the time. Gampa reproached him. 'What's the point of flogging the water, Tom? Wait for a rise.' I found it quite funny but a bit disorientating to hear my father told off like a small boy. Then my float bobbed. I did nothing. I knew from catching perch at Coniston that you didn't strike until it went under. It was most likely to be an eel. Gampa said I'd probably only catch eels. The float bobbed again a few times and then moved steadily down towards the bottom. I struck and gave an excited yelp as the rod bent double and the line came screaming off the reel. Tom and Gampa, shouting advice, ran towards me along the bank.

Twenty minutes later my first trout, three pounds in weight, lay on the grass in all its speckled glory. How responsible was I for landing it? Very little I should think, but they never took the rod off me. I believe my father stood behind me, his hands over mine, guiding them as to when to reel in, when to hold, when to let the fish run. Gampa netted it. When we got back to Hafod, Gampa wrote down in his fishing book:

DATE	RIVER	FISH	FLY	WEIGHT	REMARKS
Aug. 15 1935	Clwyd	Brown trout	worm	3lb.	G.M.'s first trout

After that Tom taught me to fly-fish, but I didn't have much success to begin with. The year we took Lount, there was a little stream at the bottom of the concrete gnome-ridden garden. I was convinced there were trout in it, and cast away there hour after hour. One day Tom told me he thought the trouble was there were too many leaves and too much rubbish floating down the stream. He bought wire netting and some posts and we spent a morning erecting a barrier across it, both at the top end and, more mysteriously, at the bottom. Two days later I hooked and landed a trout unaided. It was only six inches long but I had done it all by myself and insisted on having a photograph taken. It came out rather blurred, but you can just see the trout. I am holding it up by the tail, the rod in my other hand, and looking very proud and solemn. What Tom didn't tell me for ages was that there were no trout in that stream. He'd gone out one evening to a trout farm and bought half a dozen. The wire-netting barriers had nothing to do with either leaves or rubbish. They were to prevent the trout he'd bought from swimming away.

There was a terrible plague of wasps in the Clwyd Valley that year. At dinner at Hafod everybody was complaining and Maud said she'd found a way to deal with them. She'd put jam jars everywhere, half-full of water with some jam smeared round the inside rim, and the wasps went into the jars for the jam, fell into the water and slowly drowned. Later that night Old Nell drew Maud aside. Had we got a maid with us at Lount? Yes. Were we on the phone? Yes. Well, would Maud mind ringing up the maid before she went to bed to ask her to make *quite* sure that all the wasps were properly drowned? Maud actually refused. She said she'd have felt too much of a fool.

Towards the end of our stay that last year Aunt Eva was taken ill. Before we left for Trearddur the three of us went in to see her in bed. There was some purple clematis that grew round her window at Hafod. I remember thinking how pretty it looked framing the 'ambitious' hills beyond. She looked very flushed and was wearing one of those buttoned-up Victorian night dresses which were to become so fashionable thirty years later. Then Tom honked the horn outside and we went downstairs. She died at Chatham Street that November aged eighty-three. Within a fortnight Gampa, seventeen years her junior, was also dead. Aunt Eva left Andrée, then five, a hundred pounds, 'because she looks like me'. She didn't look like her at all, but it was kind of her. Having lost a brother and a sister in under a month, Uncle Willy sank even deeper into lethargy. With no one left to run it, he never again took a house for the summer. In 1938 we went to Coniston for a few weeks and spent the rest of the holidays in Trearddur Bay.

Anglesey is an island off the north-west coast of Wales. A sensational bridge, flung across the beetling Menai Straits, links it to the mainland. It has few trees and what there are have been bent almost double by the strong prevailing winds. There are fine beaches, mile after mile of golden sand fringed by dunes, and steep cliffs honeycombed by caves. The farms are white-washed and crouch low against the ground as though afraid of being blown away in the winter storms. There was little attempt to encourage the trippers and there were then no caravan sites. The only port of any size is Holyhead where the ferries set off for Ireland full of drunk men with red faces and bright blue suits and potentially seasick nuns. There are many golf courses.

For all these reasons, except for the presence of the Irish who anyway got straight off the train and into the boats, it was fashionable among the *haute bourgeoisie* of the North of England. 'It's like Brittany', they told each other, 'or Normandy.' Certainly there was fine sea-food: lobsters, crabs, even local whitebait. We went to Anglesey year after year after leaving Uncle Willy's, and Tom, who tended in part to commute from Hafod or Bodrhydden, took his main holiday there. The Griff too would spend a fortnight with us, and Uncle Fred and Alan would come down for a weekend or two. We usually rented a house, one of those basic white seaside villas with the hall full of sand and metal windows corroded by salt. When I said I preferred the country to the seaside I was thinking particularly of Anglesey. It was healthy, 'unspoilt' and bracing and it bored me stiff.

Trearddur Bay itself is only a few miles from Holyhead. Many friends of my parents were nearby and there was a great deal of golf and bridge, neither of which interested Maud, and a lot of drinking which she feared and detested. I think she disliked holidays in Anglesey as much as I did.

Every day, unless it was raining hard, we went swimming. We were meant to like that, but the sea was always freezing. We came out with our teeth chattering and Maud was waiting with one of those rough towels with yachts printed on it and a ginger biscuit which was meant to warm you up. We had a raft one year and Bill, who was about four, climbed on it just before the tide turned and began to drift out to sea. He sat there perfectly calmly, seemingly unaware of being in danger. I drew Maud's attention to his diminishing figure. She was fully dressed and wearing a heavy mackintosh but she plunged in, swam after him and pushed the raft back to shore. A man congratulated her, as she stumbled, wet and exhausted, up the beach: 'Very brave of you,.Madam, to rescue that little boy.' Maud, although out of breath and on the point of collapse, could never resist a good curtain line. 'Little boy?' she said. 'It's my son!'

It would be unfair to say I experienced no moments of pleasure at Trearddur. In fine weather it could be dazzlingly beautiful. Once, walking inland, I passed a windmill and found myself in a long gentle treeless valley, its slopes bright with clover and stained with poppies, fading into a blue haze in the distance. Whenever I think of the line 'Over the hills and far away', I think of that valley.

I was interested in rock pools too. I would lie full length on the damp seaweed, popping the little bladders in the long fronds and staring down into the water at the transparent shrimps, the tiny dark green crab and the rose-pink sea-anemones which closed up into little balls of jelly if you threatened them with a stick.

We did a lot of fishing, although after my three-pound trout and in comparison to casting a fly, it seemed far too easy with its big hooks, strong traces, and a wooden frame with the line wound round it instead of a delicate split cane rod. Tom and I, when he wasn't knocking them back at the golf-club, used to go and sit on a ledge just below a cliff top and pull up inedible multi-coloured fish, apparently some species of rock-bass. I didn't much like putting on the worms we used either. They were segmented with many horrid little legs and they bit. We bought them from a man with a wooden leg in Holyhead.

Sometimes we went out after mackerel in a motor-boat. I liked the getting there: bounding over the water with the cliffs and houses bobbing and lurching away behind us and the people on the beach getting smaller and smaller. But once we'd stopped and hit a shoal it soon became monotonous. The fish were beautiful – striped, streamlined, blue, green and silver – but they were so eager to get caught that they grabbed the feathered lures almost before you could get them back into the water. It was too easy to be satisfactory. I preferred prawning: scraping the straight wooden edge of the net up the underside of rocks and lifting it out of the water to find out how many hopping crustacea I'd dislodged.

We were also taught riding by a Mr Jones, a handsome black-eyed Welshman with a great deal of patience. He needed it with me. The horse I tried to ride was in no way temperamental, just obstinate. Despite trying to follow Mr Jones's advice about using my knees and letting him know who was boss, it did exactly as it wanted, turning right when I wanted to go left, and grazing whenever it chose, no matter how hard I tugged on the reins. In the rough fields around Mr Jones's riding school one year there was a plague of striped black and yellow caterpillars. I put one in a match-box to take back to Parkfield to show Hurter, but somehow it escaped.

We weren't alone in Trearddur. There were several of our contemporaries, the children of our parents' friends, some of whom I liked in Liverpool. Here all they ever wanted to do was play ball games on the beach which was exactly what I hated. Sometimes they chanted 'Sissy Parkfield' at us. It seemed hard when I loathed Parkfield so much to have to defend it during the holidays.

One morning in a hen-run on the edge of the garden of the house we rented, I came across a disturbing spectacle. On the grass in the middle of the run squatted a large toad, although how it got there I couldn't imagine. The hens, about half a dozen in number, were pecking it to death, but not in any concentrated way. They would strut around for a bit, making their stupid noises, preening their feathers, scratching here or there and then one of them, quite casually, would stab at it a few times with its beak. The toad just sat, seeming to grin, gradually coming to bits but still breathing. I could do nothing. If I rescued the toad, I thought, it was too far gone to live. I couldn't kill it either – that would mean associating myself with its beady-eyed assassins. I remained, watching in rapt horror, until it was obviously dead. Whenever I read of gratuitous cruelty I see that toad.

18

As the thirties drew to a close, Ginger's arsehole was under increasing threat. Sitting in the Tatler, waiting for the latest Disney, I saw Spain bombed, Hitler and Mussolini, Auden's 'fashionable madman', strutting and ranting. Because of my mother's blood we were more aware of the increasing persecution of the Jews than most middle-class Liverpudlians. I don't know how it came about but for a few months we even took in a Jewish refugee. Vicki was a young man from Berlin, neatly dressed and speaking perfect if pedantic English. He told us what made him decide to leave Germany: the burning of synagogues, the looting of shops, university professors forced to clean out lavatories in front of jeering crowds, the casual use of rubber truncheons. Hearing this did Tom no harm. He'd been inclined, like a lot of people, to dismiss much of what he'd heard or read as exaggerated. Nevertheless, on a personal level, Vicki drove my parents mad. Humourless and pompous, he constantly 'held the floor', the gravest crime in Maud's almanac. Much to their relief he didn't stay very long. Highly qualified in chemistry, he landed an excellent job in Leicester.

Somehow, although it was increasingly likely there would be a war, people managed to put it out of their minds most of the time. My parents continued to entertain. I went five times to see *Snow White and the Seven Dwarfs*. My mother organized a successful appeals year for the Personal Service, including a sale of work in a house belonging to Toc H in Rodney Street. Gangie and Gaga, still Mrs Melly and Mrs Isaac to each other, each ran a stall. Gangie was in charge of knitware, Gaga sold home-made chutnies and jams. There was something about sales of work which very much irritated Tom. He was obliged to go, of course, but explained to me sarcastically, when I asked him what a sale of work was, 'It's your grandmothers playing shop.'

From being unable to read, I had now become an obsessive reader, but my parents' library was no treasure trove. There were Maud's prizes from Belvidere High School for Girls: *Hiawatha* in blue leather, *The Works of Tennyson* in limp calf, and a number of theatrical memoirs by people she'd known, many of them dedicated to 'Darling Maud' in extrovert calligraphy.

Tom's contribution to the shelves was mainly Leslie Charteris's 'Saint' books, and a number of 'dossiers' of imaginary crimes with little cellophane envelopes in them containing 'real' clues: a lipstick-smeared cigarette butt, a torn-off button. There were, however, as always with Tom, a few surprises: the short stories of Damon Runyon for instance, which he bought as they came out, and a first edition of Waugh's *Vile Bodies*, his favourite book. It was typical of him that he never read, or was curious to read, any other book by Waugh, or at any rate not until *The Loved One* was published in the late forties. Maud even had difficulty in persuading him to read *Rebecca*. 'I knew he'd love it,' she'd tell people, 'so I kept leaving it about, even in the lavatory at Trearddur, but he wouldn't open it. When he did, of course, he read it cover to cover at one sitting.' She told this story a lot. She seemed to believe it reflected some credit on her.

Although my parents didn't buy books, they both subscribed to Boots. Maud liked Warwick Deeping, Gilbert Frankau (brother of Ronnie), and J.B.Priestley. Tom read mostly thrillers and detective stories: Edgar Wallace, Dorothy Sayers, and Agatha Christie but only if Poirot wasn't in them. Maud, too, could sometimes break out of her middle-brow corral; she adored *The Diary of a Nobody* and instantly saw the point of *Cold Comfort Farm*. I read all these; sometimes Maud and Tom had to fight to get their own library books back; I read the William books, E.E.Nesbit and Arthur Ransome, any collections of ghost stories I could get my hands on, and *The Story of San Michele* which I thought a masterpiece.

From being relieved that I had learned to read, Maud became worried at what had become an addiction. 'No books!' she'd shout through the bathroom door, and she'd come into the 'boys' room' several times each night to make sure I hadn't turned the light on again.

The other thing that worried her was my stomach. Given that I was eating a cooked breakfast, a substantial if disgusting lunch at school, a huge tea and a grown-up dinner at night, it was hardly surprising that, while remaining rather skinny in general, my stomach had swollen up like a tight balloon. Fearing a tumour, she took me to the doctor. While he was examining me he asked me what I ate on an average day. I told him. He didn't bother to go on with the examination. I was advised to eat rather less and my stomach disappeared for twenty years.

Maud was also much preoccupied during the later thirties with the difficulty of finding suitable 'staff'. 'Going into service' was becoming less popular and she was forced to employ girls she would have rejected instantly a few years earlier. There were two Irish sisters, for example, who gave her a great deal of trouble. They were called Nelly and Norah and had very thick Dublin brogues. Nelly, the parlour-maid, was handsome in a bold raw-boned way. Norah, the cook, was fat, dumpy and hysterical. They fought all the time. There'd be a crash in the night followed by screaming and shouting. Maud would get up and rush into their bedroom to find out what on earth had happened. Usually Nelly had thrown a water carafe at Norah or vice versa.

Nelly liked mischief. She read the Bible as if it were a dirty book because, back in Ireland, her parish priest had told her it was a sin for lay Catholics to do so. Swearing me to secrecy, she would wait until my parents were out and then use 'the green bathroom' instead of 'the blue'. Eventually Nelly scored a bull's-eye with the water carafe, cutting Norah so badly that she had to have stitches, and Maudie decided that enough was enough.

Molly, the house parlour-maid who followed, was, as Maud admitted, a very hard-worker, but she was extremely noisy and had a very strong Liverpool accent. She was also enormous. She sneezed a great deal about the house too, making no effort to control it, despite Maud asking her continuously if she could possibly use a handkerchief. 'A-a-a-a-CHEW-ER!' was what it sounded like.

I was especially fond of Molly as on her day off she would take me to the pictures. We often went twice; to the matinée at the Gaumont and the evening performance at the Mayfair, and had fish and chips in between. It never occurred to me that it was odd for a twenty-year-old girl to choose to spend her day off with a twelve-year-old boy, but in retrospect I suppose it was because she was so fat that no one of her own age ever invited her out. She was very cheerful, though, and good fun too. If we both liked a film very much we'd sit through it again. Molly left to work in a factory where they paid a great deal more money.

Then Auntie Min came back as 'cook-housekeeper', and was given the flat upstairs. Her husband Tom moved in too, still working on the railways and as silent as ever. Once Maud and Tom, after a party, brought back several members of the ballet for bacon and eggs (I don't know who cooked them – it certainly wasn't Maud) and found Tom Roberts, just off shift, drinking tea in the kitchen.

'I thought', 'darling Bobbie' told Maud later, 'that it must be your handy man, but then I thought, "What was he doing being handy at four in the morning?"'

Bella, too, returned after Jack's death, bringing Beryl with her. This was lovely for Andrée as it meant she had someone more or less her own age to play with. Beryl was very good at playground games, especially one that involved bouncing a ball against a wall, and gradually increasing the number of actions performed between each bounce. 'One, two, three, a footsie. Four, five, six, a footsie. Seven, eight, nine, a footsie. Ten, a footsie, post the ball,' she chanted. 'Darling Bobbie' happened to catch this too. 'The child's a genius!' he cried.

In 1937 Tom gave Bill and me a choice. Cousin Emma had offered to pay for us to go to London for three days to watch, from a balcony in the Mall, the Coronation procession of King George VI, or, if we preferred it, we could spend a whole week in London on a later date. It was typically generous of Cousin Emma to offer such a treat, and typically imaginative of her to give us an alternative. It didn't take us long to decide we'd prefer a whole week and no Coronation to only three days and a view from the Mall. Tom was to go with us and we were all going to stay with Aunt Maud Bradley who lived at Hammersmith. Bill and I both got very, very over-excited as the day drew closer.

I've never discovered exactly who Aunt Maud Bradley was. She came at least once a year to stay with Gangie so I suppose she may have been a sister. She didn't look at all like her though, because Gangie was very pretty, and Aunt Maud Bradley wasn't at all. 'An old boiler' was the rather unkind phrase people used to describe elderly ladies who looked like Aunt Maud Bradley in those days. She didn't actually live in Hammersmith either. She had a flat in a mansion block in Barnes but overlooking the river and Hammersmith Bridge. I thought the bridge was lovely, like a bridge in a pantomime, but the Thames itself was one of the few things in London I found really disappointing. I thought everything there must be bigger as well as better, but the Thames turned out to be far narrower than the Mersey.

I suppose Tom paid some of Cousin Emma's money to Aunt Maud Bradley to have us to stay, but she didn't spend much of it on food. For pudding, every time we ate in, which was as often as Tom could get away with it, there was always the same bowl of fruit salad and all Aunt Maud did was to empty another tin on top of what was left. Tom said he was surprised and indeed disappointed that it hadn't fomented. We didn't actually see all that much of her except when we got home. Her own 'treat' was to take us to *Gunga Din* at a cinema in Hammersmith Broadway. I was pleased to see it, because I'd read about it in Fat Molly's *Picturegoer* and knew it wouldn't be on in Liverpool for ages, but the picture house impressed me even less than the Thames. It wasn't anything like as grand as the Mayfair or the Gaumont. It was more like the Rivoli.

Aunt Maud Bradley also came with us to the Zoo, the highspot of the visit as far as I was concerned. It was a boiling day (the whole week coincided with a heat wave) and we wanted to see everything. That is to say that Bill and I wanted to see everything. We rushed from Mappin Terrace to the sealions. We banged on the glass in the reptile house although it said we shouldn't, and made the cobra rear up and open its hood as in *The Jungle Book*. We fed buns to the bears and had a ride on an elephant. We not only exhausted Aunt Maud Bradley but Tom too. When it was almost time to go we discovered we'd missed out the hippopotomi which were in the North Gardens and this meant running through a tunnel under the road. Tom and Aunt Maud Bradley were sitting on a bench near the Aquarium. We were amazed that he'd rather sit on a bench than see a hippo, but he said he would.

It was a London I was never to experience again – tourists'

London. We went to the Tower, and Madame Tussaud's where I was critical of the Chamber of Horrors. There was only one proper torture – you pulled back a curtain and there was a Turk hanging from a hook through his stomach – and the murderers looked quite like ordinary people. We enjoyed being taken to the Regent Palace Hotel for lunch afterwards, though. One of Maud's 'boyfriends' who had moved to London took us. For five shillings each you could eat as much as you liked and there were fifteen courses. Bill and I managed twelve apiece. Tom said it made him feel quite liverish just to watch us. Maud's ex-boyfriend said, 'What appetites, dear.'

Tom took us to see a review at a big theatre. The star was an actress called Frances Day. She was very pretty and imitated several film stars. Tom had chosen this review because he'd met Frances Day on a boat going to Portugal where he had a client in the wool business. He said they became quite friendly and she'd called him 'Mr Woolly Man'. I asked if we were going to go round and see her later as we did with friends of Maud's. He said no. She mightn't remember him and besides Aunt Maud Bradley was tired and wanted to get back to Hammersmith.

One afternoon we had tea at the House of Commons with David Maxwell-Fyfe, our local MP. Afterwards we went and watched a debate from the visitors' gallery. It was an important debate to start with and I recognized several of the members from the cartoons in the newspapers and the newsreels at the Tatler. Churchill was there, and Neville Chamberlain, and Lloyd George with his long white hair and moustache. After a while, though, a man got up and spoke with a Welsh accent about snobbery in the British Navy, and most people, rather rudely I thought, walked out.

At the end of the week we thanked Aunt Maud Bradley and caught the tube train back to Euston, changing in the middle onto another line. Tom got into a panic on tube trains because he always worried that we'd get lost and go to the wrong station, but we didn't. Bill and I recognized several of the names on the map above the window of the carriage from having played Monopoly. On the train back to Liverpool I suddenly wanted to eat an orange more than anything in the world. I didn't usually like oranges very much, but I could hardly wait to get to Lime Street so that I could peel one and pop the segments in my mouth.

I didn't get back to London until almost ten years later. It was a different place, scarred with bomb damage, grey, its paint peeling, everything rationed.

In a way we got to see the Coronation after all. When we went back to Parkfield Twyne told us that he was going to break his own rule and take the whole school to the Mayfair to watch it in colour. I was absolutely amazed, but immediately asked him if we were going to stay and see the whole programme. He said he'd have to find out if the main film was suitable, and told us a few days later that it was not. It was a comedy with Tom Walls and Ralph Lynn, and I was furious at missing it, but there was nothing to be done. On the appointed afternoon we filed in to the Mayfair, me displaying my *savoir-faire* by making it obvious I knew my way around, and listing the films I'd seen there since it opened. We sat through the Coronation which was very long and quite boring, and then filed out again as the titles came up for the main feature. Hoping to catch at least a glimpse of the suave Walls with his little moustache and Ralph Lynn with his monocle and 'silly ass' laugh, I looked over my shoulder until we were right out in the foyer.

Munich happened: Chamberlain in the Tatler waved his piece of paper, and most people thought it marvellous. Bill and I discovered a new milk-bar where you could ask for a free sample. Tom dug a shelter into a high bank in the garden well away from the house. It had sandbags round the entrance and a tin roof on which he piled the earth back. It was useful to play in. Fred, Alan and Tom volunteered to become air-raid wardens if there was a war. The authorities tried out the sirens a few times.

The weekend that war was declared, the ballet was back in Liverpool. 'Darling Bobbie' and Freddie Ashton were spending the day with us. We listened to Chamberlain on the radiogram. The grown-ups seemed very sad, not a bit excited. Ginger, beyond helping us now, rubbed against Maud's legs. She smiled a lot at us, but they weren't proper smiles.

Tom told us that next day he and Maud were going to drive us down to Cousin Arthur Bromilow's in Shropshire and then that Mr Twyne had arranged for Bill and me and the rest of the boys

200

from Parkfield to go to a public school nearby, at any rate for the following term, and that Andrée would stay with the Bromilows and go to the same school as their granddaughter Bridget. He'd obviously known all this in advance.

An hour after the war was announced the siren wailed, and we all went and sat in Tom's air-raid shelter, the only time it was ever used, waiting for the sound of the bombers. After a while the all-clear sounded, and we went back into the house and had lunch. Tom said perhaps it was just a trial to make sure that people didn't panic.

Next day we got up early. All the staff had gone and Maud, for the first time in her life, tried to cook sausages for breakfast. She didn't know about pricking them, and turned the grill on full to make it quicker, so that they all exploded. We thought this was very funny, but then Maud burst into tears so we stopped laughing.

We drove down to Cousin Arthur's in the old 1920s car Tom had bought for the summer. He never bought a new car; he'd spend about £10 on what he called 'a heap' and then sell it again after we got back from Trearddur, although this year we hadn't been there. It was a beautiful day. We got to Cousin Arthur's in time for tea in the garden. We sat under a cedar of Lebanon eating toast and honey in front of the pretty Georgian house in the bright sunlight. The grown-ups listened to the news all the time. I drew a caricature of Hitler which I thought was quite good. I showed it to Maud who said she didn't know why I wanted to draw such a horrible man. Somehow the Bromilows managed to find us all somewhere to sleep that night. Next morning Maud and Tom said goodbye to us and drove back to Liverpool in 'the heap'.

Tom said later that neither of them expected to see any of us again.

19

That same afternoon Cousin Arthur drove Bill and me to Oakridge, a minor public school on the Welsh borders, and over the next day or two the boys from Parkfield reassembled in this unfamiliar place. Twyne was already there to greet us, although that is certainly an inappropriate word for his gloomy if uncharacteristically restrained presence. He told us that once the term had started, which was still ten days off, we would be subject to the rules and regulations of Oakridge, although of course initially under his supervision. He also explained that in a few weeks he would be leaving us to find premises in order to reopen Parkfield as soon as possible. He hoped we would work hard and play hard. We slept that evening in a dormitory which had been set aside for us, and wondered if the bombers were over Liverpool, some sixty miles away.

Oakridge was a comparatively new seat of learning but was determined to overcome this by embracing the public school ethos at its most unyielding. Beating and fagging were held to be sacred principles; there was a school song made up from those lush Victorian harmonies guaranteed to bring a tear to the eye of the managers of rubber plantations at sundown; and a great number of rules about which piece of grass you could walk on and what buttons you could do up. The headmaster was a towering Olympian figure with a raw red face, and the buildings were unfashionably Gothic and already convincingly choked with ivy.

On the first morning of term we went down to breakfast in the usual place only to find we were expected in a different hall on the other side of the school. Those of us who had cut it fine were in consequence five minutes late. Immediately after breakfast we were sent for by our new housemaster and given three strokes of the cane. He was a jovial and savage little man called Shorte and appeared to think we should enjoy the beating almost as much as he did. It was like that all term. I'd never been beaten with a cane before, or heard the dreadful preliminary swish as it parted the fusty tobacco-laden air of Mr Shorte's study. I was to learn to know that sound well before I'd mastered the complicated structure of rules in a large school, and even after that for comparatively trivial offences.

In time we settled in. There was a school chaplain who fascinated me. He was very High Church – even Gangie might have had reservations about the amount of incense and lace he favoured – and he wore a soutane at all times. He was also very unprepossessing with a leathery yellow face and a soft insinuating voice, but what distinguished him most was his Rabelaisian relish in lavatorial and excretory jokes. I'd no objection to this – on the contrary, but I didn't hesitate to use it as a Twyne-tease. 'The chaplain', I told him with a mixture of mock horror and surprise, 'tells us lots of jokes about lavatories, sir. Why is that, sir?' Twyne was as shocked as I'd hoped, but he couldn't of course say much. 'Disgusting,' he mumbled, and turned away.

With all of us sleeping in the same dormitory, our sexual activities were resumed and indeed extended. One night I was in somebody's bed when the door was flung open and there stood Twyne silhouetted against the dim light from the stone passage. I slid out of the bed and began to crawl towards my own, wondering if I could possibly make it before Twimbo, who was walking down the dormitory on a tour of inspection, discovered it empty except for Little Ted. Under one of the intervening beds I fortunately encountered a pair of rollerskates, which went crashing out across the wooden floor like a runaway train. Twyne, with a cry of, 'My Godfathers!' ran back to the entrance of the dormitory to find the light switch and, by the time he did, I was safely back in my own bed, apparently asleep.

A week or two later he left and we heard that he had rented a house on the outskirts of Southport in the suburb of Birkdale which, being fifteen miles from Liverpool and a completely residential town, was considered fairly safe should the bombing eventually start. He would reopen Parkfield in its new premises the following term. Towards the end of the current term at Oakridge, the Olympian headmaster descended from the clouds and began to address himself benignly to us Parkfield boys. He indicated that he would be far from displeased if we chose to suggest to our parents that he might be willing to accept us into the school, even those of us rather younger than was usual. 'In the heart of the country . . .' he stressed, 'not a major city within sixty miles and, in the case of brothers, special arrangements . . .' Bill and I talked this over and decided we'd rather go back to Twyne. In the end I think only two or three boys, *proditores* it goes without saying, took advantage of the headmaster's offer.

It may seem perverse that I should prefer to return to Parkfield, but I had several sound reasons. Apart from the fact that the slipper was minimally less painful than the cane, I'd only two terms left to go. If I were transferred to a public school, and one which I actively disliked, I would find it that much more difficult to leave and go elsewhere. Also I hadn't liked the way the headmaster beamed at us and patted our heads and recruited us to solicit our parents. All I hoped was that wherever Maud and Tom did decide to send me, it would be nothing like Oakridge.

As there was still no sign of any bombing we went back to Liverpool for the holidays; something no one would have thought remotely possible only three months before. Singing the syrupy Oakridge school song in the chapel, while the scatological Chaplain ponced about genuflecting like a weasel, the only tears I felt were those of relief.

Parkfield's new premises were a large detached Edwardian house of red brick, white plaster, intricate half timbering and ill-proportioned little towers. The staff, apart from Twyne himself, was reduced to two: an eccentric Maths master called Mr Corelli who looked like Einstein, and loved his subject so much that he managed to make it interesting, even to me; and a depressive Lancastrian who taught everything else except Latin. There was no games field, but we shared one with several other schools a quarter of a mile away. There were no extras: no art, no music, and the food was almost inedible.

Twyne seemed for him comparatively restrained, but he had his moments. We petitioned for a wind-up gramophone, and most of us brought some records. Among my contribution from the nursery pile was a very old and scratchy recording which had probably once belonged to Gampa. It was called 'Yes, we have no bananas'. We were playing this one evening when Twimbo burst into the room.

'Take that record off, Melly Major,' he shouted, 'it's distinctly vulgar.'

'But, sir,' I said resorting to my usual tactic, 'my mother chose it.'

Twyne's reply very much amused Maud and Tom when I repeated it to them. 'Mrs Melly', he said, 'is a very Bohemian woman.'

We were allowed, at our parents' request, to go home sometimes for the weekend, but Twyne hated it. Although not one bomb had yet fallen on Liverpool, he would tell us, as we set off for Birkdale Station, that we were 'entering the lion's jaws'.

The summer term of 1940 was my last at Parkfield. I had passed, on the strength of my English and History papers, my common entrance and that September left Lime Street Station on my way to Stowe.

Twyne had very much disapproved of my parents' choice of school. In his view, as far as the public schools went, it was practically on a par with the Montessori System. There were, he understood, no traditions and the headmaster, J.F.Roxburgh, was not only a dandy but addressed the boys by their first names. While games were played, they were in no way a fetish. The arts were encouraged, and so on.

He was more or less right, and the reasons for his censure were exactly why my parents had chosen it. There was still some beating, but I was beaten less in the whole of my time at Stowe than I was in one term at Oakridge. As for fagging it didn't involve the master-slave relationship of the more traditional schools, but just meant that you dusted a senior boy's study twice a week for your first few terms.

On my arrival J.F. sought me out, called me 'George', and said he hoped they'd make me happy. Most of the boys and masters were friendly, and in the Art School I found a heady and experimental atmosphere which suited me down to the ground. For some reason, to have come from Liverpool and to sing its praises excited some teasing, but otherwise there was nothing that didn't delight me. I came home for my first holiday right over the top, spouting Eliot and Auden and raving about Picasso and Matisse. I calmed down in time but I was, for the moment, what Maud called 'an affected bit of goods'.

During the preceding term the bombing of London had started in earnest and that August it was the turn of the provincial cities. Up until then Tom, Fred and Alan, as chief air-raid wardens, had little to do except make sure that people observed the black-out. They'd spent a great deal of time in a rather rough pub down by the docks where Tom had become almost as much a fixture as at The Albert, while Fred and Alan scored a great hit at a War-dens' hot-pot supper by singing a parody, written by Fred, of 'Side by Side'. The middle eight bars went,

> We'd rather have our wardens
> Than any other wardens in town.
> We're touched by their loyalty and devotion,
> And very often touched for half-a-crown.

The conclusion was especially well liked,

> When you knock and ask a man to put his light out,
> He feints with his left and puts his right out.
> So wardens in blue, always march two by two,
> Side by side.

Now, however, with heavy raids every night and the docks on fire there was no time for hot-pot suppers. My father and uncles were up all night and returned grey with fatigue and covered in dust for a few hours' sleep before setting out again at dusk.

We didn't use the shelter Tom had dug in the garden, but took refuge in the Griff's cellar together with those other residents of York Mansions who had remained in their flats. The Griff took it all very calmly, largely I think because she couldn't believe that Hitler would have the nerve to harm her. One night Mary, the Griff's parlour-maid, was coming down with a tray of tea having left the door at the top of the cellar steps open, when a bomb fell somewhere in Park Road. The blast blew her down the last few steps and the tray flew up into the air. Mary wasn't hurt at all and the Griff, having first briefly commiserated with her, then expressed her satisfaction that it wasn't the best china.

After a week or two of this Tom decided that we ought to be

evacuated again, preferably somewhere not too far away so that he could join us when not on duty. His solution, while practical, appalled me. He rented Parkfield for the rest of the school holidays with Twyne *in situ*. Having just escaped, I was going to find myself again under that hated roof. I would much sooner have sat out the blitz in the Griff's cellar.

In fact it wasn't too bad because I realized, almost at once, that Twimbo had no jurisdiction over me whatsoever. He was like a sorcerer who had lost his power, whereas I could make quite certain that everything he had suspected about Stowe was absolutely true. He twice offered to 'coach' me in Latin and I refused outright. After that he left me alone. Tom, during one of his weekends off, made a discovery about Twimbo.

'Do you know what he does every evening?' he said. 'He goes down to the Scarsdale Hotel, sits in the bar and soaks up whisky.' Drink would, of course, explain a great deal of his behaviour. Twyne, though none of us had ever suspected it, was a serious boozer.

I had lunch some years ago with a publisher a few years younger than myself and discovered that he had been a boy at Parkfield in the early 1950s, during its final years at Birkdale (for Twyne never moved back to Liverpool). Once we'd established this, our publishing venture was forgotten. People at nearby tables were rather startled to hear two apparently sane men shouting 'My Godfathers!' and 'Ye Gods and little fishes!' at each other. What the publisher told me – of which I'd no idea – was of Twyne's end. He had written to all the parents saying that, for various reasons, he was in financial difficulties, but if they could see their way to advance a term's fees all would be well. Most of them had, and during the holidays Twyne had drunk himself to death.

That evacuated holiday in Birkdale, I decided one afternoon to dress up in some of Maud's clothes, make my face up, and walk with Andrée, then eight, into Southport. I've no idea why I wanted to do this. I have never been attracted by transvestism and, with this solitary exception, have only worn drag at fancy dress parties where it was requested and once, as a joke, during the last evening of a season at Ronnie Scott's. This day, however, I went to pick up Andrée and we set off down Waterloo Road, me tottering along on Maud's court shoes, Andrée with strict instructions to remember to call me 'Auntie'. On the outskirts of Southport proper were two back-to-back public toilets sited on an island in the middle of the road. Holding Andrée firmly by the hand, I entered and used the Ladies. We then walked on into Southport, where we had an ice in a fashionable café in Lord Street and returned home.

During the writing of this book several events have taken place, on both a public and personal level, which have made parts of it no longer currently accurate.

In Liverpool, during the Toxteth riots, the Rialto cinema, which I passed with Carol Ann, and the Racket Club, where I learnt to play tennis on the wooden court, were both burnt down.

Just before Christmas 1982, Alan Isaac, eighty-five years old, had a heart attack and died in hospital four days later. He had been active right up to the end. His final message to me, transmitted by a friend of his during the interval at Ronnie Scott's, was, 'Tell George I'm still battling.'

A few months later, in a nursing home in Surrey, Maud died at ninety-one. Her memory had been going for some time; whole areas of it drifting away like icebergs from a thawing ice-cap. Brighton, where she'd lived for fifteen years after Tom's death, gone. Cranleigh, where she'd spent the last five, gone. Most of her sixty-eight years in Liverpool, cracking up, melting.

At her ninetieth birthday party, Andrée, Bill and I, and most of our families were there. She seemed a little unsure about what exactly was going on but after we'd had tea, I said to her, 'Now Maudie, if you've had enough birthday cake, I'll tell S. Le Kessin he can come in and do his conjuring tricks.' Maud paused for a moment, and then began to laugh quite heartily. 'S. Le Kessin,' she said, 'I haven't thought of him for years.'

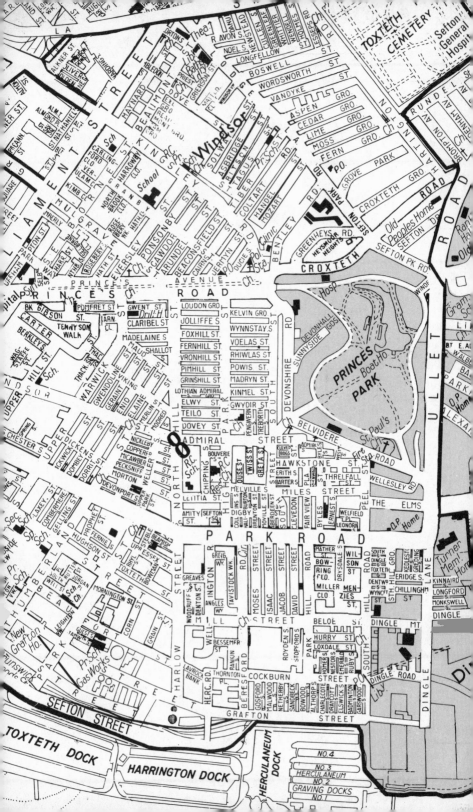